Good Luck with
your Security!

Forensic Discovery

Addison-Wesley Professional Computing Series

Brian W. Kernighan, Consulting Editor

Matthew H. Austern, *Generic Programming and the STL: Using and Extending the C++ Standard Template Library*

David R. Butenhof, *Programming with POSIX® Threads*

Brent Callaghan, *NFS Illustrated*

Tom Cargill, *C++ Programming Style*

William R. Cheswick/Steven M. Bellovin/Aviel D. Rubin, *Firewalls and Internet Security, Second Edition: Repelling the Wily Hacker*

David A. Curry, *UNIX® System Security: A Guide for Users and System Administrators*

Stephen C. Dewhurst, *C++ Gotchas: Avoiding Common Problems in Coding and Design*

Erich Gamma/Richard Helm/Ralph Johnson/John Vlissides, *Design Patterns: Elements of Reusable Object-Oriented Software*

Erich Gamma/Richard Helm/Ralph Johnson/John Vlissides, *Design Patterns CD: Elements of Reusable Object-Oriented Software*

Peter Haggar, *Practical Java™ Programming Language Guide*

David R. Hanson, *C Interfaces and Implementations: Techniques for Creating Reusable Software*

Mark Harrison/Michael McLennan, *Effective Tcl/Tk Programming: Writing Better Programs with Tcl and Tk*

Michi Henning/Steve Vinoski, *Advanced CORBA® Programming with C++*

Brian W. Kernighan/Rob Pike, *The Practice of Programming*

S. Keshav, *An Engineering Approach to Computer Networking: ATM Networks, the Internet, and the Telephone Network*

John Lakos, *Large-Scale C++ Software Design*

Scott Meyers, *Effective C++ CD: 85 Specific Ways to Improve Your Programs and Designs*

Scott Meyers, *Effective C++, Second Edition: 50 Specific Ways to Improve Your Programs and Designs*

Scott Meyers, *More Effective C++: 35 New Ways to Improve Your Programs and Designs*

Scott Meyers, *Effective STL: 50 Specific Ways to Improve Your Use of the Standard Template Library*

Robert B. Murray, *C++ Strategies and Tactics*

David R. Musser/Gillmer J. Derge/Atul Saini, *STL Tutorial and Reference Guide, Second Edition: C++ Programming with the Standard Template Library*

John K. Ousterhout, *Tcl and the Tk Toolkit*

Craig Partridge, *Gigabit Networking*

Radia Perlman, *Interconnections, Second Edition: Bridges, Routers, Switches, and Internetworking Protocols*

Stephen A. Rago, *UNIX® System V Network Programming*

Eric S. Raymond, *The Art of UNIX Programming*

Marc J. Rochkind, *Advanced UNIX Programming, Second Edition*

Curt Schimmel, *UNIX® Systems for Modern Architectures: Symmetric Multiprocessing and Caching for Kernel Programmers*

W. Richard Stevens/Bill Fenner/Andrew M. Rudoff, *UNIX Network Programming Volume 1, Third Edition: The Sockets Networking API*

W. Richard Stevens, *Advanced Programming in the UNIX® Environment*

W. Richard Stevens, *TCP/IP Illustrated, Volume 1: The Protocols*

W. Richard Stevens, *TCP/IP Illustrated, Volume 3: TCP for Transactions, HTTP, NNTP, and the UNIX® Domain Protocols*

W. Richard Stevens/Gary R. Wright, *TCP/IP Illustrated Volumes 1-3 Boxed Set*

John Viega/Gary McGraw, *Building Secure Software: How to Avoid Security Problems the Right Way*

Gary R. Wright/W. Richard Stevens, *TCP/IP Illustrated, Volume 2: The Implementation*

Ruixi Yuan/W. Timothy Strayer, *Virtual Private Networks: Technologies and Solutions*

Visit www.awprofessional.com/series/professionalcomputing for more information about these titles.

Forensic Discovery

Dan Farmer

Wietse Venema

✦✦ Addison-Wesley

Upper Saddle River, NJ • Boston • Indianapolis • San Francisco
New York • Toronto • Montreal • London • Munich • Paris • Madrid
Capetown • Sydney • Tokyo • Singapore • Mexico City

The publisher offers excellent discounts on this book when ordered in quantity for bulk purchases or special sales, which may include electronic versions and/or custom covers and content particular to your business, training goals, marketing focus, and branding interests. For more information, please contact:

> U.S. Corporate and Government Sales
> (800) 382–3419
> corpsales@pearsontechgroup.com

For sales outside the U.S., please contact:

> International Sales
> international@pearsoned.com

Visit us on the Web: www.awprofessional.com

Library of Congress Cataloging-in-Publication Data
Farmer, Dan.
  Forensic discovery / Dan Farmer, Wietse Venema.
     p. cm.
  Includes bibliographical references and index.
  ISBN 0-201-63497-X (pbk. : alk. paper)
  1. Computer security. 2. Data recovery (Computer science) 3. Forensic sciences. I. Venema, Wietse.
  II. Title.

QA76.9.A25F34 2004
005.8—dc22   2004024189

ISBN 0-201-63497-X

Text printed in the United States on recycled paper at Courier in Westford, Massachusetts.

First printing, December 2004

For feminists
—Dan

For the people who refuse to stop learning
—Wietse

CONTENTS

Today, only minutes pass between plugging in to the Internet and being attacked by some other machine—and that's only the background noise level of nontargeted attacks. There was a time when a computer could tick away year after year without coming under attack. For examples of Internet background radiation studies, see CAIDA 2003, Cymru 2004, or IMS 2004.

With this book, we summarize experiences in post-mortem intrusion analysis that we accumulated over a decade. During this period, the Internet grew explosively, from less than a hundred thousand connected hosts to more than a hundred million (ISC 2004). This increase in the number of connected hosts led to an even more dramatic—if less surprising—increase in the frequency of computer and network intrusions. As the network changed character and scope, so did the character and scope of the intrusions that we faced. We're pleased to share some of these learning opportunities with our readers.

In that same decade, however, little changed in the way that computer systems handle information. In fact, we feel that it is safe to claim that computer systems haven't changed fundamentally in the last 35 years— the entire lifetime of the Internet and of many operating systems that are in use today, including Linux, Windows, and many others. Although our observations are derived from today's systems, we optimistically expect that at least some of our insights will remain valid for another decade.

What You Can Expect to Learn from This Book

The premise of the book is that forensic information can be found everywhere you look. With this guiding principle in mind, we develop tools to collect information from obvious and not-so-obvious sources, we walk through analyses of real intrusions in detail, and we discuss the limitations of our approach.

Although we illustrate our approach with particular forensic tools in specific system environments, we do not provide cookbooks for how to use those tools, nor do we offer checklists for step-by-step investigation. Instead, we present a background on how information persists, how information about past events may be recovered, and how the trustworthiness of that information may be affected by deliberate or accidental processes.

In our case studies and examples, we deviate from traditional computer forensics and head toward the study of system dynamics. Volatility and the persistence of file systems and memory are pervasive topics in our book. And while the majority of our examples are from Solaris, FreeBSD, and Linux systems, Microsoft's Windows shows up on occasion as well. Our emphasis is on the underlying principles that these systems have in common: we look for inherent properties of computer systems, rather than accidental differences or superficial features.

Our global themes are problem solving, analysis, and discovery, with a focus on reconstruction of past events. This approach may help you to discover *why* events transpired, but that is generally outside the scope of this work. Knowing *what* happened will leave you better prepared the next time something bad is about to occur, even when that knowledge is not sufficient to prevent future problems. We should note up front, however, that we do not cover the detection or prevention of intrusions. We do show that traces from one intrusion can lead to the discovery of other intrusions, and we point out how forensic information may be affected by system-protection mechanisms, and by the failures of those mechanisms.

Our Intended Audience

We wrote this book for readers who want to deepen their understanding of how computer systems work, as well as for those who are likely to become involved with the technical aspects of computer intrusion or system analysis. System administrators, incident responders, other computer security professionals, and forensic analysts will benefit from reading this book, but so will anyone who is concerned about the impact of computer forensics on privacy.

Although we have worked hard to make the material accessible to non-expert readers, we definitely do not target the novice computer user. As a minimal requirement, we assume strong familiarity with the basic concepts of UNIX or Windows file systems, networking, and processes.

Organization of This Book

The book has three parts: we present foundations first, proceed with analysis of processes, systems, and files, and end the book with discovery. We do not expect you to read everything in the order presented. Nevertheless, we suggest that you start with the first chapter, as it introduces all the major themes that return throughout the book.

In Part I, "Basic Concepts," we introduce general high-level ideas, as well as basic techniques that we rely on in later chapters.

- Chapter 1, "The Spirit of Forensic Discovery," shows how general properties of computer architecture can impact post-mortem analysis. Many of the limitations and surprises that we encounter later in the book can already be anticipated by reading this chapter.

- Chapter 2, "Time Machines," introduces the concept of timelining, using examples of host-based and network-based information, including information from the domain name system. We look at an intrusion that stretches out over an entire year, and we show examples of finding time information in non-obvious places.

In Part II, "Exploring System Abstractions," we delve into the abstractions of file systems, processes, and operating systems. The focus of these chapters is on analysis: making sense of information found on a computer system and judging the trustworthiness of our findings.

- Chapter 3, "File System Basics," introduces fundamental file system concepts, as well as forensic tools and techniques that we will use in subsequent chapters.

- Chapter 4, "File System Analysis," unravels an intrusion by examining the file system of a compromised machine in detail. We look at both existing files and deleted information. As in Chapter 2, we use correlation to connect different observations, and to determine their consistency.

- Chapter 5, "Systems and Subversion," is about the environment in which user processes and operating systems execute. We look at subversion of observations, ranging from straightforward changes to system utilities to almost undetectable malicious kernel modules, and detection of such subversion.

- Chapter 6, "Malware Analysis Basics," presents techniques to discover the purpose of a process or a program file that was left behind after an intrusion. We also discuss safeguards to prevent malware from escaping, and their limitations.

In Part III, "Beyond the Abstractions," we look beyond the constraints of the file, process, and operating system abstractions. The focus of this part is on discovery, as we study the effects of system architecture on the decay of information.

- Chapter 7, "The Persistence of Deleted File Information," shows that large amounts of deleted file information can survive intact for extended periods. We find half-lives on the order of two to four weeks on actively used file systems.

- Chapter 8, "Beyond Processes," shows examples of persistence of information in main memory, including the decrypted contents of encrypted files. We find large variations in persistence, and we correlate these variations to operating system architecture properties.

The appendices present background material: Appendix A is an introduction to the Coroner's Toolkit and related software. Appendix B presents our current insights with respect to the order of volatility and its ramifications when capturing forensic information from a computer system.

Conventions Used in This Book

In the examples, we use `constant-width font` for program code, command names, and command input/output. User input is shown in **`bold constant-width font`**. We use $ as the shell command prompt for unprivileged users, and we reserve # for super-user shells. Capitalized names, such as Argus, are used when we write about a system instead of individual commands.

Whenever we write "UNIX," we implicitly refer to Solaris, FreeBSD, and Linux. In some examples we include the operating system name in the command prompt. For example, we use `solaris$` to indicate that an example is specific to Solaris systems.

As hinted at earlier, many examples in this book are taken from real-life intrusions. To protect privacy, we anonymize information about systems that are not our own. For example, we replace real network addresses with private network addresses such as 10.0.0.1 or 192.168.0.1, and we replace host names or user names. Where appropriate, we even replace the time and time zone.

Web Sites

The examples in this book feature several small programs that were written for the purpose of discovery and analysis. Often we were unable to include the entire code listing because the additional detail would only detract from the purpose of the book. The complete source code for these and other programs is made available online at these Web sites:

> **http://www.fish.com/forensics/**
> **http://www.porcupine.org/forensics/**

On the same Web sites, you will also find bonus material, such as case studies that were not included in the book and pointers to other resources.

Acknowledgments

We owe a great deal of gratitude to Karen Gettman, Brian Kernighan, and the rest of Addison-Wesley for their patience and support over the many years that this book has been under construction.

While we take full responsibility for any mistakes, this book would not be what it is without our review team. In particular, we would like to thank (in alphabetical order): Aleph1, Muffy Barkocy, Brian Carrier, Eoghan Casey, Fred Cohen, Rik Farrow, Gary McGraw, Brad Powell, Steve Romig, Douglas Schales, and Elizabeth Zwicky. Ben Pfaff and Jim Chow helped with a chapter, and Dalya Sachs provided valuable assistance with editing an early version of the text. Tsutomu Shimumura inspired us to do things that we thought were beyond our skills. Wietse would like to thank the FIRST community for the opportunity to use them as a sounding board for many of the ideas that were developed for this book. And contrary to current practice, the manuscript was produced as HTML draft with the vi text editor plus a host of little custom scripts and standard UNIX tools that helped us finish the book.

Dan Farmer
zen@fish.com

Wietse Venema
wietse@porcupine.org

ABOUT THE AUTHORS

Dan Farmer is the author or coauthor of a variety of security programs and papers. He's currently the chief technical officer of Elemental Security, a computer security software company.

Wietse Venema is the author of widely used software such as the TCP Wrapper and the Postfix mail system. Originally from the Netherlands, he is currently a research staff member at IBM Research in the United States.

The cooperation between the authors goes back many years and has resulted in famous and notorious software such as the SATAN network security scanner and the Coroner's Toolkit for forensic analysis.

Forensic Discovery

PART I

Basic Concepts

In the first two chapters, we lay out the framework and introduce the basic ideas that we will use throughout the rest of the book. What is the impact of user activity versus system activity? What is the effect of computer architectures and implementations? How long does data persist, and why? Why is the notion of time so important?

Chapter 1, "The Spirit of Forensic Discovery," is arguably the most accessible and most important chapter. At a relatively high level, it introduces the key forensic concepts of volatility, layering, and trust. We ask you to take a few things on faith until we cover them in more depth in chapters to come.

Chapter 2, "Time Machines," introduces the concept of timelining, with examples from the file system (MACtimes), from network traffic statistics, and even from the domain name service. We develop an understanding of the sources of time and where it is stored, we illustrate why we place so much emphasis on data within a host rather than what is found in networks, and we present the first examples of our out-of-the-box thinking.

Very experienced readers may want to skim over this first part rather than read it closely, but we would urge at least a cursory glance, as we rely on the concepts brought up here in the rest of the book.

The Spirit of Forensic Discovery

1.1 Introduction

> Now, a few words on looking for things. When you go looking for something specific, your chances of finding it are very bad. Because, of all the things in the world, you're only looking for one of them. When you go looking for anything at all, your chances of finding it are very good. Because, of all the things in the world, you're sure to find some of them.
>
> —Darryl Zero, *The Zero Effect*

A few years ago, a friend sent out a cry for help. Someone broke into her Solaris computer system and deleted a large number of files. To help her out, we wrote the first version of our file-recovery tools that later became part of the Coroner's Toolkit (Farmer and Venema 2004). Our friend only wanted her files back, but we had a different agenda: we wanted to actually find out what happened.

We did not expect to recover a lot of information intact. Solaris, like many UNIX systems, has no file undelete feature. The data from deleted files were lying on the disk as a giant puzzle, and we would have to put the pieces back together again. The UNIX FAQ was particularly pessimistic about our prospects (FAQ 2004):

> For all intents and purposes, when you delete a file with "rm" it is gone. Once you "rm" a file, the system totally forgets which blocks scattered around the disk were part of your file. Even worse, the blocks from the file you just deleted are going to be the first ones taken and scribbled upon when the system needs more disk space.

As we explored the destroyed file system, we found that common wisdom was overly pessimistic. First, modern file systems do not scatter the contents of a file randomly over the disk. Instead, modern file systems are remarkably successful in avoiding file fragmentation, even after years of intensive use. Second, deleted file information can persist intact for a significant amount of time. You can read more on deleted file persistence in Chapter 7.

The approach we followed is typical of how we advocate solving problems: rely on past experience, listen to advice from others, and use existing tools. But also, don't be afraid to turn common wisdom into myth, to create your own tools, and to develop your own methodology when that is needed to crack a case. Otherwise, you may end up like the person who searches for lost keys under the streetlight because the light is better there. This is the central message of our book: If you want to learn to solve problems, you must be ready to look anywhere, for anything, and you must be prepared when you find it.

The remainder of this chapter is an introduction to the major concepts that we cover in this book. We do not expect that every reader will have the patience to read every chapter in sequence. You may use this chapter as a springboard to get to the topics in which you're most interested.

Oh, and lest we forget to mention this: our friend did get many of her files back.

1.2 Unusual Activity Stands Out

What is going on with all those bits that are stored on your system? In most cases, nothing is happening at all. We collected data on various UNIX servers to see how recently their files were accessed. Table 1.1 shows the results, in ascending order of utilization and network traffic.

The vast majority of files on two fairly typical Web servers have not been used at all in the last year. Even on an extraordinarily heavily used (and

Table 1.1 *Percentage of files read or executed recently for a number of Internet servers*

	www.things.org	www.fish.com	news.earthlink.net
Over one year:	76.6	75.9	10.9
Six months to one year:	7.6	18.6	7.2
One to six months:	9.3	0.7	72.2
One day to one month:	3.6	3.1	7.4
Within 24 hours:	2.9	1.7	2.3

extensively customized) Usenet news system, fewer than 10 percent of the files were used within the last 30 days. Whether they are unused programs and configuration files, archives of mail, news, and data, et cetera, there are lots of files gathering electronic dust. Similar patterns emerge from Windows PCs and other desktop systems. We find that often more than 90 percent of files haven't been touched in the past year.

Why is this? Even a machine capable of processing one million instructions per second could generate enough new data to fill a one-terabyte drive in a short time. Computers are busy enough, certainly, but most activity accesses the same data, programs, and other resources over and over again. As a system keeps running around, handling the same files again and again, it is quite literally stepping upon its own footprints. This is why footprints from unusual activity not only stand out, but they are likely to stand out for a long time, because most information on a system is rarely touched.

Almost every chapter in this book discusses digital footprints in one form or another. Examples of footprints in file systems are found in Chapter 2, "Time Machines," and Chapter 4, "File System Analysis." For a discussion of footprints in main memory, see Chapter 8, "Beyond Processes."

1.3 The Order of Volatility (OOV)

The forensic analysis of a system involves capturing data and then processing the information gathered. The more accurate and complete the data, the better and more comprehensive the evaluation can be. The original data is safeguarded in a pristine state; analysis should be performed on a copy of the computer's data. This is somewhat analogous to taping off a murder scene to prevent physical evidence from being destroyed, which is done to preserve evidence, allow others to verify conclusions, and minimize data tampering.

Ideally, you want an exact copy of the entire system and all its data, but there are roadblocks that prevent this. As you're collecting data, other users or programs on the system may trigger changes in state or destroy valuable evidence. Intruders or miscreants may set electronic mines that might also damage data if agitated. And the mere execution of a program will disturb the computer's state as the program loads and runs.

It's because of these sorts of problems that traditional forensic analysis has focused on data from systems that aren't running at all. Doctrine directs you to power off the system and copy the data that has survived the transition: program logs, access times, the contents of files, and so on.

Analysis is then done on a copy of the data, which minimizes the danger to the original. This approach facilitates easy capturing of data and a reasonably irrefutable chain of logic when demonstrating results.

Our general philosophy recommends greater understanding instead of higher levels of certainty, which could potentially make such methodology more suspect in a court of law. Paradoxically, however, the uncertainty—primarily in the data collection methods—can actually give a greater breadth of knowledge and more confidence in any conclusions that are drawn. This process requires consistent mechanisms for gathering data and a good understanding of any side effects of the same. We strongly believe that to obtain dependable results, automation is a near-necessity for gathering forensic data.

Certainly care and planning should be used when gathering information from a running system. Isolating the computer—from other users and the network—is the first step. And given that some types of data are less prone to disruption by data collection than others, it's a good idea to capture information in accordance with the data's expected life span. The life expectancy of data varies tremendously, ranging from nanoseconds (or less) to years, but Table 1.2 can be used as a rough guide.

Following this order of volatility gives a greater chance to preserve the more ephemeral details that mere data collection can destroy, and it allows you to capture data about the incident in question—rather than simply seizing the side effects of your data gathering session! Of course, this all depends on the situation. If all you're interested in is the contents of a disk, or evidence from an event that transpired long ago, there might be little point to capturing the memory of the computer in question.

Table 1.2 *The expected life span of data*

Type of Data	Life Span
Registers, peripheral memory, caches, etc.	Nanoseconds
Main memory	Ten nanoseconds
Network state	Milliseconds
Running processes	Seconds
Disk	Minutes
Floppies, backup media, etc.	Years
CD-ROMs, printouts, etc.	Tens of years

Figure 1.1 *Werner Heisenberg, Göttingen, 1924. (Photo courtesy of Jochen Heisenberg.)*

Is there any limit to what you can gather? Why not capture all the data, all at once? Unfortunately it is not possible to record changes to processes and files accurately in real time, for as you capture data in one part of the computer, you're changing data in another.

Almost a century ago, Werner Heisenberg (see Figure 1.1) formulated one of the great principles of quantum physics, which describes the behavior of particles at atomic and smaller scales: one can accurately determine the position of a particle *or* one can accurately determine its motion, but one cannot determine both accurately at the same time.

The Heisenberg uncertainty principle is directly applicable to data gathering on a computer. It's not simply difficult to gather all the information on a computer, it is essentially impossible.[1] We dub this the Heisenberg principle of data gathering and system analysis.

---

1. Virtual machines may be used to capture activity down to the actual machine code instructions (Dunlap et al. 2002), but on a practical level, this is not possible on general-purpose computers and all their peripherals.

Nevertheless, on a realistic level, this Heisenberg principle is not the main impediment to capturing all the data on a computer. Computers aren't defined by their state at any given time, but over a continuum. Memory, processes, and files can change so rapidly that recording even the bulk of those fluctuations in an accurate and timely fashion is not possible without dramatically disturbing the operation of a typical computer system.

Take the humble `date` program, which prints the current date and time, as an example. If we monitor it with `strace`, a program that traces a program as it runs, `date` executes more than a hundred system calls in a fraction of a second (including those to get the time, check the time zone you're in, print out the result, etc.). If we went further and monitored the machine code that the CPU executes in performing this work, we would have many thousands of pieces of information to consider. But even instrumenting all the programs on a computer doesn't tell the whole story, for the computer's video card, disk controller, and other peripherals each have their own tale to tell, with memory, processors, and storage of their own.

We can never truly recover the past. But we will show that you don't need all the data to draw reasonable conclusions about what happened.

1.4 Layers and Illusions

About seventy years ago, René Magritte made a series of paintings that dealt with the treachery of images. The cover of this book shows an image of a pipe with the words "Ceci n'est pas une pipe" (this is not a pipe) below. Yes, this is not a pipe—it's only a painting of a pipe. The image could be an artist's rendering of a real pipe, but it could also be a completely imaginary one or a composite picture of many pipes. You can't tell the difference by simply looking at the image.[2]

Computer systems are subject to the treachery of images as well. The image on your computer screen is not a computer file—it's only an image on a computer screen. Images of files, processes, and network connections are only remotely related to the raw bits in memory, in network packets, or on disks. As shown in Figure 1.2, the images that you see are produced by layer upon layer of hardware and software. When an intruder "owns" a machine, any of those layers could be tampered with. Application software can lie, operating system kernels can lie, and even the firmware inside hard disk drives can lie.

---

2. Some information about René Magritte's work can be found online at
   http://www.magritte.com/.

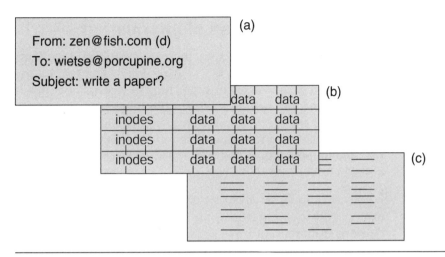

Figure 1.2 *A simplified picture of files as seen by (a) users and applications, (b) file system software in the operating system, and (c) hardware*

Computer file systems, for instance, typically store files as sequences of bytes and organize files within a directory hierarchy. In addition to names and contents, files and directories have attributes such as ownership, access permissions, time of last modification, and so on.

The perception of files, directories, and their attributes is one of the illusions that computer systems create for us, just like the underlying illusion of data blocks and metadata (or inode) blocks. In reality, computer file systems allocate space from a linear array of equal-size disk blocks, and they reserve some of that storage capacity for their own purposes. However, the illusion of files and directories with attributes is much more useful for application programs and their users.

Even the notion of a linear array of equal-size disk blocks is an illusion. Real disks have heads and platters. They store information as magnetic domains, and they too reserve some of the storage capacity for their own purposes. The illusion of a linear sequence of equal-size disk blocks has only one purpose: to make the implementation of file systems easier.

As we peel away layer after layer of illusions, information becomes more and more accurate because it has undergone less and less processing. But as we descend closer and closer toward the level of raw bits, the information becomes less meaningful, because we know less and less about its purpose. This issue of accuracy versus ambiguity is just one consequence of layering; in a later section, we will see how it affects the persistence of deleted information.

1.5 The Trustworthiness of Information

In the early days of computing, the mathematician Alan Turing devised a test for machine intelligence (Turing 1950). The test was to be carried out as an interview via teleprinters, the predecessors of today's computer displays. An interviewer would ask the subject questions without knowing whether the answers came from a machine or from a human being. If the replies from a machine were indistinguishable from replies from a real human being, then the machine must be considered as intelligent as a real human being.

Forensic computer analysis has strong parallels with the Turing test. You examine information from a computer system, and you try to draw conclusions from that information. But how do you know that the information can be trusted? Are you really looking at traces of what happened on a machine, or are you looking at something that the intruder wants you to believe? This is the Turing test of computer forensic analysis.

To avoid falling into a trap that was set up by an intruder, you have to carefully examine every bit of available information, looking for possible inconsistencies that might give away a cover-up attempt. The more sources of information you have, and the more independent those sources are from each other, the more confident you can be about your conclusions.

Listing 1.1 illustrates this process with a small example that uses the logging from typical UNIX systems. The listing shows information about a login session from three different sources: TCP Wrapper logging (Venema 1992), login accounting, and process accounting. Each source of information is shown at a different indentation level. Time proceeds from top to bottom.

Going from the outer indentation level inward:

- The TCP Wrapper logging shows that on May 25 10:12:46 local time, machine spike received a telnet connection from machine hades. The TCP Wrapper logs connection events only, so there is no corresponding record for the end of the telnet connection.

- The `last` command output shows that user wietse was logged in on terminal port ttyp1 from host hades and that the login session lasted from 10:12 until 10:13, for a total amount of time of less than two minutes. For convenience the same record is shown twice, once at the beginning and once at the end of the login session.

```
May 25 10:12:46 spike telnetd[13626]: connect from hades
|
| wietse       ttyp1     hades         Thu May 25 10:12 - 10:13  (00:00)
| |
| | hostname   wietse      ttyp1       0.00 secs Thu May 25 10:12
| | sed        wietse      ttyp1       0.00 secs Thu May 25 10:12
| | stty       wietse      ttyp1       0.00 secs Thu May 25 10:12
| | mesg       wietse      ttyp1       0.00 secs Thu May 25 10:12
. . .             .           .         .    .    .    .    .    .
| | ls         wietse      ttyp1       0.00 secs Thu May 25 10:13
| | w          wietse      ttyp1       0.00 secs Thu May 25 10:13
| | csh        wietse      ttyp1       0.03 secs Thu May 25 10:12
| | telnetd    root          __        0.00 secs Thu May 25 10:12
| |
| wietse       ttyp1     hades         Thu May 25 10:12 - 10:13  (00:00)
```

Listing 1.1 *Three sources of information about a login session*

- Output from the `lastcomm` command shows what commands user wietse executed, how much CPU time each command consumed, and at what time each command was started. The order of the records is the order in which each process terminated. The last two records were written at the end of the login session, when the command interpreter (`csh`) and the telnet server process (`telnetd`) terminated.

The records in the example give a consistent picture: someone connects to a machine, logs in, executes a few commands, and goes away. This is the kind of logging that one should expect to find for login sessions. Each record by itself does not prove that an event actually happened. Nor does the *absence* of a record prove that something *didn't* happen. But when the picture is consistent across multiple sources of information, it becomes more and more plausible that someone logged into Wietse's account at the indicated time.

In real life, login sessions leave behind more information than is shown in the listing. Some of that information can be found on the target machine itself. Each command executed may change access and modification times of files and directories. Other information can be found outside the target machine, such as accounting records from network routers, event records from intrusion detection systems, forensic information on the host that originated the login session, and so on. All that information should properly correlate with each other. Information is power, and when you are investigating an incident, you just can't have too much of it.

1.6 The Fossilization of Deleted Information

Destroying information turns out to be surprisingly difficult (Gutmann 1996, 2001). Memory chips can be read even after a machine is turned off. Although designed to read only ones and zeros, memory chips have undocumented diagnostic modes that allow access to tiny, leftover fragments of bits. Data on a magnetic disk can be recovered even after it is overwritten multiple times. Although disk drives are designed to read only the ones and zeros that were written last, traces of older magnetic patterns still exist on the physical media (Veeco 2004).

The challenge of electronic dumpster diving is to recover information that is partially destroyed: that is, to make sense of digital trash. Without assistance from the application that created a file, it can be difficult to understand that file's contents. And without assistance from a file system, disk blocks are no longer grouped together into files, so that data reconstruction can be like solving a puzzle. As more and more layers of illusion are affected by data destruction, the remaining information becomes more and more difficult to understand.

Once deleted, file contents do not generally change until they are overwritten by a new file. On file systems with good data clustering properties, deleted files can remain intact for years. Deleted file information is like a fossil: its skeleton may be missing a bone here or there, but the fossil remains, unchanged, until it is completely overwritten.

The layering of illusions has major consequences for data destruction and data recovery. Deleting a file from the file system is relatively easy, but it is not sufficient to destroy its contents or attributes. Information about the deleted file persists in disk blocks that were once allocated to that file.

This phenomenon of deletion and persistence can happen at other abstraction levels, as well. At the abstraction level of magnetic disk reading heads, overwritten information persists as analog modulations on the newer information. And at the abstraction level of magnetic domains, overwritten information persists as magnetic patterns on the sides of magnetic tracks.

At each layer in the hierarchy of abstractions that make up computer systems, information becomes frozen when it is deleted. Although deleted information becomes more and more ambiguous as we descend to lower and lower levels of abstraction, we also find that deleted information becomes more and more persistent. Volatility is an artifact of the abstractions that make computer systems useful. What we see is nothing less than OOV (order of volatility) in another guise, with a host of implications of its own. You can find more on this in Chapter 7, "The Persistence of Deleted File Information."

1.7 Archaeology vs. Geology

Over time, computer systems have become more and more complex. As seen by the user, systems become increasingly mature and stable. Under the surface, however, computer systems have become less and less predictable regarding when and where they store information, and how they recycle storage space. The information that we find on a disk, in main memory, or in network packets is affected by a multitude of processes that have trashed each other's footsteps and fingerprints.

Traditionally, these less predictable processes have been ignored by computer forensics. This book breaks with tradition and tries to learn from the way that systems manage information. As always, the challenge is to turn an apparent disadvantage, nonpredictability, into an advantage. While trying to get a grasp on this problem, we found it helpful to consider the real-world parallel shown in Table 1.3.

Just as real-world geological processes are constantly destroying archaeological sites, their cyberspace versions are constantly destroying information. For example, users have direct control over the contents of existing files; after a file is deleted, users have no direct control over the sequence of destruction. We explore these processes further in Chapter 7, "The Persistence of Deleted File Information," and in Chapter 8, "Beyond Processes," which discusses the decay of information in main memory.

Destruction of information is not the only way that user control and autonomous processes interfere with each other. Autonomous processes also leave their distinguishing mark when information is created. As we discuss in Chapter 5, "Systems and Subversion," most systems assign their process ID numbers sequentially. Some processes are permanent; they are created while the system boots up and end up with relatively small process ID numbers. Most processes, however, are transient; they are created and destroyed throughout the life of a computer system.

Table 1.3 *The differences between digital archaeology and geology*

Archaeology is about the direct effects from human activity, such as artifacts that are left behind.	Digital archaeology is about the direct effects from user activity, such as file contents, file access time stamps, information from deleted files, and network flow logs.
Geology is about autonomous processes that humans have no direct control over, such as glaciers, plate tectonics, volcanism, and erosion.	Digital geology is about autonomous processes that users have no direct control over, such as the allocation and recycling of disk blocks, file ID numbers, memory pages, or process ID numbers.

When a process records an event of interest to a log file, the record typically includes a time stamp and the process ID number. These log file records form a time series of process ID numbers, and gaps in this progression reveal that other processes were created in the meantime, even if we know nothing else about those processes. Figure 1.3 illustrates this concept.

Just as gaps in observed process ID sequences can reveal the existence of unobserved processes, similar indirect effects reveal unobserved events in file systems and in network protocols. Chapter 4, "File System Analysis," shows how file ID number analysis can reveal information about the origin of a back door program file. Indirect effects also happen with network protocols. For example, the ID field in Internet packets is usually incremented by one for each packet generated by a system. By probing a system repeatedly over the network, you can find out how many other packets that system is generating, even when you can't observe those other packets directly (Sanfilippo 1998).

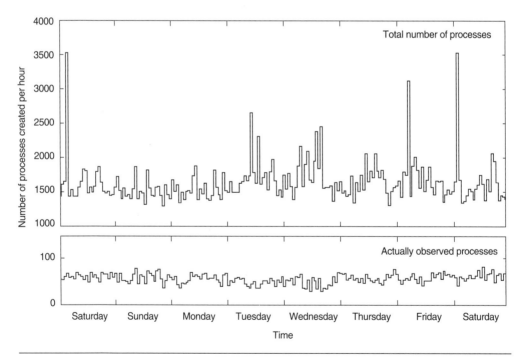

Figure 1.3 *Total process creation rate (top) and actually observed rate (bottom) for a small FreeBSD mail server. The two peaks at 02:00 on Saturday morning are caused by a weekly housekeeping job.*

Interesting phenomena happen on the boundary between autonomous processes and user-controlled processes. While digital archaeology is concerned with the direct, or first-order, effects of user activity such as processes, network connections, and files, digital geology can reveal indirect, or second-order, effects from user activity on where information is stored, and on what file ID, process ID, or network packet ID number is assigned to it.

First-order and second-order effects are just another consequence of the layered architecture of computer systems. Direct user control is limited to the upper layers of processes, files, and network connections. Activity at lower layers becomes increasingly autonomous. This book looks mainly at first-order effects that happen close to the upper layer. Higher-order effects are still waiting to be discovered at the boundaries between lower layers.

CHAPTER 2

Time Machines

2.1 Introduction

In this chapter, we introduce some basic methods of how to gather and interpret time data from the network and individual hosts—essentially constructing little time machines. Although individual events might be interesting when considered in isolation, their sequence in time gives valuable context that may change their meaning. For instance, new programs are installed on a regular basis, but if a program was introduced right after a computer was broken into, that installation takes on new meaning.

Though we deliberate over networking data and events in this particular chapter, throughout the book we focus mostly on information taken from individual systems. The sheer volume easily captured from network taps is both the investigator's best friend and his worst enemy—sometimes you can have it all, but what do you do with it all? We start the chapter by following a real incident to show how network data and host data can complement each other. We then move to show three unusual venues where time information can be found and analyzed: the raw disk, the combination of process memory and the network, and the journal part of file systems.

2.2 The First Signs of Trouble

There was trouble on the net. On August 20, 2001, Barney, a harmless Linux computer previously used as a group's multimedia jukebox, was found to have an `ssh` daemon (a program that enables encrypted network logins) listening for connections on a very strange TCP port. When no one confessed to installing the program, it seemed clear that Barney had been compromised.

In a rush to help the situation, Barney's administrators created a backup of all the directories that appeared to contain suspicious files. Then they sent an alert to the corporate computer security staff. It took three days, but finally the security team quarantined the computer, unpacked the Coroner's Toolkit (see Appendix A for more on this software), examined the suspect disk drive, and the story started to unfold. The team knew what had happened, but they wanted to know when and, if possible, why it had happened.

2.3 What's Up, MAC? An Introduction to MACtimes

At times knowing *when* something happened is more valuable than knowing *what* took place. Throughout this book, we focus on techniques for either finding or using time-related data. There are two ways to get time data: by observing activity directly and by observing that activity's secondary effects on its environment. In this section, we focus on the latter.

One of the simplest things to understand and use in an investigation is MACtimes. MACtimes are not the McDonald's version of a time zone. They are simply a shorthand way to refer to the three time attributes— mtime, atime, and ctime—that are attached to any file or directory in UNIX, Windows, and other file systems.[1]

The atime attribute refers to the last time the file or directory was accessed. The mtime attribute, in contrast, changes when a file's contents are modified. The ctime attribute keeps track of when the contents or the meta-information about the file has changed: the owner, the group, the file permissions, and so on. The ctime attribute may also be used as an approximation of when a file was deleted.

For all of these attributes, however, it is crucial to note the word *last*. MACtimes only keep track of the last time a file was disturbed; once the file has been changed, historical MACtime data is impossible to uncover.[2]

---

1. Microsoft's file systems have four similar times: ChangeTime, CreationTime, LastAccessTime, and LastWriteTime (MSDN 2004). Linux also has the dtime attribute, which is set when a file or directory has been deleted. In particular, this doesn't affect files in the visible file system, only deleted files. We'll discuss more about how the file system keeps track of all this information in Chapter 3, "File System Basics."

2. At least, most of the time. Journaling file systems can reveal recent history that would otherwise be lost in the system. For more, see Section 2.8.

On UNIX systems, these times may be viewed with the humble `ls` command (see the `ls` man page for more details). For NT file systems, various third-party tools are available. In real situations, however, it's often easier to use the Coroner's Toolkit's `mactime` tool or to simply rely on the `lstat()` system call (which `mactime` itself uses), as evidenced by this simple Perl code fragment:[3]

```
($dev, $inode, $mode, $nlink, $uid, $gid, $rdev,
 $size, $atime, $mtime, $ctime, $blksize, $blocks) = lstat($filename);
print "$filename (MAC): $mtime,$atime,$ctime\n";
```

If you've never looked at MACtimes before, it can be surprising how useful they can be. Listing 2.1 shows a bit of what the security team found when Barney was investigated.

It's no coincidence that the output in Listing 2.1 looks very similar to UNIX's `ls -l` output. The big difference here is the inclusion of the "MAC" column. This shows which of the three file time attributes (mtime, atime, and ctime) correspond to the dates and times in the first column.

This output shows that on July 19, just before 5:00 p.m., a user with root privileges created and unpacked a tar file (a popular UNIX file archive format) with a file name suspiciously looking like it contained a replacement

```
Jul 19 2001
time        size MAC permissions   owner file name
----        ---- --- -----------   ----- ---------
16:47:47  655360 m.. -rw-r--r--    root  /usr/man/.s/sshdlinux.tar
16:48:13  655360 ..c -rw-r--r--    root  /usr/man/.s/sshdlinux.tar
16:48:16     395 ..c -rwxrw-r--    2002  /usr/man/.s/ssh.sh
             880 ..c -rw-r--r--    2002  /usr/man/.s/ssh_config
             537 ..c -rw-------    2002  /usr/man/.s/ssh_host_key
             341 ..c -rw-r--r--    2002  /usr/man/.s/ssh_host_key.pub
16:48:20    1024 m.c drwxr-xr-x    root  /usr/man/.s
16:51:31    1024 m.c drwxr-xr-x    root  /home
            1422 m.c -rw-r--r--    sue   /home/sue/.Xdefaults
              24 m.c -rw-r--r--    sue   /home/sue/.bash_logout
             230 m.c -rw-r--r--    sue   /home/sue/.bash_profile
             124 m.c -rw-r--r--    sue   /home/sue/.bashrc
16:57:57    1024 m.c drwx------    sue   /home/sue
               9 m.c -rw-------    sue   /home/sue/.bash_history
```

Listing 2.1 *Slightly edited* `mactime` *program output from Barney*

---

3. MACtimes returned by the Perl `lstat()` function call are displayed as the number of seconds since January 1, 1970, 00:00:00 UTC. NTFS keeps file times in 100-nanosecond chunks since January 1, 1601; thankfully, Perl converts this for you.

for `ssh` server. The file itself was in an even more suspicious location (he or she might as well have named the directory "Kilroy was here"). Finally, soon after the file was created, user "sue" logged off.

You might have noticed that there were no atimes listed in the MACtime output. This is because the "helpful" administrator who copied all the files for safekeeping also destroyed a wide variety of evidence at the same moment. Backing up files before gathering other evidence is a very poor idea, because it runs against the *order of volatility* (also known as the OOV—we mentioned the OOV briefly in Chapter 1; see Appendix B for a more thorough discussion). The OOV demands that more ephemeral data be harvested before more stable data. In this case, reading (or copying) the files changed their atime attributes to the time the file was read. Directories also have atimes; accessing a directory's contents updates its atime as well. Note, too, that running a program changes the atime of its executable file, because the contents of the executable file must be read before execution.[4]

2.4 Limitations of MACtimes

We return to MACtimes throughout the book. Though not as comprehensive as network data, they have the advantage that they may be gathered after an incident—indeed, long after, as we'll see in Chapter 7, "The Persistence of Deleted File Information." However, as useful as they can be for discovering what happened after the fact, MACtimes are not without problems. Collecting and analyzing them must be done with caution, because they are extremely ephemeral: a stiff electronic breeze can destroy any hope of recovering them. We saw how a well-intentioned user who simply backed up some files destroyed evidence by resetting the file access times.

While `lstat()`'ing a file does not change the MACtimes, opening a directory for reading will change the atime, so you must be certain to `lstat()` directories before opening them and examining their contents. Be cautious if using GUI-based file system management tools: many such tools change the atime even when only listing files, because they read the file to figure out which icon to display in the file listing. Digital hashes of file contents are commonly used for a variety of forensic and adminis-

---

4. Many systems allow root to disable atime updates, which is something to remember when examining time stamp information. When investigating a system, turning off atimes can also be useful to avoid destroying atime information when it is not possible to mount a disk as read-only.

trative purposes, but they must be done *after* the `lstat()`, because reading a file changes the atime of that file.

For a serious investigation you'll want to work from a duplicate of the media rather than the original data. Failing that, mount the media as read-only, or at the very least, turn off atime updates so that you don't inadvertently destroy or alter the data and come up with incorrect conclusions.

MACtimes' most obvious shortcoming is that they only report on the last time a file was disturbed, and hence they have no way of revealing the historical activity of a file or directory. A program could run a thousand times and you'd only see evidence of a single occurrence. Another limitation is that MACtimes show you only the result of an action—not who did it.

MACtimes also degrade over time, displaying a sort of digital Alzheimer's. As the activity goes further back in the past, you're fighting a losing battle. MACtimes are less useful on busy multi-user systems, because user activity becomes difficult to distinguish from intruder activity. MACtimes also don't help much when normal system activity resembles the kind of trouble that you wish to investigate.

Finally, MACtimes are easily forged. UNIX systems have the `touch` command, which can change atimes and mtimes. Both Microsoft's NTFS and UNIX file systems can also use the `utime()` system call to change those two times, as this simple Perl fragment demonstrates:

```
$change_to = time();                    # set to current time
utime($change_to, $change_to, $file);   # atime, mtime, file name
```

The ctime attribute is more difficult to change on UNIX systems, because the ctime value is always taken from the system clock. (NT provides the `SetFileTime()` system call, which can be used to change all three times at once.) However, if an intruder has privileged user access, he or she can reset the system clock and then change the ctime or, alternatively, bypass the file system and write the time directly to the disk. (We talk more about this in Section 3.9.) Changing the system clock can cause other warning sirens to sound, however: most systems don't like time going backward or hopping around, and log files or other signs might tip off such activity.

2.5 Argus: Shedding Additional Light on the Situation

According to legend, some 2,300 years ago, Ptolemy III gave the order that all ships stopping at Alexandria under the watch of its great lighthouse were to be searched for books (Wikipedia 2004). All found were commandeered and copied. The duplicates were returned to the ship masters, and the originals were put into the Library of Alexandria. Capturing information this way, from ships passing by an ancient hub, might be viewed as an early version of network packet capturing.

Modern network instrumentation is significantly easier to implement and can be accomplished with network-sniffing software, preferably on a dedicated host, and ideally with the network transmit wire physically severed. Perhaps the biggest benefit of network instrumentation compared to host data capture is the ease in which the former can be accomplished. For instance, though it can require specialized software to capture keystroke or log activity at the host level, it's fairly simple to record keystrokes or the contents of sessions at the network level.

Due to the volume of traffic, however, sites that monitor the network typically don't—can't—keep all the raw network data. Unlike, say, a honeypot or other controlled experiments, in the real world networks can carry staggering amounts of traffic. For example Ohio State University, a large Midwestern college, currently carries about 300 Gbytes of Internet traffic per hour, enough to fill the largest currently available hard drive.[5] And with disks and data traffic continuing to grow at proportional rates (Coffman and Odlyzko 2002), this reality seems unlikely to change soon.

So instead of keeping raw data it is more common to summarize it as connection logs and statistics. No matter what method is used, however, preparing for disaster on the network level isn't important—it's mandatory. Networks are transport, not storage elements, so all data must be captured and stored in real time, or else it will be lost forever. And while we would be among the last people to say that being prepared isn't a good idea, the sad truth is that most people aren't. This lack of preparation is the primary reason that we generally don't discuss networks in this book and focus instead on incidents in a post-mortem fashion on individual hosts.

Fortunately, the corporate security staff in our example had the foresight to have Argus in place before the Barney incident. Argus—which stands for Audit Record Generation and Utilization System (Argus 2004)—is software that reports on network status and traffic. The security team had been running Argus for a couple of years and had kept all the logs since they had started using the tool.

There were two things to look for: connections to the rogue `ssh` daemon (the port the program was listening to, TCP 33332, was unusual enough that it could be readily spotted even in large quantities of data; ironically,

---

5. Private communication with Steve Romig, 2004.

if the intruder had simply placed it on ssh's normal port, it might have never been noticed) and a file transfer that might have placed the tar file onto Barney.

In this example, Barney's IP address was 192.168.0.1, and the intruder came from 10.0.0.1. Finding the first session to the new ssh daemon was easy: it lasted 17 minutes, as seen in the following slightly edited Argus output. Argus appends the port number to the IP address, and the "sSEfC" status flags indicate a complete TCP connection:

```
Jul 19 2001
start      end          proto   source           destination       status
===========================================================================
16:30:47-16:47:16      tcp    10.0.0.1.1023    192.168.0.1.33332   sSEfC
```

Using that information, it was simple to spot further connections and track the incident. Just prior to the ssh connection, the intruder entered from a second system and downloaded something to Barney with FTP from 10.0.1.1. (An FTP server uses TCP ports 20 and 21 to send data and receive commands.) This is quite possibly the ssh tar file that was downloaded earlier.

```
Jul 19 2001
16:28:34-16:29:36    tcp   192.168.0.1.1466      10.0.1.1.21       sSEfC
16:29:30-16:29:36    tcp    10.0.1.1.20       192.168.0.1.1467     sSEfC
16:30:47-16:47:16    tcp    10.0.0.1.1023     192.168.0.1.33332    sSEfC
```

Comparing the various sources of data revealed that the time on the Argus system and Barney's time differed by some 17 minutes (purely coincidental to the duration of the initial ssh connection). Clock skews such as this are very common and can provide endless amounts of frustration when trying to correlate evidence from different sources.

If we scan the Argus logs further back, we see the computer at 10.0.0.1 scanning the network for back doors on TCP port 110 (the POP3 mail service) and TCP port 21 (the FTP port). We note that all the connections are from TCP source port 44445—presumably such an unusual occurrence is not merely a coincidence. An FTP connection lasting four and a half minutes suggests that there might have been a back door previously installed on Barney (the "sR" status flags mean a connection has been refused):

```
Jul 19 2001
16:25:32             tcp 10.0.0.1.44445  192.168.1.1.110  s
16:25:49             tcp 10.0.0.1.44445  192.168.0.1.110  sR
16:25:53-16:30:26    tcp 10.0.0.1.44445  192.168.0.1.21   sSEfR
```

At times Argus will miss a packet or connections will not gracefully terminate, so you'll see lack of acknowledgments and errant packets (such as the single initial request and the longer connection without the "C" indicating a completed connection).

The unusual port numbers used by the attackers warranted additional searching, and certainly, finding additional connections from TCP port 44445 was easy enough. Not only did we find the preceding traffic, but we also discovered another suspicious trail involving the same Barney machine, starting almost a year earlier, on August 22, 2000. Barney was apparently compromised through the name daemon port (TCP port 53) by what was probably a server vulnerability.

```
Aug 21-22 2000
23:59:55-00:29:48   tcp     10.0.3.1.1882    192.168.0.1.53     sSEfR
Aug 22 2000
00:08:32-00:09:04   tcp 192.168.0.1.1027        10.0.2.1.21     sSEfC
00:08:42-00:09:04   tcp     10.0.2.1.20    192.168.0.1.1028     sSEfC
00:11:08-00:13:26   tcp 192.168.0.1.1029        10.0.2.1.21     sSEfC
00:12:07-00:12:13   tcp     10.0.2.1.20    192.168.0.1.1030     sSEfC
00:13:38-00:13:35   tcp     10.0.2.1.44445 192.168.0.1.21       sSEfR
```

Barney's DNS server on port 53 was initially broken into from 10.0.3.1; this session extends over the entire time slice shown here. The intruder then used FTP to pull a set of tools from another compromised system (10.0.2.1), and finally tried out the newly installed back door using the TCP source port 44445. When the MACtime evidence was reexamined for activity during this time frame, many signs of the first break-in were found. Knowing there is a problem makes finding things much, much easier! The case was finally closed after all the holes were patched.

Of course, the forensic data was there all along. They could have found all of this immediately after the initial break-in by looking at the Argus logs or the MACtime output. Alas, that's not how it usually works. In this case there was simply too much data to review on an ongoing basis. It was only having some initial idea of where to look or what to look for that made the analysis possible. We revisit this idea repeatedly: detecting events when they occur is often much harder than analyzing them after you know something is amiss.

So what was discovered? Barney was broken into almost a year before, and a crude back door was put in place. The intruders apparently wanted a better user experience and installed `ssh`—thinking, perhaps, that the encrypted traffic might hide their tracks better. If this hadn't been done, the intrusions might have never been found. Figure 2.1 is a timeline of the incident.

For a variety of reasons, individual host data is fairly untrustworthy, primarily because it is exposed to the digital elements and to attackers. Host data erodes over time with normal system behavior, and it may also be modified by miscreants. Network data, on the other hand, can have much higher fidelity, especially if steps have been taken to protect it and

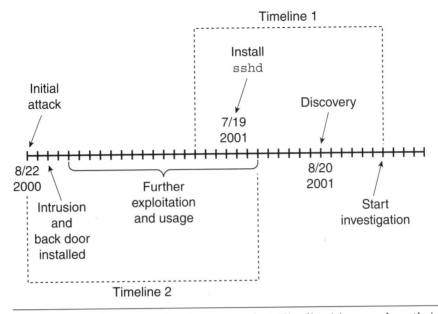

Figure 2.1 *A full timeline of the Barney incident. Timeline 1 is covered mostly in Section 2.5; Timeline 2, further in the past, is discussed in this section.*

if others don't know that it exists or know where it is. Note, though, that even if you could capture all the traffic that flows through a network, interloper activity might still go undetected or undeciphered. Encryption; covert channels; connectionless traffic; back doors hidden in legitimate protocol traffic (such as HTTP, SMTP, and so on); incorrect, broken, or fragmented network packets; and a host of other issues (see Ptacek and Newsham 1998 for more) can all hide activity.

However, even if the network data is encrypted, traffic analysis can still be very useful, especially when combined with other types of information, as shown in this chapter.

2.6 Panning for Gold: Looking for Time in Unusual Places

Some of the more interesting—but difficult to capture—wellsprings of time reside in the dark corners of the system. Though there is no single way to access them all, many places, such as kernel and process memory, unallocated disk space, removed files, swap files, and peripherals, will have a time stamp here, an audit record there, or other fragments of time hidden within.

This type of time data is some of the most pernicious, undependable, and difficult for black hats and white hats alike to use, destroy, or even know about. Ignoring such data, however, should only be done at your peril. Barring a complete wipe of the system, there is essentially no way that anyone can ever be certain that such data isn't still out there . . . somewhere. Based almost completely on undocumented and unpredictable locations and processes, this information is both very interesting and very frustrating to work with. However, text-based records in particular can be useful, even if the data is incomplete or partially obliterated.

Besides, who needs file names to find data? We give labels to files only to make them easier to use and manipulate; file names have nothing to do with the contents within. It's actually quite simple to view data on disk or in memory by just looking outside of the box, at the raw bits. A text pager that can handle binary data can display the raw data. For instance, less can be used to look at the physical memory of many UNIX systems:

```
solaris # less -f /dev/mem
```

Trying to find what you want from any system of significant size, however, can be a Herculean—but at times unavoidable—task. The hardest part of working with data is often not merely collecting it, but also winnowing out the useless data. Raw memory can be particularly difficult, because some of the most interesting data is stored in compact binary data representations. These formats are almost impossible to decipher, because all context concerning what wrote the data or why it is there has been lost (although see Chapter 8, "Beyond Processes," for more).

However, even raw and hard-to-process data may be a very useful source of information for the dedicated investigator. Any and all information that has ever resided on a computer can be placed in memory or get swapped from memory to disk. Furthermore, as noted in Chapter 1, this information storage is a geologic process, not something an intruder or a user can directly control or even know about. As a result, investigators just might be able to find information that was thought to be destroyed or otherwise lost. As we discuss in Chapter 7, once data is on the disk, it's nearly impossible to completely eliminate these mischievous bits, barring physical destruction.

Certain types of data, such as those found in log files and file headers, are stored in repetitive and simple formats without a great deal of variety. Simple filters or searches can be one of the most efficient and effective methods for recovering such data.

For example, if you wanted to see all the system log file records (which might start with the month, day, and time) on the disk from the first week of January, sorted by date, you could use the UNIX `strings` and `grep` commands, combined with a text pager:

```
linux # strings /dev/sda1 | egrep \
        '^Jan [1-7] [0-9][0-9]:[0-9][0-9]:[0-9][0-9]' | \
        sort | less
```

This code would display not only your log files, but also any deleted data on the disk. Because this command searches through the entire disk, it can be quite slow. More concise regular expressions or programs may be used to further separate the digital wheat from the chaff.

Many times, however, you would like to examine or search a part of a system rather than a relatively large subsection of it. The Coroner's Toolkit's `pcat` command, which captures the raw memory contained in a process, can be used to find any date strings within the currently running `syslogd` process:

```
linux #  ps axuww|grep syslog
root 337 0.0 0.0 1156 448 ? S Feb10 15:29 syslogd -m 0 linux
# pcat 337 | strings | egrep '[0-9][0-9]:[0-9][0-9]:[0-9][0-9]' |
egrep 'Jan|Feb|Mar|Apr|May|Jun|Jul|Aug|Sep|Oct|Nov|Dec'
Sat Oct 13 09:57:00 2001 tsunami.trouble.org inetd[187]: \
     telnet[17637] from 216.240.49.170 4514
Aug 12 03:08:53 ipmon[135]: 03:08:52.883456 hme0 @0:8 p \
     211.78.133.66,655 -> 216.240.49.180,53 PR udp len 20 54  K-S IN
Oct  5 15:03:23 tsunami.trouble.org inetd[187]: telnet[6997] \
     from 216.240.49.165 62063
Sep 22 11:55:20 tsunami.trouble.org sendmail[1059]: LAA01057: \
     to=zen@fish.com, ctladdr=root (0/1), delay=00:00:01, \
     xdelay=00:00:00, mailer=relay, relay=fish.com. [216.240.49.170],\
     stat=Sent (Ok: queued as 60101179E6)
[. . .]
```

This output shows what is currently in the processes' memory. As you can see, we have log entries spanning several months! Although the quantity and type of data in a running process can vary wildly from system to system, from process to process, and depending on the activity levels of the computer in question, this data can be an invaluable source of information. Here the log entries in memory could be checked against the actual system logs; if the entries in memory are not present in the log file, then something is amiss.

For those who are really serious about making sense of data that has no shape or defining boundaries, the Coroner's Toolkit's `lazarus` automatically categorizes data based on the contents that it finds. This program can be useful not only for finding time-based data, but also for giving form to arbitrary contents, based on how it looks and smells to `lazarus`.

2.7 DNS and Time

Some programs keep their time-related data in memory, but often they can be coaxed into divulging their secrets in an orderly fashion. For instance Bind, the standard UNIX domain name system (DNS) daemon, is perhaps the most widely relied upon program on the Internet. Almost anytime an e-mail is sent, a Web site is visited, a music file is down-loaded, and so on, Bind is used to translate the name of a server (such as "fish.com") to an IP address (such as those in the Barney investigation).

DNS has several types of records, perhaps the most widely used being PTR (pointer records, which map an IP number to a host name), A (address records, which map the computer's name to an IP number), and MX (mail exchange records, which tell mail agents where e-mail should be sent). Bind maintains an in-memory cache of recent lookup results. On request, it can dump this cache in an orderly manner. The request is made via the ndc or rndc command, or by sending a SIGINT signal (such as "kill -INT *bind-pid*").

Although Bind doesn't keep the explicit time for each lookup, it does display the time the data has left in the cache before it will discard the data (this is called its *time to live*, or TTL). Listing 2.2 shows a snippet from an rndc dump of the Bind program.

If you were able to obtain the real TTL value and subtract Bind's time left for a specific request in the cache, you would—in theory—know how long ago the query happened. We can look at TTLs on the Internet for any DNS resource record, using the host command:

```
linux #  host -t soa -v porcupine.org
[. . .]
porcupine.org 10823 IN SOA spike.porcupine.org wietse.porcupine.org(
                  2004071501      ;serial (version)
                  43200    ;refresh period
                  3600     ;retry refresh this often
                  1209600  ;expiration period
                  86400    ;minimum TTL
                  )
[. . .]
```

If you were running your own caching name server, it would save the TTL (86,400 seconds, in this case), and subsequent requests would show the TTL counter decrementing (normally this value will remain the same from query to query). When the cached TTL reaches zero, the cache entry for the resource record is cleared and any network requests must again

```
$DATE 20040822164741
[. . .]
165.49.240.10.in-addr.arpa.    479   PTR   rainbow.fish.com.
209.in-addr.arpa.            86204   NS    chill.example.com.
rasta.example.com.           10658   A     192.168.133.11
al.example.com.              86298   NS    ns.lds.al.example.com.
4.21.16.10.in-addr.arpa.     86285   PTR   mail.example.com.
[. . .]
```

Listing 2.2 *A fragment of in-memory dump of a* Bind *database (version 9), with the respective TTLs (measured in seconds) in bold*

ask the network for a new TTL. To get a definitive value for a TTL, you must ask an authoritative name server and then look at the TTL that comes back with your request. Alternatively, you can use your own server. Figure 2.2 depicts the process.

Taking the difference between the two TTL values and the time of the Bind cache dump gives you the approximate time of the query (it's not the exact time because the original TTL could have changed in the meantime). To do this effectively, we need to write a program. One of the big differences between an expert investigator and merely a good one is the ability to react to new situations. For instance, here we have to write a small program to better understand the situation after a scan. The ability to come up with small programs or do back-of-the-envelope analysis on data can be invaluable in an investigation. (A classic text on the spirit of writing small tools is *Software Tools* [Kernighan and Plauger 1976].)

We're big fans of scripting languages like awk, Perl, and others. The Perl code in Listing 2.3 processes the database dump results of Bind and prints out a sorted version of the lookup times. It first consults the local name server's cache to see how much time is left, and then it looks up the full TTL from a remote name server.

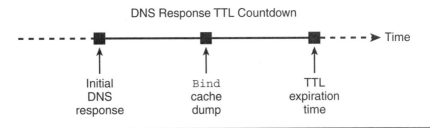

Figure 2.2 *How DNS MACtimes are generated and collected*

```perl
#!/usr/bin/perl
use Time::Local;
while (<>) {
    if (/^\$DATE/) { $dump_time = &parse_date(); next; }

    # look for interesting DNS records
    ($r, $ttl, $type) = &parse_record_data();
    next unless $r =~ /^[-._a-zA-Z0-9]+$/;

    # get the initial TTL from the authority record
    open(HOST, "host -v -t soa $r|") || die "Can't run host\n";

    $init_ttl = "";
    while (<HOST>) {
        if (/^\s+(\d+)\s*;\s*minimum ttl/i) { ($init_ttl = $1); last; }
    }
    close(HOST);

    # save the difference between the two
    if ($init_ttl > $ttl) {
        $t = $dump_time - ($init_ttl - $ttl);
        if (! defined($time{"$t,$type"})) { $time{"$t,$type"} = $r; }
        else { $time{"$t,$type"} .= "\n" . " " x 29 . "$r"; }
    }
}

# output the sorted logs
for $_ (sort keys %time) {
    ($time, $type) = split(/,/, $_);
    print localtime($time) . " ($type) " . $time{"$_"} . "\n";
}
```

Listing 2.3 *A Perl program to print out MACdns records. The full implementation, which includes the* parse_date() *and* parse_record_data() *functions, is available on the book's Web site.*

On most sites, DNS is very busy; even on our personal domains, we get
lots of requests and attacks. We dumped our own Bind cache and ran the
program against it. The output in Listing 2.4 shows a brief slice of time
when someone took an interest in us. You might think of this as a
MACdns measurement, an indicator that shows you when someone has
looked at your systems. Just like MACtimes, MACdns records may not
provide much value in isolation. However, if you were to spot additional
network activity on your system after seeing records similar to those in
Listing 2.4, they could give a clue as to when the first probes began.

The A records here show when our SMTP mailer wanted to send mail to
another site and needed to look up the destination site's IP address from the
host name. The PTR record indicates that a computer was probing our ssh
daemon, which logged the IP address along with the resolved host name.

```
Date          Time      Type    Name
Sun Aug 22 09:56:05 (A)        5.167.54.10.in-addr.arpa.
                               mail.earthlink.example.com.
                               230.253.168.192.in-addr.arpa.
Sun Aug 22 09:56:07 (A)        7.32.4.10.in-addr.arpa.
Sun Aug 22 09:56:08 (A)        ens2.UNIMELB.example.com.
                               mx1.hotmail.example.com.
Sun Aug 22 09:56:09 (PTR) 86.90.196.10.in-addr.arpa.
```

Listing 2.4 *A fragment of* Bind's *processed memory cache*

With busy DNS servers interesting activity can be hard to spot—but it's not impossible, or even improbable. And yes, intruders can play games by juggling their own DNS server's TTL to fool such a ploy. But many network services automatically look up the name of any connecting system. To destroy the evidence once that information is in memory, the process must either be killed or have its memory flushed or recycled—perhaps via a restart or by waiting for the program to forget what has happened in the past. This is also made difficult because name servers are often in protected areas of the network. And the mere fact that programs have been restarted or killed is suspicious to the watchful eye. And so the game continues.

Bind is simply one program—albeit an important one—on a UNIX system; it is not going to solve many problems by itself. We've discussed Bind here as an example of a broader class of programs and opportunities, each with its own implementation. Time is everywhere, but sometimes you must hunt it down.

2.8 Journaling File Systems and MACtimes

Journaling file systems have been a standard feature of enterprise-class systems for a long time and have more recently become available for popular systems such as Linux and Microsoft Windows. Examples are Ext3fs, JFS, NTFS, Reiserfs, XFS, Solaris UFS, and others. With a journaling file system, some or all disk updates are first written to a journal file before they are committed to the file system itself (Robbins 2001). Although at first this seems like extra work, it can significantly improve the recovery from a system crash. Depending on what optimizations the file system is allowed to make, journaling does not need to cause loss of performance.

Why does the world need journaling file systems? Every nontrivial file system operation, such as creating or appending a file, results in a sequence of disk updates that affect both file data (that is, the contents) and file metadata (such as the location of file contents, and what files belong to a directory). When such a sequence of updates is interrupted due to a system crash, non-journaling file systems—such as FFS,[6] Ext2fs, and Windows FAT—can leave their file metadata in an inconsistent state. The recovery process involves programs such as `fsck` and `scandisk` and can take several hours with large file systems. By comparison, recovery with a journaling file system is almost instantaneous: it can be as simple as replaying the "good" portion of the journal to the file system and discarding the rest.

Journaling file systems differ widely in the way they manage their information, but conceptually they are very easy to understand. There are two major flavors: those that journal metadata only, and those that journal both data and metadata. In this section, we look only at MACtimes—that is, metadata—although we are aware that journaled file contents have great forensic potential, too.

From a forensics point of view, the journal is a time series of MACtime and other file information. It is literally a time machine by itself. Whereas normal MACtimes allow us to see only the last read/write operation or status change of a file, journaled MACtimes allow us to see repeated access to the same file. Listing 2.5 shows an example of repeated access that was recovered more than 24 hours after the fact from an Ext3fs file system.

Regular system activity can act as a heartbeat, showing up in logs and in other locations such as the file system journal. Here it turns out that `cron`, the scheduler for unattended command execution, is running a maintenance program every ten minutes. Besides the information that we have learned to expect from normal MACtimes, the MACtimes from the journal also reveal how log files grow over time, as shown by the file sizes of `/var/log/cron` and `/var/log/sa/sa19`.

Rather than trying to cover all the major journaling file system players, we'll take a brief look at the Ext3fs implementation. Ext3fs is particularly easy to use because of its compatibility with its predecessor, Ext2fs, and it has become the default file system in many Linux distributions. Although Ext3fs stores the journal in a regular file, that file is usually not referenced by any directory, and therefore it cannot be accessed by name. The Linux `tune2fs` command reveals where the journal is kept:

```
linux# tune2fs -l /dev/hda1 | grep -i journal
Filesystem features:   has_journal filetype needs_recovery sparse_super
Journal UUID:          <none>
Journal inode:         8
Journal device:        0x0000
```

---

6. FFS versions with soft metadata updates avoid this consistency problem by carefully scheduling their disk updates, so that most of the file system check can be run in the background while the system boots up (McKusick and Neville-Neil 2004).

```
time         size MAC permissions owner file name
19:30:00   541096 .a. -rwxr-xr-x  root  /bin/bash
19:30:00    26152 .a. -rwxr-xr-x  root  /bin/date
19:30:00        4 .a. lrwxrwxrwx  root  /bin/sh -> bash
19:30:00      550 .a. -rw-r--r--  root  /etc/group
19:30:00     1267 .a. -rw-r--r--  root  /etc/localtime
19:30:00      117 .a. -rw-r--r--  root  /etc/mtab
19:30:00      274 .a. -rwxr-xr-x  root  /usr/lib/sa/sa1
19:30:00    19880 .a. -rwxr-xr-x  root  /usr/lib/sa/sadc
19:30:00    29238 m.c -rw-------  root  /var/log/cron
19:30:00   114453 mac -rw-r--r--  root  /var/log/sa/sa19

19:40:00   541096 .a. -rwxr-xr-x  root  /bin/bash
19:40:00    26152 .a. -rwxr-xr-x  root  /bin/date
19:40:00        4 .a. lrwxrwxrwx  root  /bin/sh -> bash
19:40:00      550 .a. -rw-r--r--  root  /etc/group
19:40:00     1267 .a. -rw-r--r--  root  /etc/localtime
19:40:00      117 .a. -rw-r--r--  root  /etc/mtab
19:40:00      274 .a. -rwxr-xr-x  root  /usr/lib/sa/sa1
19:40:00    19880 .a. -rwxr-xr-x  root  /usr/lib/sa/sadc
19:40:00    29310 m.c -rw-------  root  /var/log/cron
19:40:00   115421 mac -rw-r--r--  root  /var/log/sa/sa19
```

Listing 2.5 *Journaled MACtimes showing repeating activity, recovered more than 24 hours after the fact from an Ext3fs file system journal. For the sake of clarity, dynamically linked libraries were omitted. Files with the same time stamp are sorted alphabetically.*

This output shows, among other things, that the journal is stored as a regular file with inode number 8 (see Chapter 3 for an introduction to inodes). What it does not show is that the journal has a fixed size of 32 Mbytes. As part of an investigation, it is therefore worthwhile to save the contents of the journal with the Coroner's Toolkit's icat command early, before the data is overwritten with newer information. However, be sure to save this new file to a different file system; otherwise the journal may end up destroying itself with its own contents.

```
linux# icat /dev/hda1 8 >journalfile
```

The Linux debugfs file system debugger may be used to examine the file system journal in some detail. The following command dumps recent access times for the /etc/passwd file:

```
linux# debugfs -R 'logdump -c -i /etc/passwd' /dev/hda1 | grep atime
    atime: 0x4124b4b8 -- Thu Aug 19 07:10:00 2004
    atime: 0x4124b5e4 -- Thu Aug 19 07:15:00 2004
    atime: 0x4124b710 -- Thu Aug 19 07:20:00 2004
    [. . .]
```

To examine a saved journal file, we would specify "-f journalfile" on the logdump command line.

The standard `debugfs` command is sufficient if we want to look at only one file at a time, and if we already know what file we are looking for. However, to produce multi-file reports such as the one in Listing 2.5, we had to use a modified version that allows us to see all the MACtime information in the journal. This software is available via the book's Web site.

As with all tools that are used for unintended purposes, `debugfs` can produce unexpected results at times. The version that we used (1.35) did not always recognize where the journal terminates, and thus it would misinterpret the remainder of the journal file. So you need to use some judgment when interpreting the results.

The amount of MACtime history that can be recovered from a file system journal depends on the type and amount of activity in the file system, as well as file system implementation details. With file systems such as Ext3fs that can journal both data and metadata, the amount of recoverable MACtimes can be disappointingly small. On the other hand, systems with little activity can have records that go back more than an entire day. In such cases, reading a file system journal can be like watching a tree grow, one ring at a time.

2.9 The Foibles of Time

> A man with a watch knows what time it is. A man with two watches is never sure.
>
> —Segal's Law

By now, you might be thinking that timeline reconstruction is simply a matter of collecting, sorting, and neatly printing information. However, there are many potential problems along the way.

To start, let's consider how we represent time. Usually when we think of time we think of hours and minutes and seconds, or perhaps in a more calendrical sense, we think about days, weeks, months, and years. Time zones are another consideration, as are leap years. Unfortunately, in computing systems as in real life, there is no single method of representing time—even recognizing some time formats can be a challenge, let alone converting them to a universal format.

Would that these were the only problems. Another trio of chronological gremlins is accuracy, drift, and synchronization. No real-world clocks keep perfect time (as defined by various agencies around the world), and there is always an opportunity for errors in records. Uncorrected, computers are notoriously poor time-keeping devices and will usually lose seconds, if not minutes or more, each day. After all, no one will pay more for a computer simply because it has a particularly accurate clock—instead, they'll buy a good clock!

This isn't a big issue for most users, but in an investigation, it can become a large complication, especially if multiple computers are involved. The Network Time Protocol (NTP) and other time synchronization efforts can certainly help with this, but they will not solve all problems.[7]

Systems that act as a central repository for logs will often get log messages from systems in other time zones, yet they log the activity in the local time zone. There are many other sources of trouble: computers are relocated to another time zone, clocks go bad, intruders attempt to inject false or spurious times into logging mechanisms, systems lose power, backup clock batteries lose power, and so on. Dealing with time is almost certain to be a hair-pulling experience.

And none of this addresses the malleability of digital evidence. Simply because a file or record reports a given time doesn't mean it hasn't been changed, nor does a clock that is accurate now guarantee that it hasn't been incorrect in the past.

We dodge most of these issues in this book, because we're mostly writing about data coming from a single system. However, in real investigations, there are often many computers involved, and accurate time will often be an issue—especially when the computers in question are out of your control and you can't tell how they've been maintained.

2.10 Conclusion

Perhaps no other form of data is more interesting, frustrating, relied upon, and untrustworthy than time. Provably accurate or consistent time can be extraordinarily difficult to obtain and should generally be trusted only when several events or points of view are correlated.

Systems generate a wealth of data about all kinds of activity, and as we cast our information-retrieval net wider and wider, it becomes easier to catch anomalies or problems. Some forms of time data recovery and processing are difficult to automate and impractical for general use—the system will often reveal its secrets only under duress. Additional work has to be done investigating, documenting, and providing methods to collect such data.

---

7. See the official NTP Web site at http://www.ntp.org/.

Because computers use time for almost all their actions and decision-making processes, perhaps it shouldn't come as a surprise to see it permeate the system so completely. It was enlightening to us, however, to see firsthand not only some of the different locations where time is kept (and the near-random success that one has in finding it), but also how redundant the data can be. With time data being so valuable to understanding and reconstructing the past, as well as a golden opportunity to detect modified or deleted records, great care and effort should be taken to try to uncover the gems of time scattered throughout the system.

PART II

Exploring System Abstractions

In the second part of the book, we explore the abstractions of files, processes, and systems. We start at the surface with the visible abstractions, and then we explore the less visible abstractions underneath. As we go deeper, we must remain aware of those higher-level abstractions to retain the context of the data at hand. In this part of the book, our main motivation to look under the hood is not so much to discover information, but rather to judge the trustworthiness of our observations.

In Chapter 3, "File System Basics," we present the principles and implementation strategies behind popular UNIX file systems, and we look at their properties from a forensic analyst's point of view.

Chapter 4, "File System Analysis," builds on Chapter 3 and unravels an intrusion in great detail. We look at existing and deleted information, and then we correlate our observations to determine their consistency.

Chapter 5, "Systems and Subversion," is about the environment in which user processes and operating systems execute. We look at subversion of observations, ranging from straightforward changes to system utilities to almost undetectable malicious kernel modules, and we discuss the possibilities and impossibilities of detecting such subversion.

In Chapter 6, "Malware Analysis Basics," we present techniques to discover the purpose of a process or a program file that was left behind after an intrusion. To do so in a responsible manner, we first discuss safeguards to prevent malware from escaping, and the limitations of those safeguards.

This part of the book is not for the faint of heart. We expect familiarity with UNIX or UNIX-like file systems, and with the general principles of computer system architecture.

## CHAPTER 3

File System Basics

3.1 Introduction

In this chapter, we explore some fundamental properties of file systems. As the primary storage component of a computer, the file system can be the source of a great deal of forensic information. We start with the basic organization of file systems and directories, including how they may be mounted on top of each other to hide information. We then move on to various types of files, along with their limits and peculiarities, as well as the basic relationship between inodes and data blocks. Next, we outline the lowest levels of the file system: partitions, zones, inode and data bitmaps, and the superblock. Along the way, we discuss a variety of tools and methods to facilitate our exploration and analysis.

Forensic data must be captured at the appropriate abstraction level. For example, tools that use the normal file system interface will be able to access only existing files. To capture information about the unused space that exists between files, one has to use lower-level tools that bypass the file system. Such tools have additional benefits: they eliminate the possibility of false reports by maliciously modified file system code. This chapter will lay the groundwork for more serious analysis in the next chapter, "File System Analysis."

3.2 An Alphabet Soup of File Systems

There are more file systems than there are operating systems. Microsoft has several, and UNIX certainly has its share, in typical acronymic fashion: FFS, UFS, Ext2fs,[1] XFS, and more. Much has been written about these (in McKusick et al. 1984, Card et al. 1994, Nemeth et al. 2002, and others), and we aren't trying to write the definitive file system reference. The purpose of this chapter is to illustrate general file system properties and their relevance to forensic analysis, irrespective of their origin. However, to keep the discussion succinct, we focus on file systems that are either based on or very similar to the UNIX Fast File System (FFS). The design of FFS was done well and is fairly easy to understand; as a result, FFS has influenced many other file systems.

The original UNIX file system dates back to the early days of UNIX evolution. Though many improvements have been made over time, the fundaments of the design have not changed in thirty years. That is amazing, considering that disk capacity has increased by a factor of ten thousand, and it means that the initial design was done by very smart people (Ritchie and Thompson 1974).

3.3 UNIX File Organization

All UNIX file systems are organized within a single tree structure underneath one root directory. Leaves, or nodes, in the tree are separated by slashes, and they have names like `/home/you/mailbox`. There is no forest of directory trees beginning with host or network names, nor does each disk have its own name space, as in some other systems (A:, B:, and C:, anyone?). Even non-file devices, such as terminals, printers, and disks themselves, are abstracted and accessed via names in the file system.

To make files on a disk partition accessible, the disk partition has to be mounted at some directory in the file system tree. As Figure 3.1 demonstrates, when a disk partition is mounted over a directory, its contents overlay that directory, much like roof tiles overlapping each other.

You may mount many different types of file systems on top of each other: not only the UNIX standards, but also those accessed across the network

---

1. Ext3fs is Ext2fs with journaling added. Though there are other differences, in this chapter on basics, we treat them as the same, and you may consider "Ext2fs" and "Ext3fs" interchangeable in the text wherever journaling is not discussed. See Section 2.8 for more on file system journaling.

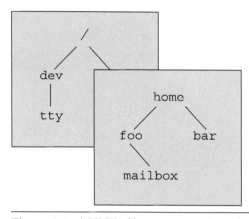

Figure 3.1 *A UNIX file system tree built from multiple disk partitions*

(such as NFS and AFS) and those from completely different vendors (such Microsoft, Apple, and so on) and operating systems. Unfortunately, although all these file systems will behave somewhat as standard UNIX file systems, this beauty is sometimes only skin deep. When foreign file systems are mounted onto UNIX, you sometimes get only a subset of the vendor's semantics. The network abstraction usually strips off even more lower-level details of the file system. You can even mount files containing block file system formats onto special devices (such as the loopback file or vnode pseudo-disk device drivers, which we talk about in Chapter 4).

Disks can contain many file systems, and the file system tree can be built from multiple disk partitions. Note that the tiling effect mentioned above means that you can hide things underneath a mount point. In the following output, df shows the mounted file systems before and after a file system is stacked on top of the /research directory; see how the contents of a file underneath a mount point cannot be read with cat.

```
# df
Filesystem    1k-blocks      Used  Available Use% Mounted on
/dev/sda1      1008872    576128     381496  60%     /
/dev/sda5     16580968  15136744     601936  96%     /home
# ls /research
foo
# cat /research/foo
hello, world
# mount /dev/sdb1 /research
# ls /research
lost+found      src      tmp
# cat /research/foo
cat: /research/foo: No such file or directory
```

The file system provides little help when you want to know the details of where and how it stores information; indeed, the entire purpose of file systems is to hide such specifics. To look under the file system, you have to bypass the file system code and use tools that duplicate some of the file system's functionality.

If a mounted file system isn't currently being used, the umount command can remove it from the directory tree. File systems are dubbed busy and cannot be unmounted when they contain files that are currently open or have running processes whose current directory or executable file is within the file system. Under Solaris, FreeBSD, and Linux, you may try to force the file system to unmount by using the -f option with umount, but doing so can crash processes that have their virtual rug pulled from underneath them. The fuser and lsof commands may be used to determine which processes are preventing us from unmounting a busy file system. In the next section we also reveal how to peer under mount points, when we discuss inodes in more detail.

Another fine way to conceal information is not by ensconcing it under another file system, but rather by neglecting to mount the file system at all, so that it doesn't appear in the directory structure. There is no easy way to find all the file systems (or all the hardware, in general) that may be attached to a system—especially because they may not even be turned on while you're examining the computer. Being in the same physical location as the computer is helpful (so you may see the devices in question), but with components getting smaller every day (such as keyboards and mice with USB or memory sockets), even this is not a foolproof solution.

However, a UNIX computer usually records the existence of hardware attached to it as it boots, writing the information to a ring buffer of kernel memory. (It's called a ring because the buffer will overwrite older messages with more recent entries as the buffer is filled.) Linux and FreeBSD, as well as older versions of Solaris, have the dmesg command to print out this buffer. (With recent Solaris versions, the dmesg command displays information from system log files that are updated by syslogd.) Though the records vary from system to system, you may get valuable information by poring over this record. See Listing 3.1 for an illustration of this.

After the system has completed its start-up phase, newly added hardware will be reported to the ring buffer, or it will cause the UNIX kernel to log a message via the syslogd (Solaris and FreeBSD) or klogd (Linux) daemons. Keeping an eye on dmesg or these log files can be the only way to detect that the configuration has changed.

```
freebsd# dmesg
[. . .]
ppi0: <Parallel I/O> on ppbus0
ad0: 114440MB <WDC WD1200JB-75CRA0>[232514/16/63] at ata0-master \
    UDMA100
ad1: 114440MB <WDC WD1200JB-75CRA0>[232514/16/63] at ata0-slave UDMA100
ad3: 114473MB <WDC WD1200BB-00CAA0>[232581/16/63] at ata1-slave UDMA33
acd0: CDROM <LTN526S>at ata1-master PIO4
Mounting root from ufs:/dev/ad0s2a
/dev/vmmon: Module vmmon: registered with major=200 minor=0 tag=$Name: \
    build-570$
/dev/vmmon: Module vmmon: initialized
[. . .]
```

Listing 3.1 *Elided* dmesg *output, displaying three hard disks and a CD-ROM on a FreeBSD system. It also shows the capacity of the disks, potential mount points, and additional miscellaneous information.*

FreeBSD and Linux also have the fdisk command (each, of course, with its own set of options), which displays any partitions on a given disk, while Solaris's prtvtoc command prints out a disk's geometry and the partitions contained in the volume table of contents (VTOC).

In the following example, df shows what file systems are mounted, while fdisk uncovers a hidden Linux partition named /dev/sda5:

```
linux# df
Filesystem    1k-blocks     Used  Available Use% Mounted on
/dev/sda1      1008872    576128    381496  60%     /
linux# fdisk -l /dev/sda
Disk /dev/sda: 64 heads, 32 sectors, 17501 cylinders
Units = cylinders of 2048 * 512 bytes

   Device Boot    Start      End    Blocks   Id  System
/dev/sda1    *        1     1001   1025008   83  Linux
/dev/sda2          1002    17501  16896000    5  Extended
/dev/sda5          1002    17452  16845808   83  Linux
```

We can then mount the hidden file system and explore its contents.

```
linux# mount /dev/sda5 /mnt
linux# df
Filesystem    1k-blocks      Used  Available Use% Mounted on
/dev/sda1      1008872     576128    381496  60%     /
/dev/sda5     16580968   15136744    601936  96%   /mnt
```

We talk about how to capture file system data in Chapter 4.

3.4 UNIX File Names

File names are stored in directories (which we discuss in Section 3.6), and they may contain any character except the "/" or the null character. Some systems disallow character values above 127. (Non-UNIX types of mounted file systems can possess file names with these illegal characters.) The POSIX standard specifies a minimum upper bound for file names of 255 bytes, which is the current limit for most implementations of UFS, FFS, and Ext3fs.[2]

This flexibility can cause problems with unprepared programs that trust the input they receive to be well behaved. For instance, the `touch` command can create a file name with a newline character embedded in it:

```
$ touch '/tmp/foo
/etc/passwd'
```

If such a file name exists and someone with root privileges is foolish enough to try the following housekeeping command (which attempts to remove files in the temporary directory that were modified a day or more ago), the password file will be deleted—probably not what was wanted:

```
# find /tmp -mtime +1 | xargs rm -f
```

This example mirrors a bug that was found in several UNIX distributions. The `cron` program, which allows users to schedule periodic execution of programs, had just such a command that was executed with super-user privileges. Because of this problem, many implementations of `find` and `xargs` now include an option (usually "`-print0`" or "`-0`") to separate file names by a null character, which should be relatively safe, because nulls, as previously noted, cannot be in a file name.

3.5 UNIX Pathnames

As mentioned earlier in this chapter, pathnames are built from strings separated by "/" characters. Although directory and file pathnames may generally be of arbitrary length, there is a limit on the length of a pathname you can specify when accessing a file. Solaris and FreeBSD currently allow 1024 characters, while Linux can go up to 4096.

These size limits for directory and file pathnames are rarely a concern for day-to-day operations, but they open up opportunities to hide information or to prevent programs from working. For instance, consider a file

---

2. For more on the POSIX and POSIX.1 standards, see the FAQ at
   http://www.opengroup.org/austin/papers/posix_faq.html.

named "foo", with a complete pathname length of 1028 bytes, composed of four directories of 255 characters each:

```
/111 . . . 111/222 . . . 222/333 . . . 333/444 . . . 444/foo
```

This file is a tricky one to access in both Solaris and FreeBSD—and if the file name were a bit longer, in Linux as well. You cannot specify the full pathname, because its length is over the limit that you may use in a system call such as `open()`. For the same reason, you cannot directly change into a very long directory pathname, because the `chdir()` system call is subject to the same restriction on pathname length as other system calls.

Programs like `find` suffer from limits that are imposed by their environment. Even without hard limits built into the software itself, such programs will ultimately fail when the directory tree is sufficiently deep, as the system runs out of memory to keep track of nesting or runs out of file descriptors for reading directories.

The basic problem is not that UNIX allows long file names and deeply nested directory trees but that you—as a programmer or a user—should be wary of trusting anything outside your sphere of control. When investigating a system, it is important to understand how that system and your tools will behave under stress or unusual circumstances. All tools have a breaking point; good ones will fail gracefully and then report the failure, along with its causes. When in doubt always exercise extreme diligence and caution.

3.6 UNIX File Types

From a user's point of view, the UNIX file system is made up of directories and an assortment of files of various types. To UNIX, however, a directory is just another type of file, one that ordinary users cannot modify directly. On a typical UNIX system, you will find regular files, directories, symbolic links, inter-process communication (IPC) endpoints, and device files.

Regular Files

A regular file is the most common type of file on a UNIX system. It contains data or software.

Directories

A directory is another type of file, but users cannot update a directory directly. Instead, this is done via primitives that create, rename, or remove a directory entry.

A directory contains all the names of files and directories within it. The basic ls(1) command is therefore easy to understand—and code—even if you know nothing about the underlying low-level details. You simply open the directory (via the opendir() function) and read the contents with the readdir() system call. The Perl program in Listing 3.2 does just that.

Symbolic Links

A symbolic link is an alias for another file name or directory. Removing a symbolic link doesn't affect the file being referred to, but be aware that any output directed at the symbolic link will affect the target, not the symbolic link.

IPC Endpoints

IPC endpoints in the file system[3] allow one process to talk to another process running on the same machine. A FIFO (also called a named pipe) may be created with the mkfifo() system call, which provides a one-way communication channel. A socket can be created with the socket() system call, which provides a two-way channel each time a connection is made.

```
$ cat ls.pl
#
# Usage: "program [directory-name]"
#
# Defaults to reading the current directory unless we give it an argument
#
$ARGV[0] = "." unless $#ARGV >= 0;

opendir(DIR, $ARGV[0]) || die "Can't open directory $ARGV[0]\n";

# read the directory, one file name at a time, and print it out
while (($next_file = readdir(DIR))) {
        print "$next_file\n";
        }
$
$ perl ls.pl /tmp
.

..
ps_data
ups_data
```

Listing 3.2 *Executing a trivial* ls *command, which prints out a directory's entries*

3. As opposed to other IPC endpoints, such as Internet sockets.

Named pipes can be trouble if they aren't connected to a data source, because a process that attempts to read the contents of such a named pipe will hang, waiting for data.

Device Files

UNIX uses device files to access hardware. The two types of device file—character and block—give access to device drivers that control disks, terminals, and so on. Typically, they are found below the /dev directory, they are created with the mknod command, and they are protected via the same file system permission bits as other files.

Block devices access the hardware via the block structure that the physical medium uses, and they employ buffering in the kernel. Disks are the primary example of a block device. Character devices can use (generally smaller) buffers as well, but they allow byte-level access (either virtual or real) to hardware, and they are not buffered as block devices are. Terminals, line printers, and physical memory are some of the more common character devices, but many block devices also have a character-device interface. Disk and tape character devices are called raw devices, and they are not buffered in the kernel.

The interface between hardware and software can cause a variety of problems. When a device has both a character and a block device interface, you may run into trouble when trying to access data through the character device, because the kernel is buffering the data and may not have written it to the actual device. We show an example of this in the next section. Device files may also be duplicated and placed anywhere on a file system. Users who have system privileges may place a normally restricted device in an unusual or hidden location that has weaker-than-desired file permissions. The FreeBSD and Linux mount command has a "nodev" option, which forbids access to block or character device files. Care must also be taken when memory-mapped devices are present on the system (for example, when registers in graphics cards are mapped to the virtual address space to improve performance. Probing or searching these memory locations—say, via /dev/mem or /dev/kmem, or the pcat command from the Coroner's Toolkit—can cause the system to freeze or even crash. (See Appendix A for details on the Coroner's Toolkit and the tools within.)

3.7 A First Look Under the Hood: File System Internals

To discuss the more unusual properties of the UNIX file system, we need to peel back its outer layer and examine some of the internals.

A UNIX directory is organized as a sequence of directory entries that are not necessarily sorted. Each directory entry consists of at least two parts: a name and a number. Directory entries in Ext3fs and modern FFS file systems also list the file type, unlike Solaris's UFS. The file name is what humans and programs normally use to access a file. The number refers to the file's inode, which is what UNIX uses internally. This number is an index into a table of so-called inode blocks, which describe all file properties except the file name. The inode block has references to the data blocks that contain the actual contents of the file. Figure 3.2 illustrates these relationships.

The inode itself contains a wealth of information about a file. At minimum, it includes the following:

- **Ownership.** The numerical user and group ID of the owner (the name and numerical user and group IDs are stored in the password and group databases).

  Some UNIX versions allow unprivileged users to transfer the ownership of files that they own to another user. This rather dangerous practice is disallowed altogether in FreeBSD and Linux systems, but the POSIX RSTCHOWN parameter can be used in Solaris and other systems to control this behavior (it is turned off by default).

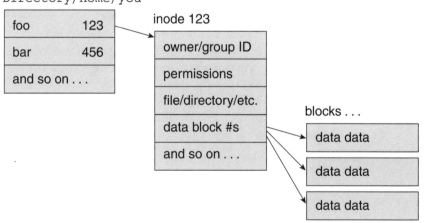

Figure 3.2 *The structure of the UNIX file system (simplified)*

- **Permissions.** For owner, group, and other access, the system examines the read, write, and execute bits associated with a file. In addition to these bits, there are the infamous set-uid and set-gid bits (allowing execution of a program with the user or group privileges of the file owner); and the sticky bit (useful only in directories), which restricts the rename or remove operations to the owner of the directory or files within the sticky directory.

  Command interpreters with set-uid or set-gid file permissions are frequently left behind by intruders as a way to regain privileged access. Always be wary of set-uid or set-gid files, but especially those that weren't installed with the vendor's operating system. The `find` command may be used to locate such files, but it's best to rely on the `nosuid` option when mounting untrusted file systems: this flag takes away the special properties of set-uid and set-gid files.

  Some file systems include support for immutable or append-only bits. The former disallows changing, moving, or deleting such a file; the latter is an immutable file that also allows data to be appended to its end (McKusick and Neville-Neil 2004).

- **File type.** There are directories, regular files, symbolic links (a file name alias), devices, named pipes (also called FIFO), sockets, and so on.

- **Hard link count.** The number of directory entries that refer to this inode. In other words, one inode may have multiple file names. A hard link should not be confused with a symbolic link, which is an alias for another file name. Hard links are also referred to simply as links.

  UNIX file systems allow a file to be removed even while it is still being accessed or executed. The directory entry is removed, but the file's inode and data blocks are still labeled as "in use" until the file is no longer needed. The Coroner's Toolkit's `ils` and `icat` may be used together to recover files that are open but have been removed.

  A file can even have entries in directories not owned by the file owner. Thus, when a file is found in a directory, the file hasn't necessarily been put there by the file's owner. The directory owner could have created the hard link with the `ln` command. It also means that a file does not necessarily go away when it is deleted! The file is deleted only when the link count is zero.

- **File size, in bytes.** With regular files, the file size is the number of bytes that can be read before reaching the end of the file. The UNIX file system has no overhead for record boundaries that silently add to a file's size.

- **Time stamps.** As we briefly saw in Chapter 2, UNIX maintains three time stamps, which we call MACtimes:

  - *Last modification time.* For directories, the last time an entry was added, renamed, or removed. For other file types, the last time the file was written to.

  - *Last access (read) time.* For directories, the last time the directory was searched. For other file types, the last time the file was read.

  - *Last status change.* Examples of status change include change of owner, change of access permission, change of hard link count, and an explicit change of any of the MACtimes.

  Ext3fs and UFS2 have two additional time stamps of interest:

  - *Deletion time.* Ext3fs records the time a file was deleted in the dtime stamp.

  - *Birth time.* UFS2, available with FreeBSD 5, records the time an inode was created in the birthtime stamp.

  We talk more about MACtimes in Chapter 4.

- **Data block addresses.** The location of the actual contents of a regular file, symbolic link, or directory. Actually, this is a bit of a simplification. For files larger than 12 blocks, the 13th data block address refers to a disk block that is dedicated entirely to storing disk block numbers. This disk block is called a *singly indirect block*; when it fills up, the 14th data block address refers to a disk block that contains the block numbers of singly indirect blocks. This disk block is called a *doubly indirect block*. UNIX file systems support up to three levels of indirection, where one data block contains the addresses of data blocks or indirect blocks.

FreeBSD and Solaris don't come with any programs to query inodes (Linux has the `stat` command, which prints the inode contents), but you may construct your own. The `stat()`, `fstat()`, and `lstat()` system calls return most of the information just described, as illustrated by this Perl code fragment:

```
($dev, $inode, $mode, $nlink, $uid, $gid, $rdev, $size,
     $atime, $mtime, $ctime, $blksize, $blocks) = lstat($filename);

print "$filename: $dev, $inode, $mode, $nlink, $uid, $gid, $rdev, $size,
     $atime, $mtime, $ctime, $blksize, $blocks\n";
```

Further information on specific inode information can be found in its corresponding file system header file or in the `stat(2)` man page.

The Coroner's Toolkit contains two programs that delve into inodology. The `ils` command reads inode contents, and the `icat` command reads the data blocks to which an inode refers. The `icat` command may be used exactly like `cat`, except that instead of accessing a file by name, `icat` accesses a file by its device name and inode number. A third tool, `fls` (Carrier 2004a), lists file and directory names similarly to `ls`. Again, instead of a pathname, one specifies a device name and an inode number.

All three tools bypass the file system and access disk blocks directly, and this is why they use device names and inode numbers instead of path-names. The tools can be used to examine not only a disk partition that contains a file system, but also a file system image—that is, a regular file that contains the contents of a disk partition. More information about how disk images are created and how they are used can be found in Chapter 4.

Earlier in this chapter, we showed how files could be hidden from `cat` under a mount point, but the dynamic duo of `fls` and `icat` will not be fooled, because they bypass the file system by utilizing a lower-level abstraction.

To demonstrate this, we show two different ways to access a file. First, `ls` reads the directory entry of a file named "foo" to recover the file name and inode number, while `cat` prints the contents via the file name. Next, `fls` and `icat` bypass the file system altogether to read directly the inode number and contents of "foo".

```
# df
Filesystem              1k-blocks       Used Available Use% Mounted on
/dev/sda1                 1008872     576128    381496  60% /
/dev/sda5                16580968   15136744    601936  96% /home
# ls -lia /research
32065      .
2          ..
96741      foo
# fls -ap /dev/sda1 32065
-/d 96193:   .
-/d 2:       ..
-/r 96741:   foo
# cat /research/foo
hello, world
# icat /dev/sda1 96741
hello, world
```

We now mount a second file system on top of the directory file "foo" lived in. When we look again, `ls` and `cat` cannot see the file, but `fls` and `icat` have no problems peering underneath the mount point.

```
# mount /dev/sdb1 /research
# ls -lia /research
      2 .
      2 ..
     11 lost+found
  32449 tmp
# fls -ap /dev/sda1 32065
-/d 96193:   .
-/d 2:       ..
-/r 96741:   foo
# cat /research/foo
cat: /research/foo: No such file or directory
# icat /dev/sda1 96741
hello, world
```

As previously mentioned, directories are simply another type of file; most file systems allow direct reading of a directory (via `strings` or `cat`), but Linux requires `icat` or some other program to directly access its contents.

Directories mounted over the network (as with NFS) often cannot be directly accessed at all. This loss of low-level detail is one of the main reasons why forensic and other serious investigative data should always be gathered directly on the computer hosting the data, rather than accessed across a network.

To further confound matters, sometimes `icat` won't get you what you want . . . but `cat` will! Watch what happens when we create a simple file and try to access the contents via the file name rather than the inode:

```
solaris# df
 Filesystem              kbytes     used    avail capacity  Mounted on
/dev/dsk/c0t0d0s7     2902015 1427898 1416077     51%    /export/home
solaris# echo hello, world > test-file
solaris# ls -i test-file
119469    test-file
solaris# cat test-file
hello, world
solaris# icat /dev/dsk/c0t0d0s7 119469
solaris# icat /dev/rdsk/c0t0d0s7 119469
hello, world
```

This is all possible because of how the file system buffers data; we see more about this in Chapter 8. In this case, the data blocks pointed to by inode number 119469 have not been written to disk yet. Trying to access them via the raw device bypasses file system buffers, so `icat` sees nothing.

An interesting feature of UNIX file systems is that when an application skips over areas without writing to them, the data blocks will not be allocated for this empty space. This happens when a program writes data after seeking past the end of a file; after the write, this hole is read as though it were full of null bytes. The Berkeley DB files (such as "file-name.db") and DBM files (such as "filename.pag"), used in USENET news history, Sendmail maps, and the like, are examples. They are sometimes called *sparse files*.

To see the difference, we use a Perl program to create two files, one with a hole and one without:

```
$ cat hole.pl
#!/usr/local/bin/perl

# Create two files, F1 and F2
open(F1, ">F1") or die "can't open F1\n";
open(F2, ">F2") or die "can't open F2\n";

# With holes
print F1 "Text before test";
seek(F1, 100000, 2);      # boldly seek where no data has gone before
print F1 "Text after test";

# Without holes
print F2 "Text before test";
print F2 "\000" x 100000;      # output 100,000 NULLS
print F2 "Text after test";

close(F1);
close(F2);
```

After executing this Perl program, look how `ls` shows the different block allocation sizes of the sparse and regular files. But when the files are run through `cmp` (a file content comparison program), no difference is shown.

```
linux $ ./hole.pl
linux $ ls -ls F1 F2
  12 -rw-------   1 zen      root          100031 May 30 15:09 F1
 104 -rw-------   1 zen      root          100031 May 30 15:09 F2
linux $ cmp F1 F2
linux $ hexdump -c F1
0000000   T   e   x   t       b   e   f   o   r   e       t   e   s   t
0000010  \0  \0  \0  \0  \0  \0  \0  \0  \0  \0  \0  \0  \0  \0  \0  \0
*
00186b0   T   e   x   t       a   f   t   e   r       t   e   s   t
00186bf
linux $
```

In particular, holes can cause problems when a program tries to read the data via the file system. It is nearly impossible to tell which nulls were written to disk and which weren't (Zwicky 1991). Also, the size of the file read and what is actually stored on the disk can be quite different. Programs that can bypass the file system (such as `dd` and `dump`) have no problems with holes, but when using the normal file system interface to copy or read the file, additional null bytes will be read. The result will be larger than what is actually on the disk.

3.8 UNIX File System Layout

Below the abstraction of inodes and data blocks lies the abstraction of zones, labels, and partitions. The typical UNIX disk partition is organized into equal-size zones, as shown in Figure 3.3. Typical zone sizes are 32768 blocks; the block size depends on the file system type, and with some systems, it also depends on the file system size. UFS, FFS, and Ext3fs use a block size that is a multiple of 1024 bytes.

Storage space is divided into multiple zones, each of which has its own copy of the superblock, allocation bitmaps, file data blocks, and file attribute (inode) blocks. Normally, information about a small file is stored entirely within one zone. Disk labels hold disk geometry data about the disk's cylinders and tracks, as well as the disk's sector and partition layout.

Excessive disk head motion is avoided by keeping related information close together. This not only reduces the fragmentation of individual file contents, it also reduces delays while traversing directories in order to access a file. Good file system locality can be expected from any file system that doesn't fragment its information randomly over the disk. The Coroner's Toolkit's `lazarus` program takes advantage of this property when attempting to reconstitute the structure of deleted or lost file system data.

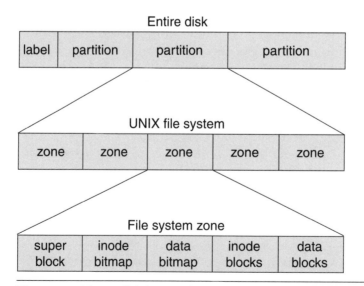

Figure 3.3 *The on-disk layout of a typical UNIX file system. The figure is not drawn to scale, and files may appear larger in your rearview mirror than they do in real life.*

3.9 I've Got You Under My Skin: Delving into the File System

When data is accessed or modified through the file system, evidence of the activity may exist in MACtime bits or in any system or kernel accounting. Instead of modifying a file through the file system, however, you may change the data blocks by writing directly to the device that contains the data in question, bypassing the file system in order to avoid leaving behind traces of file access. You'll remember that we used `fls` and `icat` to read underneath a file system; the program in Listing 3.3 modifies data by directly accessing the disk device itself and changing logs that might register an attacker's presence. It does so by reading until it sees the attacker's system name ("evil.fish.com") and replacing this with an innocuous log entry ("localhost").

Only people who are a bit carefree or on death row should attempt this with any regularity, because serious file corruption could happen when the program and the system race to write to the same block. Intruders, of course, might not care about your data as much as you do.

```
#
# Usage: "program device-file"
#

# open the device or file for both reading and writing
open(DEVICE, "+<$ARGV[0]") || die "can't open $ARGV[0]\n";

# make sure the change is the same length!
$TARGET    = "connection from \"evil.fish.com\"";
$MUTATE    = "connection from \"localhost\"      ";

$BYTESIZED = 4096;
$n = $position = 0;

while (($num_read = read(DEVICE, $block, $BYTESIZED))) {
    if ($block =~ /$TARGET/) {
        $current = tell(DEVICE);
        $block =~ s/$TARGET/$MUTATE/g;
        seek(DEVICE, $position, 0) || die "Can't seek to $position\n";
        print DEV $block;
        seek(DEVICE, $current,  0) || die "Can't seek to $position\n";
        }
    $n++;
    $position = $n * $BYTESIZED;
    }
```

Listing 3.3 *Those with guts—or using someone else's system—can bypass the file system with this Perl program.*

Unless your logs or files are kept in multiple locations or on different hosts, low-level countermeasures such as FreeBSD's `securelevel(7)` are required to truly defend against this sort of obnoxious behavior (see Section 5.6 for more about this). The changes can be detected, but even that may be difficult. Files may be compared with backups that have been saved either entirely off-line or on a different computer. Performing digital signatures on individual blocks of files is another possible tactic—you know that last week's records of log files, for instance, should rarely change after the events in question—but this approach is very cumbersome in practice. Schneier and Kelsey (1998) describe a method of protecting log files so that intruders cannot read or undetectably modify log data that was written before the system was compromised—but of course, you must have this type of mechanism in place *before* any incident occurs.

Data may be kept from disclosure or undetected modification by utilizing encryption, but in a rather unusual approach, the Steganographic File System goes even further (Anderson et al. 1998). The Steganographic File System is a way of hiding data by encrypting the data and writing it multiple times to random places on a disk. It not only keeps the data encrypted but also provides plausible mathematical deniability that data is even there. It also includes multiple layers of encryption, where the unused blocks of layer N may contain the data of a hidden file system $N + 1$. This means an investigator cannot find out if all the keys for all the levels have been surrendered. StegFS, a modified implementation of the system, uses unallocated blocks of an Ext2fs file system to hide its data (McDonald and Kuhn 1999).

3.10 The Twilight Zone, or Dangers Below the File System Interface

We've traveled up and down the file system, but there are still a few dark corners we haven't visited yet. Most UNIX computers never utilize significant amounts of space on a disk even if it is reaching "full." This is mostly due to the layers of abstraction that have been laid on top of the underlying disk: many of the things that make systems easier to use also sacrifice a bit of performance and introduce some amount of waste. For normal usage this side effect may be easily ignored—when you have a terabyte of storage, what does it matter if some amorphous gigabytes are wasted or unaccounted for? However, for someone with something to hide, the more capable a system is, the more attractive it becomes. Faster systems, with more space to store data, make it easier to conceal information and programs—and make break-ins harder to detect. And though some methods allow more room than others, all give plenty of space for malware and hidden data to rest comfortably.

Although UNIX file systems have an efficient set of algorithms that prevent serious fragmentation or wasted space under most situations, there will be a certain amount of overhead and waste in any file system. Because UFS, FFS, and Ext2fs will not write data to the disk in multiples of less than their block size, any file whose size is not an exact multiple of the block size will leave a bit of unused room (often called slack space) at the end of the data block. With a block size of 1024 bytes, a file will, on average, waste 512 bytes of space—about 50 Mbytes for each 100,000 files. The `bmap` tool can read, write, and wipe data in the slack space at the end of Ext2fs files.[4]

When a UFS, FFS, or Ext2fs file system is created by `newfs`, it reserves about 3 percent of the disk blocks for use by inodes. This is a one-size-fits-all scheme, however. There are only so many inodes to go around, and once you're out of them, you cannot create files or new inodes. For the vast majority of systems, this is more than enough; however, it also means that the majority of inodes are never used. When we examined some seventy UNIX workstations, we found that about 2.5 percent of the inodes were used (and only one system used more than half its maximum inodes). So in a 100-Gbyte file system, there will be about 3 Gbytes of virgin territory that will never be touched by the file system.

We've already seen how entire disks or partitions may be hidden or unused, and how to detect this with `fdisk` or `prtvtoc`. However, there is often a bit of space left over between disk partitions or at the tail end of a disk that may be exploited for hidden storage. Swap files or swap partitions may also be used as a potential cache, because as the prices of memory chips have fallen dramatically and their storage space has risen, swap is probably being used less frequently. Swap space could be used for some time without being overwritten.

3.11 Conclusion

The basic hierarchical file system model used by UNIX and other file systems has proven to be remarkably resilient and adaptable over the years, and we foresee it continuing to be so for some years to come.

---

4. The `bmap` tool was written by Daniel Ridge. A discussion on how to use it is available at http://www.linuxsecurity.com/feature_stories/data-hiding-forensics.html.

Some might wonder why we talk about various minutiae concerning UNIX file systems when what they really want for post-mortem analysis is the ability to copy the entire disk using a low-level software program such as dd, or using a hardware solution. The file system abstraction is useful not only in the day-to-day operations of a computer, but also in the analysis of a system, as we see in the next chapter, "File System Analysis." In addition, content-based examinations may easily be derailed by data that has been encrypted, compressed, or simply fragmented into various pieces over the disk.

As reported elsewhere (Miller et al. 2000, Zwicky 1991), UNIX system tools are prone to unexpected failure modes that result in inaccuracy or even corruption of information. Given the need for accuracy and the often serious nature of investigations, that file systems and forensic tools appear to be no different is even more alarming. Our own work is not immune. While writing this chapter, we discovered (and fixed) some problems in our own forensic software, the Coroner's Toolkit; presumably there are more problems and issues as yet undiscovered. As people try to push these complex systems to their limits—and beyond—things will break unless we are very careful indeed. Tread lightly and keep your eyes open.

CHAPTER 4

File System Analysis

4.1 Introduction

In the previous chapter, we introduced the fundamentals of UNIX file system architecture, as well as basic tools to examine information in UNIX file systems. In this chapter, we show how to apply these tools to post-mortem intrusion analysis. We use information from a real break-in, slightly edited to protect the guilty and the innocent.

After a brief introduction to the break-in, we describe how to duplicate (that is, image) a disk for analysis and how to access a disk image for off-line analysis on another machine. We examine existing and deleted file information, and we correlate the information for consistency. Our reconstruction includes such fine detail that we can even see where a file was created before it was renamed to its final location. In the end, we reveal how our case study differs from the average intrusion.

The analysis described in this chapter is based on an older version of the Linux Ext2fs file system. Some data recovery details have changed in the meantime, as file system software has evolved. We keep you informed where these differences matter as we walk through the analysis.

4.2 First Contact

On September 25, at 00:44:49 in the U.S. Central time zone, someone sent a nastygram to a Red Hat 6.2 Linux machine belonging to an acquaintance. The attack was aimed at the `rpc.statd` service, which is part of the family of NFS file-sharing protocols. NFS was popularized in the mid-1980s by Sun Microsystems, and implementations exist for many UNIX and non-UNIX systems. The intruder gained access to the system

59

within seconds and came back later that same day. The following information was found in the system log files:

```
Sep 25 00:44:49 dionysis rpc.statd[335]: gethostbyname error for
    [. . . a very long, nonconforming host name . . . ]
Sep 25 00:45:16 dionysis inetd[473]: extra conf for service
    telnet/tcp (skipped)
Sep 25 00:45:28 dionysis in.telnetd[11554]: connect from 10.83.81.7
Sep 25 01:02:02 dionysis inetd[473]: pid 11554: exit status 1
Sep 25 17:31:47 dionysis in.telnetd[12031]: connect from 10.83.81.7
Sep 25 17:32:08 dionysis in.telnetd[12035]: connect from 10.83.81.7
```

This was a popular break-in technique, involving a well-known "format string" vulnerability in the `rpc.statd` service (CVE 2000). The intruder's exploit program overwrote some memory and took full control over the `rpc.statd` process. This in turn gave full control over the entire system because, like many services, the `rpc.statd` process runs with super-user privileges, whether it needs them or not.

4.3 Preparing the Victim's File System for Analysis

When doing a post-mortem analysis, we make trade-offs that depend on how much time and other resources are available. At one extreme, we're given very little time to gather information while the compromised machine is left running. The `grave-robber` tool in the Coroner's Toolkit is optimized for this scenario. It captures volatile information about processes and network connections, file attributes such as access time stamps, configuration files, log files, and assorted other files. The result is stored in a database that is meant to be transferred to an analysis system. This approach captures the volatile state of processes and networks, but it also has disadvantages. The accuracy of the information depends strongly on the integrity of the compromised machine. For example, if the kernel has been subverted, then process, network, or file information may be incomplete or even misleading. Furthermore, if the machine has been booby-trapped with a logic bomb, our actions may result in the destruction of information. We cover the basics of subversion in Chapter 5.

Another limitation of "live" data collection is that the procedure cannot be reproduced, because information changes due to system activity and due to our own irreversible actions. These side effects may raise questions about the integrity of the evidence collected, an issue that needs to be weighed against the value of the evidence itself.

At the other extreme is the more traditional approach: halt the machine, remove the disks, and make copies of the data for forensic analysis. This approach can be 100 percent reproducible but has the obvious disadvantage that it misses all the dynamic state information. However, if something is rapidly destroying information by deleting or overwriting data, then losing the dynamic state is preferable to losing everything. For more discussion on the options for capturing system information after an incident, refer to Appendix B.

The approach taken in this chapter lies closer to the second extreme. The owner of the compromised system provided us with copies of disk partitions for analysis, but he gave us no dynamic state information. The disk partition copies were made while the disks were attached to the compromised machine. The use of a relatively low-level copying procedure (as we discuss in the next section) limited the possibility of data corruption by the compromised machine. So our results are only slightly less accurate than what they could have been in the ideal case. Leaving the disks attached to the compromised machine avoids the need to arrange for compatible controller hardware and driver software in order to access the victim's disk drives, which can be a problem with RAID systems or with non-PC hardware, for example.

4.4 Capturing the Victim's File System Information

There are several ways to duplicate file system information. Which method is available depends on circumstances. Both authors remember capturing information by logging in to a compromised machine, listing files to the terminal, and recording the session with a terminal emulator program. In order of increasing accuracy, here are some methods to capture information:

- **Copying individual files.** This is the least accurate approach, because it captures only the contents of files. No meta-information is captured, except perhaps the file size. (Note, however, that holes in files become indistinguishable from zero-filled blocks, increasing the apparent file size; see Section 3.7 for more about files that contain holes in their block allocation map.) All other meta-information, such as file ownership, access times, permissions, and so on, is lost unless it is saved by some other means. For example, the `grave-robber` utility from the Coroner's Toolkit copies selected files (such as configuration files and logs) after saving their meta-information to a so-called `body` file.

- **Making a backup.** Depending on the backup software used, this method preserves some meta-information, such as ownership, information about hard links, and last modification time, but it does not capture the last read access time. Commonly used UNIX utilities are `tar`, `cpio`, and `dump`. The drawback of making a backup is that what you see is all you get. Backups do not capture information about deleted files.

- **Copying individual disk partitions.** This method creates a bit-for-bit, identical copy of each file system, including all the meta-information and all the information that sits in unallocated space at the ends of files, between files, in unallocated inode blocks, and so on. This is typically done with the dd command. A major benefit of this approach is that it is file system neutral. For example, the same technique can be used to copy UNIX and Windows partitions alike. The downside is that one still misses data that is stored between and outside partitions. The following command fragments read the first UNIX partition on the first disk. Then we would either direct the output to a local disk image file or send it across the network, as discussed in the next section.

```
linux#   dd if=/dev/hda1 bs=100k . . .
freebsd# dd if=/dev/da0s1a bs=100k . . .
solaris# dd if=/dev/dsk/c0t0d0s0 bs=100k . . .
```

- **Copying the entire disk.** This time, the result is a bit-for-bit, identical copy of all accessible information on the disk, including storage space before and after disk partitions. This can be necessary when suspicion exists that data could be hidden outside disk partitions. Again, dd is the preferred command for doing this. Even this method has limitations, however. It will not read disk blocks that have developed errors and that the hardware has silently remapped to so-called spare blocks. Nor will this method give access to unused spare blocks, because they lie outside the normally accessible area of the disk. The following command fragments read all accessible blocks on the first disk:

```
linux#   dd if=/dev/hda bs=100k . . .
freebsd# dd if=/dev/da0 bs=100k . . .
solaris# dd if=/dev/c0t0d0s2 bs=100k . . .
```

The accuracy of the captured information increases as our dependence on the integrity of the compromised system decreases. For example, when we capture individual files while logged in to the victim machine, subverted application or kernel software can distort the result. Subversion is much less likely when we use a low-level disk-imaging procedure, with the disk drive connected to a trusted machine.

In this chapter, we focus on the analysis of disk images that were produced by copying individual disk partitions. To find out what partitions exist on a disk, we use fdisk on Linux, disklabel on BSD, or prtvtoc on Solaris. Some operating systems (such as BSD and Solaris) have a convention in which the third partition of a disk always spans the entire disk. In that case, it can be sufficient to copy the "whole disk" partition. Of course, we still need to record how that whole disk was organized into partitions, or else we may run into problems later when trying to make sense of the disk.

4.5 Sending a Disk Image Across the Network

When the disks remain attached to the victim machine, the disk-imaging procedure can be as simple as using Hobbit's Netcat to copy the disk image across the network to a drop-off machine (Hobbit 1996). (At this time, we do not recommend using GNU Netcat, because of code maturity problems.) When possible, use a copy that is run directly from a trusted CD-ROM. For examples of bootable CD-ROMs with ready-to-run forensic tools, see FIRE 2004, KNOPPIX 2004a, or KNOPPIX 2004b.

In this section, we give two examples of creating a disk image file of the victim's /dev/hda1 partition. The first example is the simplest, but it should be used only over a trusted network. A trusted network can be created by first removing the victim machine from the network and then connecting it directly to the investigator's machine. If a trusted network is not available, we need to use additional measures—which we discuss shortly—to protect forensic data in transit against modification or eavesdropping.

A warning is in order: disk imaging over a network can take a lot of time, because the capacity of disks grows much faster than the bandwidth of local area networks. In the days when 2-Gbyte disks were common, imaging over 10-Mbit-per-second Ethernet took less than an hour. Imaging a 200-Gbyte disk over 100-Mbit-per-second Ethernet takes ten times as long. Slower networks are hopeless unless data can be compressed dramatically. (We have some suggestions at the end of this chapter, though these are applicable under limited conditions only.)

Figure 4.1 shows the disk-imaging procedure for a trusted network. To receive a disk image of the victim's /dev/hda1 file system on network port 1234, we run Netcat as a server on the receiving machine:

```
receiver$ nc -l -p 1234 > victim.hda1
```

To send the disk image to the receiving host's network port 1234, we run Netcat as a client on the sending machine:

```
sender# dd if=/dev/hda1 bs=100k | nc -w 1 receiving-host 1234
```

Imaging all the partitions on one or more disks is a matter of repeating the preceding procedure for each partition, including the swap partition and other non-file system partitions that may be present.

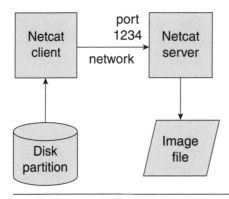

Figure 4.1 *Sending a disk partition image over a trusted network*

When the network cannot be trusted, data encryption and data signing should be used to ensure privacy and integrity. As shown in Figure 4.2, we still use Netcat to send and receive the disk image, but we use `ssh` to set up an encrypted tunnel between receiving machine and sending machine. The tunnel endpoint on the sending machine encrypts and signs the data after it enters the tunnel, while the tunnel endpoint on the receiving machine verifies and decrypts the data before it leaves the tunnel.

On the receiving host, we use the same Netcat command as before to receive a disk image of partition `/dev/hda1` on network port 1234:

```
receiver$ nc -l -p 1234 > victim.hda1
```

In a different terminal window, we set up the encrypted `ssh` tunnel that forwards the disk image from network port 2345 on the sending host to network port 1234 on the receiving host. The `-x` option is needed for

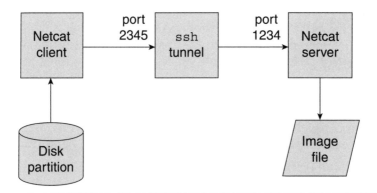

Figure 4.2 *Sending a disk image through an encrypted network tunnel*

security, and it prevents `ssh` from exposing the local display, keyboard, and mouse to the victim machine. The `-z` option enables data compression and should be used only when sending data over a nonlocal network.

```
receiver$ ssh sender -x -z -R 2345:localhost:1234
```

To set up the tunnel, we must log in from the receiving machine to the compromised machine. Doing the reverse—logging in from the compromised machine to the receiving machine—would expose a password or an `ssh` secret key to the compromised machine.

On the sending machine, we use Netcat to send the disk image to local port 2345, so that the `ssh` tunnel forwards the disk image to port 1234 on the receiving machine:

```
sender# dd if=/dev/hda1 bs=100k | nc -w 1 localhost 2345
```

The same trick can be used to deliver other data to the receiving machine, such as the output from the Coroner's Toolkit's `grave-robber` or from other commands that examine dynamic state.

As a finishing touch, we can compute a cryptographic hash of the image file and store the result in a safe off-line location. This allows us to verify later that the disk image file has not been changed. For example, to compute the MD5 hash on Linux, one would use the following:

```
receiver$  md5sum victim.hda1 >victim.hda1.md5
```

On BSD systems, the command is called `md5`. At the time of writing, the MD5 algorithm is reaching the end of its life; future applications should consider using the SHA-1 algorithm instead.

4.6 Mounting Disk Images on an Analysis Machine

Some care is needed when mounting a disk image from an untrusted machine. We recommend using the `noexec` mount option to disallow execution of untrusted programs on the disk image; this helps to prevent contamination of the analysis machine by unintended execution of malicious software. Another useful mount option is `nodev`, which disables device files in the imaged file system; this prevents all kinds of accidents when a disk image contains device file nodes. On Solaris, the `nosuid` option can be used to disable devices. And needless to say, the image should be mounted as read-only to avoid disturbing the data.

To examine the partitions of an imaged disk, we could copy each partition image to a disk partition of matching size, and then mount the file system

What If Netcat Is Not Available?

If no Netcat command or equivalent is available for the victim machine (either installed on disk or in the form of a ready-to-run executable file on a CD-ROM), then one of the least attractive options is to download 200 Kbytes of source files and compile a C program to create the Netcat executable program. Such an approach could do a lot of damage to deleted and existing information. For similar reasons, it may be undesirable to download and install a precompiled package. In such situations, instead of using Netcat, which has many features we don't need, we have found that the following minimal Perl program will do the job just fine:

```perl
#!/usr/bin/perl

# ncc - minimal Netcat client in Perl
# Usage: ncc host port

use IO::Socket;
$SIG{PIPE} = 'IGNORE';
$buflen = 102400;

die "usage: $0 host port\n" unless ($host = shift)
                                && ($port = shift);

die "connect to $host:$port: $!\n" unless
    $sock = new IO::Socket::INET(PeerAddr => $host,
                                 PeerPort => $port,
                                 proto => 'tcp');

while (($count = sysread(STDIN, $buffer, $buflen)) > 0) {
    die "socket write error: $!\n"
        unless syswrite($sock, $buffer, $count) == $count;
}
die "socket read error: $!\n" if $count < 0;
die "close socket: $!\n" unless close($sock);
```

as usual. However, this is not a convenient approach, because it requires partitioning a disk. It is more convenient to store the data from each imaged partition as an ordinary file. This works fine with low-level forensic utilities such as `ils`, `icat`, `fls`, and `unrm`. For those tools, it makes no difference whether information is stored in a file or in a disk partition.

However, before we can access a disk partition image file as a real file system, we need to trick the operating system into believing that a regular file is a disk partition. Many operating systems have this ability built in.

- Linux has a loopback device that will take a regular file and then make it accessible as a block device, so that it can be mounted as a file system:

```
# mount victim.hda1 /victim -r -t ext2 -o loop,noexec,nodev
```

This mounts the file victim.hda1 on the directory /victim, making the contents of the partition accessible as a read-only file system.

- FreeBSD has a facility called *vnode pseudo-disk devices,* which can be used to access a regular file as a block device, so that it can be mounted as a file system:

```
# vnconfig vn0 victim.sd0a
# mount -r -t ufs -o noexec,nodev /dev/vn0 /victim
```

This mounts the file victim.sd0a on the directory /victim, making the contents of the partition accessible as a read-only file system. In all respects, the result is the same as in the previous Linux section.

- Solaris version 8 and later has the lofiadm command, which can be used to mount a file system image much like FreeBSD and Linux:

```
# lofiadm -a victim.c0d0s0
    /dev/lofi/1
# mount -F ufs -o ro,noexec,nosuid /dev/lofi/1 /victim
```

This mounts the file victim.c0d0s0 on the directory /victim, making the contents of the partition accessible as a read-only file system. In all respects, the result is the same as in the previous Linux and FreeBSD sections.

The preceding examples are for image files that contain exactly one disk partition. Things get more complicated with images of entire disks that contain multiple partitions. To mount a partition from such an image file, we have to specify what part of the disk image file to mount. The Linux loopback mechanism supports the -o *offset* option to specify a byte offset with the start of the data of interest. At the time of writing, such an option is not available with Solaris or FreeBSD. A workaround is to use the dd skip=*offset* feature to copy a partition to an individual image file.

One note of caution is in order. When we mount a disk image under /victim instead of its usual place in the file system hierarchy, all file names change. While having to prepend the string /victim to every pathname is burdensome enough for the investigator, this is not an option for absolute pathnames that are embedded in the file system image itself. For example, symbolic links may resolve to the wrong file or directory, and mount points within a file system image may no longer be overlaid by another file system tree. In our experience, it is very easy to wander off into the wrong place.

4.7 Existing File MACtimes

For a post-mortem analysis of the `rpc.statd` break-in, the owner of the machine provided us with a disk image of the victim machine, in the form of one image file per file system. The disk image was made a day after the intrusion, shortly after the owner found out about it. Unfortunately, the Netcat command had to be brought into the machine first, which destroyed some evidence. We mounted the image files on a Linux analysis machine via the Linux loopback device, as described in the previous section. First we present information from existing files; we look at deleted file information later.

We used the `grave-robber` utility from the Coroner's Toolkit to examine the file system images. In the command that follows, `-c /victim` specifies that a disk image was mounted under the `/victim` directory, `-o LINUX2` specifies the operating system type of the disk image, and `-m -i` requests that `grave-robber` collect information about existing and deleted files. To bypass file permission restrictions, this part of the analysis had to be done with super-user permissions.

```
# grave-robber -c /victim -o LINUX2 -m -i
```

This command produced a `body` file with file name and numerical file attribute information. The `grave-robber` utility stored the file in a directory named after the host and the time of day. This information was subsequently sorted with the `mactime` utility from the Coroner's Toolkit, using the full command as shown next. The `-p` and `-g` options specify the disk image's user database files, which are needed to convert numerical file ownership attributes back to the correct user and group names. We specified `1/1/1970` as the time threshold because `mactime` won't produce output unless a time threshold is specified.

```
# mactime -p /victim/etc/passwd -g /image/etc/group \
  1/1/1970 >mactime.out
```

This command produces a report with times according to the default time zone. If the disk image comes from a system with a different time zone, we need to override that information. For example, the following commands cause all time conversions to be done for the U.S. Central time zone—that is, the zone where the disk image originated:

```
$ TZ=CST6CDT; export TZ   (/bin/sh syntax)
$ setenv TZ CST6CDT       (/bin/csh syntax)
```

The MACtime report in Listing 4.1 covers the time of the incident, as known from system log files. (We introduce this report format in Chapter 2.) At first sight, the report may seem overwhelming, but this should not discourage you. As we see in the next sections, the analysis becomes quite straightforward once we start to identify small chunks of related information.

```
Sep 25 00:45:15
    Size MAC Permission Owner File name
   20452 m.c -rwxr-xr-x root  /victim/bin/prick
  207600 .a.  -rwxr-xr-x root  /victim/usr/bin/as
   63376 .a.  -rwxr-xr-x root  /victim/usr/bin/egcs
   63376 .a.  -rwxr-xr-x root  /victim/usr/bin/gcc
   63376 .a.  -rwxr-xr-x root  /victim/usr/bin/i386-redhat-linux-gcc
    2315 .a.  -rw-r--r-- root  /victim/usr/include/_G_config.h
    1297 .a.  -rw-r--r-- root  /victim/usr/include/bits/stdio_lim.h
    4680 .a.  -rw-r--r-- root  /victim/usr/include/bits/types.h
    9512 .a.  -rw-r--r-- root  /victim/usr/include/features.h
    1021 .a.  -rw-r--r-- root  /victim/usr/include/gnu/stubs.h
   11673 .a.  -rw-r--r-- root  /victim/usr/include/libio.h
   20926 .a.  -rw-r--r-- root  /victim/usr/include/stdio.h
    4951 .a.  -rw-r--r-- root  /victim/usr/include/sys/cdefs.h
 1440240 .a.  -rwxr-xr-x root  /victim/usr/lib/[. . .]/cc1
   45488 .a.  -rwxr-xr-x root  /victim/usr/lib/[. . .]/collect2
   87312 .a.  -rwxr-xr-x root  /victim/usr/lib/[. . .]/cpp
    5794 .a.  -rw-r--r-- root  /victim/usr/lib/[. . .]/include/stdarg.h
    9834 .a.  -rw-r--r-- root  /victim/usr/lib/[. . .]/include/stddef.h
    1926 .a.  -rw-r--r-- root  /victim/usr/lib/[. . .]/specs
Sep 25 00:45:16
       0 m.c -rw-r--r-- root  /victim/etc/hosts.allow
       0 m.c -rw-r--r-- root  /victim/etc/hosts.deny
    3094 mac -rw-r--r-- root  /victim/etc/inetd.conf
  205136 .a.  -rwxr-xr-x root  /victim/usr/bin/ld
  176464 .a.  -rwxr-xr-x root  /victim/usr/bin/strip
    3448 m..  -rwxr-xr-x root  /victim/usr/bin/xstat
    8512 .a.  -rw-r--r-- root  /victim/usr/lib/crt1.o
    1124 .a.  -rw-r--r-- root  /victim/usr/lib/crti.o
     874 .a.  -rw-r--r-- root  /victim/usr/lib/crtn.o
    1892 .a.  -rw-r--r-- root  /victim/usr/lib/[. . .]/crtbegin.o
    1424 .a.  -rw-r--r-- root  /victim/usr/lib/[. . .]/crtend.o
  769892 .a.  -rw-r--r-- root  /victim/usr/lib/[. . .]/libgcc.a
  314936 .a.  -rwxr-xr-x root  /victim/usr/lib/libbfd-2.9.5.0.22.so
     178 .a.  -rw-r--r-- root  /victim/usr/lib/libc.so
   69994 .a.  -rw-r--r-- root  /victim/usr/lib/libc_nonshared.a
```

Listing 4.1 *A MACtime report for the time of first contact. Times are shown relative to the time zone of the compromised machine. Files are indicated by their name, with* /victim *prepended. The MAC column indicates the file access method (modify, read access, or status change). File names with identical time stamps are sorted alphabetically. To keep the example readable, very long file names are shortened with* [. . .].

The majority of the MACtimes in Listing 4.1 resulted from compiling a program with the gcc compiler. This must have been a relatively simple program: only generic include files and generic object library files were accessed. Later in the analysis, we encounter a program that was probably built at this stage of the intrusion.

4.8 Detailed Analysis of Existing Files

For a more in-depth analysis, we break up the overwhelmingly large MACtime report into smaller chunks of related information. While we explore the MACtimes, we examine other pieces of information, as appropriate.

The MACtimes revealed that the intruder left behind two new files: /bin/prick and /usr/bin/xstat. Comparison with a pristine Red Hat 6.2 system revealed that neither program is part of the system software. The presence of these two files in system directories immediately raised multiple red flags.

```
Sep 25 00:45:15    20452 m.c -rwxr-xr-x root  /victim/bin/prick
Sep 25 00:45:16     3448 m.. -rwxr-xr-x root  /victim/usr/bin/xstat
```

The file /bin/prick was identified by its MD5 hash as an unmodified copy of the original Red Hat 6.2 /bin/login program, which authenticates users when they log in to the system.

```
$ md5sum /victim/bin/prick
9b34aed9ead767d9e9b84f80d7454fc0  /victim/bin/prick
```

Cryptographic hashes such as MD5 or SHA-1 prove their value when we have to compare an unknown file against a large list of known files. Instead of comparing the files themselves, we can save a lot of time and space by comparing their hashes instead. Known file hashes are maintained in databases such as the Known Goods database (Known Goods 2004), the NIST National Software Reference Library (NIST 2004), and the Solaris fingerprint database (Dasan et al. 2001). In this particular case, we worked with our own database of MD5 hashes for all the files on a known-to-be-good Red Hat 6.2 machine.

The fact that /bin/prick was a copy of the original /bin/login program immediately raised a question: What had happened to the /bin/login program itself? To our surprise, the file status change time revealed that the /bin/login file was updated later in the day, at 17:34, when the intruder returned for another visit. It was no longer possible to see what the /bin/login file had looked like right after the initial intrusion session, which happened 45 minutes after midnight. As we found out later, the file modification time dates from before the time the file was brought into the system.

```
Aug 18 01:10:16    12207 m.. -rwxr-xr-x root  /victim/bin/login
Sep 25 17:34:20    12207 ..c -rwxr-xr-x root  /victim/bin/login
```

The strings command reveals text messages, file names, and other text that is embedded in program files or in other files. A quick inspection with this tool revealed that the file /usr/bin/xstat had references to both /bin/prick (the copy of the unmodified /bin/login program) and /bin/sh (the standard UNIX command interpreter). As we have found repeatedly, files that reference both a login program and a command interpreter program are highly suspicious. Invariably, they allow some users to bypass the system login procedure.

```
$ strings /victim/usr/bin/xstat
/lib/ld-linux.so.2
__gmon_start__
libc.so.6
getenv
execve
perror
system
__deregister_frame_info
strcmp
exit
_IO_stdin_used
__libc_start_main
__register_frame_info
GLIBC_2.0
PTRh
DISPLAY
/bin/prick
/bin/sh
```

A full reverse-engineering analysis would occupy too much space here; see Chapter 6 for an analysis of back-door software. In the case of the xstat file, the back-door password had to be provided with the DISPLAY environment variable. This information is propagated via remote logins with the telnet protocol and normally specifies the name of a user's X Windows display. The relevant C code fragment is this:

```
display = getenv("DISPLAY");
[. . .]
if (strcmp(display, "lsd") == 0)
    system("/bin/sh");
```

To be useful as a login back door, this program would have to be installed as /bin/login. Only users with the right DISPLAY setting would gain unrestricted access to the machine; other users would have to authenticate as usual, and they would be none the wiser about the login back door's existence. Entering through the back door would be a matter of typing one simple command:

```
$ DISPLAY=lsd telnet victim.host
```

Why then wasn't this xstat back-door program installed as /bin/login? Well, it probably was installed that way at some earlier time. The next

MACtime fragment shows that the `/usr/bin/xstat` file status change time was suspiciously close to the time when the intruder installed the present `/bin/login` program during the visit at 17:34:

```
Sep 25 00:45:16    3448 m.. -rwxr-xr-x root  /victim/usr/bin/xstat
Sep 25 17:34:17    3448 ..c -rwxr-xr-x root  /victim/usr/bin/xstat
Sep 25 17:34:20   12207 ..c -rwxr-xr-x root  /victim/bin/login
```

The MACtime information is perfectly consistent with the following scenario: At 00:45:16, during the initial intrusion session, an intruder installed the first `/bin/login` back-door program, with references to `/bin/prick` (the original login program) and `/bin/sh` (giving full system access). At 17:34:17, during a second visit, an intruder renamed the `/bin/login` back door to `/usr/bin/xstat`. Then at 17:34:20, only three seconds later, that intruder installed the new `/bin/login` back-door program, this time with references to `/usr/bin/xstat` (the 00:45:16 login back-door program) and `/bin/sh`. At this point, two levels of login back doors were installed on the machine. As if one back door wasn't enough . . . .

4.9 Wrapping Up the Existing File Analysis

Let's recapitulate what we have found up to this point, just by looking at existing file information. Logging shows that an intruder exploited a well-known `rpc.statd` vulnerability at 00:44:49. MACtimes of existing files reveal that the intruder installed a login back-door program at 00:45:16. As the finishing touch on the initial intrusion, all that needed to be done was to enable the back door. What follows is based on the contents of log files and configuration files.

At 00:45:16, the intruder added an entry to the `/etc/inetd.conf` configuration file, to enable logins via the telnet service.

```
Sep 25 00:45:16    3094 mac -rw-r--r-- root  /victim/etc/inetd.conf
```

This network service was already enabled at the time, causing the `inetd` process to log a warning about a duplicate service:

```
Sep 25 00:45:16 dionysis inetd[473]: extra conf for service
    telnet/tcp (skipped)
```

The duplicate telnet service entry was still present in the `/etc/inetd.conf` file, in the file system images that the system owner had provided to us:

```
$ grep telnet /victim/etc/inetd.conf
telnet  stream  tcp   nowait  root    /usr/sbin/tcpd  in.telnetd
telnet  stream  tcp   nowait  root    /usr/sbin/tcpd  in.telnetd
```

Besides changing the `inetd` configuration file to enable telnet connections, the intruder also truncated the TCP Wrapper's `/etc/hosts.allow` and `/etc/hosts.deny` files to zero length. These files normally specify policies for access from the network to services on the local machine. Presumably, the files were truncated to disable any policies that could interfere with intruder access to the telnet service.

```
Sep 25 00:45:16      0 m.c -rw-r--r-- root  /victim/etc/hosts.allow
                     0 m.c -rw-r--r-- root  /victim/etc/hosts.deny
```

At 00:45:28, a telnet connection was made to verify that the back door was functional. The connection was terminated in an abnormal manner after 994 seconds.[1] No MACtime information was found that revealed what happened in this session, if anything happened at all.

```
Sep 25 00:45:28 dionysis in.telnetd[11554]: connect from 10.83.81.7
Sep 25 01:02:02 dionysis inetd[473]: pid 11554: exit status 1
```

That was all for the night. The intruder returned later in the day at 17:34, replaced the initial login back-door program with the second one, and installed the `floodnet` distributed denial-of-service software. But let's not get ahead of things.

Our next step is to look for clues from deleted files. These clues can confirm or contradict our earlier findings, or they can even reveal completely new information. First we have to discuss what happens when file information is deleted.

4.10 Intermezzo: What Happens When a File Is Deleted?

Deleting a file has a directly visible effect: the file name disappears from a directory listing. What happens under the hood depends on system internals. Some file systems (such as Microsoft's FAT16 and FAT32 file systems) mark the file as deleted by hiding the file name in a special manner. Traditionally, the Berkeley Fast File System (FFS) breaks all the connections between directory entry, file attributes, and file data blocks. FFS descendants are commonly found on Solaris and BSD systems. With 2.2 Linux kernels, the Linux Ext2fs file system marks the directory entry as

---

1. In reality, the connection was broken after 1000 seconds. An attempt by the author to look up the client host name failed after about 5 seconds, because no proper IP address to host name mapping was set up in the DNS. Because of this, the connection was not logged until 5 seconds after it was completed. We suspect that the connection was broken after 1000 seconds as the result of a timeout, not as the result of a deliberate action.

unused, but it preserves the connections between directory entry, file attributes, and file data blocks. With 2.4 Linux kernels, deleting a file has become more destructive, so that Ext2fs no longer preserves the connections between directory entries and file attributes. On the other hand, some of the 4.4 BSD derived systems do preserve connections between directory entries and file attributes. Table 4.1 summarizes what information is preserved and what information is destroyed when a file is deleted.

The discussion in this section is limited to FFS (McKusick et al. 1984) and descendants, including Solaris UFS, as well as Linux Ext2fs (Card et al. 1994) and its descendants. In all cases, we assume access to a local file sys-

Table 4.1 *The effect of file deletion on file names, file and directory attributes, and file contents, for typical UNIX file systems. See the text for a description of the system-dependent effects.*

File Property	Location	Effect of File Deletion
Directory entry	Directory data blocks	Marked as unallocated
File name		Preserved
Inode number		System dependent
Directory attributes	Directory inode block	
Last read access time		Deletion time
Last write access time		Deletion time
Last attribute change time		Deletion time
File attributes	File inode block	Marked as unallocated
Owner		Preserved
Group ownership		Preserved
Last read access time		Preserved
Last write access time		System dependent
Last attribute change time		Deletion time
Deletion time (if available)		Deletion time
Directory reference count		Zero
File type		System dependent
Access permissions		System dependent
File size		System dependent
Data block addresses		System dependent
File contents	File data blocks	Preserved, marked as unallocated

tem. Remote file systems normally give no access to unallocated or deleted file information.

Parent Directory Entry

When a file is deleted, the directory entry with the file name and inode number is marked as unused. Typically, the inode number is set to zero, so that the file name becomes disconnected from any file information. This behavior is found on Solaris systems. Some FreeBSD UFS and Linux Ext2fs implementations preserve the inode number in the directory entry.

Names of deleted files can still be found by reading the directory with the `strings` command. Unfortunately, Linux does not allow directories to be read by user programs. To work around this restriction, one can use the `icat` utility (copy file by inode number) from the Coroner's Toolkit. The following command lists file names in the root directory (inode number 2) of the `hda1` file system:

```
# icat /dev/hda1 2 | strings
```

A more sophisticated tool for exploring deleted directory entries is the `fls` utility (list directory entries) from the Sleuth Kit software package (Carrier 2004a). This utility also bypasses the file system and any restrictions that it attempts to impose. The following command lists deleted directory entries in the root directory (inode 2) of the `hda1` file system:

```
# fls -d /dev/hda1 2
```

As we have seen in Chapter 3, `fls` can also recursively process all directories in a file system, including directories that are hidden under mount points. We use `fls` again later in this chapter.

Parent Directory Attributes

As a side effect of the directory entry update, the directory's last read, last modification, and last status change attributes are all set to the time of that update. Thus, even if the deleted file itself is no longer available, the directory's last modification time will still reveal past activity within that directory.

Inode Blocks

On UNIX systems, a deleted file may still be active. Some process may still have the file open for reading or writing, or both, or some process may still be executing code from the file. All further file deletion operations are postponed until the file is no longer active. In this state of suspended deletion, the inode is still allocated, but it has a reference count of zero. The `ils` utility (list file by inode number) from the Coroner's Toolkit has an option to find such files. The following command shows all the deleted but still active files in the `hda1` file system:

```
# ils -o /dev/hda1
```

Once a file is really deleted, the inode block is marked as unused in the inode allocation bitmap. Some file attribute information is destroyed (as shown in Table 4.1), but a lot of information is preserved. In particular, Linux 2.2 Ext2fs implementations preserve the connections between the file inode block and its file data blocks. With older and later Linux implementations, some or all data block addresses are lost.

Data Blocks

Deleted file data blocks are marked as unused in the data block allocation bitmap, but their contents are left alone. The Linux Ext2fs file system has an option to erase file data blocks upon file deletion, but that feature is currently unimplemented. As a rule, file data blocks are no longer connected with the file in any way, except on Linux 2.2 Ext2fs, where all data blocks remain connected to the inode block. On those Linux systems, the following command recovers the data blocks from a file in partition `hda1` with inode number 154881:

```
# icat /dev/hda1 154881 > recovered.hda1.154881
```

In this case, the output file should be created in a file system different from the file system from which deleted files are being recovered.

4.11 Deleted File MACtimes

To resume the intrusion analysis, let's briefly summarize our findings. MACtime analysis of existing files reveals indications that someone compiled a relatively simple C program at 00:45:15, and that he or she installed a back-door `/bin/login` program at 00:45:16. This `/bin/login` program was apparently replaced later in the day with another one when the intruder returned for a second visit, and it can still be found as `/usr/bin/xstat`.

As a first step in our analysis (see Section 4.7), we used the `grave-robber` utility to collect information from the imaged file system:

```
# grave-robber -c /victim -o LINUX2 -m -i
```

The `-i` option requested that information be collected about inodes of deleted files. Older Coroner's Toolkit releases require running an `ils2mac` utility to convert this into a format that `mactime` understands. Newer versions automatically merge the information into the `body` file.

We then ran the `mactime` command to process the deleted file information. What follows is the deleted file MACtime information that corresponds to the time of the initial intrusion session. Deleted files are indicated by the file system image file name (for example, `victim.hda8`) and by their file inode number (such as 30199). Because the victim machine used the Linux Ext2fs file system, a wealth of deleted file information is available for investigation.

```
Sep 25 00:45:15    20452 .a. -rwxr-xr-x root  <victim.hda8-30199>
                     537 ma. -rw-r--r-- root  <victim.hda8-30207>
Sep 25 00:45:16        0 mac -rw------- root  <victim.hda8-22111>
                       0 mac -rw------- root  <victim.hda8-22112>
                       0 mac -rw-r--r-- root  <victim.hda8-22113>
                   20452 ..c -rwxr-xr-x root  <victim.hda8-30199>
                     537 ..c -rw-r--r-- root  <victim.hda8-30207>
                   12335 mac -rwxr-xr-x root  <victim.hda8-30209>
                    3448 m.. -rwxr-xr-x root  <victim.hda8-30210>
```

4.12 Detailed Analysis of Deleted Files

We used the `icat` command from the Coroner's Toolkit (see Section 4.10) to recover the contents of the deleted files. Unfortunately, the two files with inode numbers 30207 and 30209 were unrecoverable: the result contained all or mostly null bytes. We searched the file system for other existing or deleted files with the same file sizes, but nothing came up that could be linked to the intrusion.

Our attempts to recover the three zero-length deleted files with inode numbers 22111 through 22113 produced the expected result: zero bytes. Examination with the Coroner's Toolkit's `ils` command revealed not only that these inodes had a zero file-length field, but also that their fields for data block addresses were all zero as well. Presumably, the files were truncated before they were deleted. If these files ever contained data, then the prospects for recovery would be grim, as their data blocks would have to be scraped from the unused disk space.

However, we noticed that these three deleted files had inode numbers (22111–22113) that were very different from those of the other deleted files (which lie around inode number 30200). This was a clue that the three files were created in a different part of the file system. See Section 4.14 for insights that can be gleaned from inode numbers.

File recovery with `icat` was more successful with the other two deleted files. The deleted file with inode number 30199 was easily identified by its MD5 hash as a copy of the Red Hat 6.2 login program. The complete MACtime information for this deleted file was this:

```
Mar 07 04:29:44    20452 m.. -rwxr-xr-x root  <victim.hda8-30199>
Sep 25 00:45:15    20452 .a. -rwxr-xr-x root  <victim.hda8-30199>
Sep 25 00:45:16    20452 ..c -rwxr-xr-x root  <victim.hda8-30199>
```

The file modification time is identical to that of the Red Hat 6.2 login program as distributed on CD-ROM. The file status change time shows that the file was removed at 00:45:16. We conclude that this was the original /bin/login file that was deleted when the first login back door was installed during the initial intrusion session. This finding is confirmed by an analysis of file inode numbers in the next section.

The deleted file with inode number 30210 was a copy of /usr/bin/ xstat, the back-door program that featured as /bin/login until it was renamed during the 17:34 intruder visit. In fact, the deleted file 30210 and the /usr/bin/xstat file had more in common: they also had the same file status change time and the same file modification time.

```
Sep 25 00:45:16    3448 m.. -rwxr-xr-x root  /victim/usr/bin/xstat
Sep 25 00:45:16    3448 m.. -rwxr-xr-x root  <victim.hda8-30210>
Sep 25 17:34:17    3448 ..c -rwxr-xr-x root  /victim/usr/bin/xstat
Sep 25 17:34:17    3448 .ac -rwxr-xr-x root  <victim.hda8-30210>
```

Why did we find two copies of the initial login back-door program with the same file modification times and the same file status change times? And why was one copy deleted and the other not? The initial login back-door program was installed as /bin/login. However, when the file was renamed to /usr/bin/xstat, it was moved from the root file system (on the hda8 disk partition) to the /usr file system (on the hda5 partition). The instance on the hda8 disk partition was removed, and a new instance was created on the hda5 partition. In this process, file attributes were preserved, resulting in the deleted file having the same attributes and contents as the existing file.

4.13 Exposing Out-of-Place Files by Their Inode Number

By now we have a pretty clear picture of what happened. Someone broke in, compiled a simple program, installed a back-door /bin/login program, and installed another back-door /bin/login program later that day (of course, different intruders could have been involved at different times). We were able to recover the deleted original /bin/login program file, as well as the deleted initial /bin/login back-door program. There are still a few deleted files that we could not identify.

Everything we have found so far appears to be consistent. Now it is time to look at smaller details, and to see if our observations still hold up after closer scrutiny. How could we be so certain that the deleted file with inode number 30199 was the original Red Hat 6.2 /bin/login program file, and not some copy of that file? The inode number, 30199, provides the clue.

As an operating system is installed on the disk and as files are created, the inode numbers are assigned by the file system. Normally, the base operating system, with standard system commands in /bin and in /usr/bin and so on, is installed one directory at a time. Thus, successive entries in system directories tend to have successive inode numbers. Red Hat 6.2 Linux is no exception.

A file listing of the /bin directory, in order of directory entry, revealed a neat sequence of inode numbers. In the listing that follows, the first column of each line contains the file inode number. The remainder of each line is standard "ls -l" formatted output:

```
$ ls -fli /victim/bin
[. . . skipped . . .]
30191 -r-xr-xr-x     1 root        60080 Mar   7  2000 ps
30192 -rwxr-xr-x     1 root       886424 Mar   1  2000 rpm
30193 -rwxr-xr-x     1 root        15844 Feb   7  2000 setserial
30194 lrwxrwxrwx     1 root            3 Aug  26  2000 gtar -> tar
30195 -rwxr-xr-x     1 root       144592 Feb   9  2000 tar
30196 -rwxr-xr-x     1 root         2612 Mar   7  2000 arch
30197 -rwxr-xr-x     1 root         4016 Mar   7  2000 dmesg
30198 -rwxr-xr-x     1 root         7952 Mar   7  2000 kill
60257 -rwxr-xr-x     1 root        12207 Aug  18  2000 login
30200 -rwxr-xr-x     1 root        23600 Mar   7  2000 more
30201 -rwxr-xr-x     1 root          362 Mar   7  2000 vimtutor
30202 lrwxrwxrwx     1 root            2 Aug  26  2000 ex -> vi
30203 lrwxrwxrwx     1 root            2 Aug  26  2000 rvi -> vi
30204 lrwxrwxrwx     1 root            2 Aug  26  2000 rview -> vi
30205 -rwxr-xr-x     1 root       346352 Mar   7  2000 vi
30206 lrwxrwxrwx     1 root            2 Aug  26  2000 view -> vi
30208 -rwxr-xr-x     1 root        20452 Sep  25  2000 prick
```

Clearly, the directory entry for /bin/login was out of place. It should have inode number 30199. And that is exactly the inode number of the deleted login program that we found in the previous section.

The directory entry for /bin/prick (the copy of the original login program) also revealed that something was out of order, though not as dramatically as with /bin/login. The inode number sequence shows a hole at inode number 30207. This again is consistent with the deleted MACtime analysis in the previous section, which shows that a file with inode number 30207 was created and removed in the course of the initial intrusion session.

4.14 Tracing a Deleted File Back to Its Original Location

In the previous section, we noticed a few deleted files with inode numbers in the 22111–22113 range, which is well outside the range of inode numbers of the other deleted files that were involved with the initial intrusion session. Because of this difference, we suspect that the files were not created in the /bin directory but must have been created in a very different place. But where?

With some Linux Ext2fs or FreeBSD UFS file system implementations, there is a quick way to trace a deleted file back to its directory. This approach exploits a property that does not work on systems such as Solaris. When the Linux Ext2fs or FreeBSD UFS file system removes a file, it marks the directory entry as unused, but it leaves the deleted file name and inode number intact. See Section 4.10 for more information.

We used the fls utility from the Sleuth Kit to produce a MACtime report for all deleted directory entries within the hda8 file system image. In the command that follows, -m /victim prepends the string /victim to any recovered file name, victim.hda8 is the file that contains the hda8 file system image, and 2 is the inode number of the root directory of the hda8 file system.

```
$ fls -m /victim victim.hda8 2 >>grave-robber-body-file
```

The syntax has changed in the meantime, and the command would now look like this:

```
$ fls -f linux-ext2 -r -m /victim victim.hda8 >>grave-robber-body-file
```

The output from fls is compatible with the body file format that is expected by the mactime command. The following MACtime fragment shows all the deleted entries in the /tmp directory that were found by fls, including their deleted file names, inode numbers, and file attributes:

```
Sep 25 00:45:16
    0 mac -rw-r--r-- root  /victim/tmp/ccpX2iab.ld <22113> (deleted)
    0 mac -rw------- root  /victim/tmp/ccWxNYYa.o  <22112> (deleted)
    0 mac -rw------- root  /victim/tmp/ccXJHPza.c  <22111> (deleted)
```

This result confirmed that the inodes 22111–22113 once belonged to deleted files in the /tmp directory. The names of the deleted files suggest that they were temporary files produced by the gcc compiler.[2] We already

---

2. If this observation is correct, then we may have uncovered a minor privacy problem in the compiler software. Note that the deleted file named /tmp/ccpX2iab.ld appears to be world readable, whereas the other apparent compiler temporary files are not.

knew from the MACtime analysis that the files were created when the initial back door was installed.

The Sleuth Kit's `ffind` tool can be used to find all the deleted directory entries that refer to a specific inode. With larger numbers of deleted inodes, `fls` is probably more convenient.

On systems such as Solaris that do not preserve inode numbers in deleted directory entries, `fls` will not be able to pair the deleted inode number with a deleted file name. But we don't have to give up. It is still possible to find out the disk region where a file was initially created, just by looking at the inode number.

4.15 Tracing a Deleted File Back by Its Inode Number

In Chapter 3, we explain that many UNIX file systems are organized into discrete zones. As a rule, all the information about a small file can be found in the same zone: the directory entry, the file inode block, and the file data blocks. This approach achieves good performance by avoiding unnecessary disk head movement.

Thus, to trace deleted files back to their initial parent directory, we have to look for files or directories in the same file system zone as the deleted files. In other words, we have to look for files or directories with inode numbers in the same inode number range as the deleted files. We sorted all the files and directories in the `hda8` file partition image by their inode number and looked at the numbers in the region of interest. The `-xdev` option prevented `find` from wandering across file system mount points into information from different disk image files.

```
$ find /victim -xdev -print | xargs ls -id | sort -n
[. . .]
22104 /victim/etc/autorpm.d/autorpm-updates.conf
22105 /victim/etc/autorpm.d/autorpm.conf.sample
22106 /victim/etc/autorpm.d/redhat-updates.conf
22107 /victim/etc/autorpm.d/autorpm.conf
22108 /victim/tmp/dd
24097 /victim/dev
24098 /victim/dev/printer
24099 /victim/dev/null
[. . .]
```

We found that the inode numbers 22111–22113 were in the same range as the `/tmp/dd` file, which was created by the owner of the system while preserving the file systems with `dd` and Netcat. This suggests that the three deleted files with inode numbers 22111–22113 were probably created in the `/tmp` directory. This is consistent with the `fls` results shown earlier.

4.16 Another Lost Son Comes Back Home

What can be said about the origin of the `/bin/login` program that the intruder installed in the course of the second visit, and whose inode number, 60257, was so wildly out of sequence with its neighboring files? Inode sequence number analysis suggests that the intruder's file was created in a very different file system zone before it was moved to the final location `/bin/login`. The following command reveals the inode numbers and file names around the region of interest:

```
$ find /victim -xdev -print | xargs ls -id | sort -n
[. . .]
60256 /victim/etc/.tmp/.tmp
60257 /victim/bin/login
60261 /victim/etc/.tmp/.tmp/install
60262 /victim/dev/.1
60263 /victim/etc/.tmp/.tmp/.m.list
60264 /victim/etc/.tmp/.tmp/install2
[. . .]
```

This suggests that the present back-door login program was created somewhere under `/victim/etc/.tmp/.tmp` and then renamed to `/bin/login`. Again, the `fls` utility was able to recover the deleted file name, as the following fragment from a MACtime report shows:

```
Sep 25 17:34:20
  12207 ..c -rwxr-xr-x root  /victim/etc/.tmp/.tmp/1 <60257> (deleted)
```

The files and directories with such suspicious names as `.tmp` and `.1` were created when the intruder returned for a second visit at 17:34. But instead of proceeding with an analysis of that episode, we have to take a step back and put the intrusion in its proper context.

4.17 Loss of Innocence

This intrusion was a quick and automated job. The whole break-in, from first contact to back-door test, was completed in less than a minute. The intruder did not attempt to erase any traces. No log files were edited, no padding was added to the back-door login program to match the file size and file checksum of the original login program, and no attempts were made to forge file time stamps. In fact, the intruder tried none of the cool tricks that we mention elsewhere in this book.

This absence of concern for detection is typical of intrusions that automatically set up large distributed denial-of-service (DDOS) software networks. For such a network to be effective, an intruder needs control over thousands of systems. When you have a whole army of systems at your disposal, the loss of a few soldiers is not a problem. Any casualties are easily replaced with new recruits.

At this point, we would continue the post-mortem analysis by looking at MACtimes from the second intruder's visit. We would find some of the tools that the intruder left behind, including the `floodnet` denial-of-service software. This would lead us into another round of reverse engineering, inode analysis, and so on. But doing so would take up too much space in this book, and it would not be fair to you, the reader.

We have a confession to make: the machine described in this chapter was not really an innocent victim of an evil intruder. In reality, the machine was a *honeypot*; that is, it was set up for the sole purpose of being found and compromised (see the sidebar). The owner of the machine kindly asked us if we were willing to do a post-mortem analysis and share what we could learn from the file system image and from a very limited subset of his network sniffer recordings. We took up the challenge. What we discovered from the system exceeded our expectations, although some of our findings had little to do with our initial assignment.

Honeypots

A honeypot machine is a trap for intruders. In "An Evening with Berferd," Bill Cheswick describes how he and colleagues set up their jail machine, also known as a roach motel (Cheswick 1992). They monitored the intruder in an environment where he could do no harm, while at the same time they lured him away from more precious resources.

In *The Cuckoo's Egg*, Cliff Stoll describes how he invented a complete governmental project with realistic-looking documents and memoranda (Stoll 1989). The intruder(s) spent long hours examining and downloading the information, giving Cliff plenty of opportunity to practice his tracing skills.

The machine that we feature in this chapter was part of the Honeynet Project (Honeynet Project 2004). While we examined the data that the owner of the system made available to us, we could not fail to notice how tricky it can be to operate a honeypot. In this sidebar, we point out the real or potential pitfalls that were most obvious to us.

Disk images of a similar break-in are available for analysis. You can find them online at the Honeynet Project's Web site (Honeynet Project 2001). The lessons described in this chapter were applied when preparing this material.

Downstream Liability

It may be exciting to lure an intruder into your honeypot. Other people will be less amused when they find out that you are providing the intruder with a launchpad for attacks on their systems. Unless you have the resources to watch your honeypot around the clock in real time, you have to severely limit its ability to connect to other systems.

History Keeps Coming Back

As we discuss elsewhere in this book, computer systems can be like tar pits, with the bones, carcasses, and fossilized remains of the past accumulating in the unallocated storage areas. Using the low-level techniques described in Chapter 3, we found files from operating systems that were installed previously on the same disk, including firewall configuration files and other items that could be of interest to an intruder.

With a network honeypot machine, erasing history is simply a matter of writing zeros over the entire disk before installing the operating system from installation media. After that, no remote intruder will ever see files from the machine's previous life. Overwriting with zeros also has the benefit that disk image copies compress better and deleted files are easier to find.

Information Leaks

A not-so-obvious pitfall is using the honeypot machine for real work. Even a remote login from the honeypot into a sensitive machine can be enough to expose information to intruders. If you let sensitive information into the honeypot via any means, then it may stick forever in unallocated storage space or in swap space until you explicitly erase it.

False Evidence

It can be really tempting to use the honeypot machine for your own break-ins and other security exercises. After all, the machine exists solely for the purpose of being broken into. The problem with using a honeypot machine for target practice is that you're shooting yourself in the foot, by producing massive amounts of false evidence. It quickly becomes difficult to distinguish between the acts from random (or not-so-random) intruders and the acts from your own personnel.

4.18 Conclusion

The case described in this chapter follows a general pattern. The initial signal that something was amiss came from network logging. Local log files provided the host-side view of what happened.

The post-mortem analysis was driven almost entirely by MACtime information. While unraveling the pattern of existing file MACtimes, we came upon a suspected login back-door program. A simple reverse-engineering analysis confirmed our initial suspicion. Existing file MACtimes also indicated that the login back-door program was replaced in a later intruder session. The analysis of deleted file MACtimes provided additional insights and confirmed many details that we already knew from existing file MACtimes and contents.

Similarly, analyzing the inode sequence numbers gave us more details, and again strengthened our suspicions. On Solaris systems, only inode sequence number analysis would provide information about the initial location of a deleted file. Inode sequence numbers yield another piece of forensic information that is hard, but not impossible, to forge.

Our approach to post-mortem analysis is straightforward. The bulk of the work entails painstakingly verifying each finding, by examining all available sources of information and by comparing them for consistency. The techniques demonstrated here offer a great deal of insight into what happened. But none of this would have helped us to look outside the box. Once we had figured out the general sequence of events in this particular intrusion, we started to look between the cracks. By straying from the beaten path, a path that we ourselves had beaten in the past, we learned new and unexpected things, such as how tricky it can be to operate a honeypot machine.

CHAPTER 5

Systems and Subversion

5.1 Introduction

In the last two chapters, we looked at information that can be found in file systems. Such information is static in nature and is typically examined after the fact. In this chapter, we turn our attention from static data to the more dynamic world of running code, and we look at system state in real time.

After an overview of the basic elements of computer system architecture, we walk through the system life cycle from start-up to shutdown, and we present some measurements of the complexity of today's operating systems. We cannot fail to observe how this complexity introduces opportunities for subversion.

Before we turn to system subversion, we recapitulate the essential kernel and process concepts that are often involved with subversion. There is a lot more to kernels and processes than we can describe in the context of this book, and the interested reader is referred to any good book on UNIX and UNIX system administration (such as Nemeth et al. 2000).

Subversion is the subject of the second half of this chapter. We present the mechanisms behind several generations of so-called *rootkit* software, and we show examples of their detection. This is an ongoing cat-and-mouse game of making observations, subverting observations, and detecting subversion. And because none of the popular systems today can offer strong security guarantees, this game is likely to continue until a radical change is made to system architecture.

5.2 The Standard Computer System Architecture

Over the past 35 years, the basic architecture of computer systems has not changed significantly, despite major advances in hardware and in operating systems. The main principle that underlies this architecture is separation of concerns. We distinguish two main levels: process and system. At the process level, software runs in an environment that is relatively independent of the details of the hardware and the operating system. At the system level, hardware and software provide the environment in which processes execute. Within each level, we distinguish some additional structure, as shown in Figure 5.1.

Going from top to bottom, we encounter the following layers:

- **The executable program.** Each running instance of a program file runs in what appears to be its own virtual memory. Once a process starts execution, it is usually linked with one or more run-time libraries, as described next.

- **Libraries with standard utility routines.** These routines run as part of the process into which they are linked. Library code provides generic services to application programs, such as computing a square root, looking up an IP address, and so on.

- **Resident operating system kernel.** (We use the term *kernel* although the implementation may use multiple cooperating processes.) The kernel manipulates the hardware and provides an interface to processes in terms of files, directories, network connections, other processes, and so on.

- **The hardware.** This layer presents an interface in terms of memory pages, disk blocks, network packets, device registers, I/O ports, interrupts, and more. Beyond these low-level interfaces lies another universe of processors and operating systems that are embedded inside hardware. Regrettably, we won't be able to cover hardware-level forensics in this book.

The benefits of this architecture are portability and simplicity. Portability means that the exact same application software can be used on multiple versions of similar operating systems, and on multiple configurations of similar hardware. Simplicity means that processes do not have to be aware that they share one machine with other processes. The operating system deals with all the complexities of resource management, and the hardware does the work.

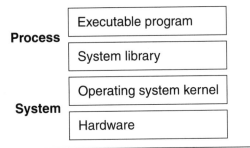

Figure 5.1 *The general relationship between hardware, the operating system kernel, system libraries, and executable program files*

5.3 The UNIX System Life Cycle, from Start-up to Shutdown

Having introduced the basic layers of the computer system architecture, we now take a bottom-up approach from hardware to executable programs, and we watch how different layers take control of the machine at different points in time. Figure 5.2 shows a simplified picture of the entire system start-up procedure.

When a computer system is powered up, resident firmware (often called BIOS, EEPROM, and so on) performs a hardware self-test and some low-level configuration. This includes finding out the type and capacity of installed random-access memory; locating additional resident firmware in, for example, disk or network interface controllers; configuring plug-and-play devices; and so on. Meanwhile, intelligent peripherals may execute their own power-up self-test and configuration sequences.

After completion of the power-up self-test and low-level configuration, the resident firmware loads a boot program from disk or from the network and gives it control over the machine. The boot program loads either the operating system kernel or the next-stage boot program. Boot programs and operating system kernels often have their own configuration parameters, as discussed in Section 5.5.

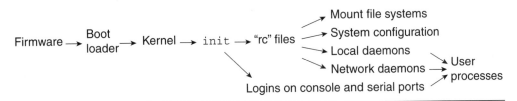

Figure 5.2 *A simplified process genealogy of a typical UNIX system*

The kernel probes the hardware for devices such as disk or network interface controllers and may load kernel modules to access and initialize those devices. Once the kernel completes its initialization, it creates the `init` process and passes control to it. From this point onward, the kernel becomes dormant. Kernel code executes only in response to hardware interrupt events and in response to system call requests from processes.

The `init` process executes the system start-up and shutdown procedures. These procedures are implemented by a multitude of "rc" files (shell command files) that are usually located under the `/etc` or `/sbin` directory. The start-up shell command files mount file systems; configure kernel modules and kernel parameters (more about those in Section 5.5); configure network interfaces; and start daemon processes, including the window system that presents the graphical console login window. The `init` process also controls nongraphical logins via hardwired and dial-up terminal ports. The shutdown shell command files stop specific processes in a controlled manner, before all the leftover processes are forcibly terminated.

An important function of `init` is to implement the *run levels*. In BSD-like systems, these are called single user (administrative access only) and multi-user. Solaris and Linux run levels are called S (single user) and 0–6, where 0 and 6 are for system shutdown and 1–5 are for increasing levels of service. For example, different run levels may enable multi-user logins, network logins, graphical console logins, or file sharing; the exact details of run level functionality differ per system.

5.4 Case Study: System Start-up Complexity

In the previous section, we talked about multitudes of files that are involved with start-up and shutdown sequences. To find out how complex these sequences are, we measured the number of different files that systems attempt to access during boot procedures. The measurements were done with generic i386 Solaris and Red Hat Linux systems and include booting up system configurations with and without a graphical user interface. For system configurations with a graphical user interface, the file counts include one login/logout with the default user interface. The results are shown in Table 5.1.

To get these numbers, we recorded all file access requests by all `init` child processes in real time, including file accesses that happened while file systems were still mounted as read-only. Tools that can monitor file access and other system call requests are discussed in Chapter 6. Playing with system start-up sequences is fraught with peril, especially when

Table 5.1 *The number of different file names accessed while booting generic Linux and Solaris systems, with and without a graphical user interface (GUI). The Red Hat and Solaris counts include all accesses after* init *start-up. Program files include executable files as well as run-time libraries and other files with executable machine code.*

System Type and Configuration	Program Files	Other Files	Nonexistent Files
Red Hat 4.1 boot, no GUI	81	290	217
Red Hat 5.2 boot, no GUI	86	494	289
Red Hat 6.1 boot, no GUI	76	639	262
Red Hat 6.1 boot and default GUI login/logout	107	1667	1090
Solaris 2.5.1 boot, no GUI	65	250	229
Solaris 7.0 boot, no GUI	77	344	273
Solaris 7.0 boot and default GUI login/logout	150	1153	1986

playing games with a critical process such as init. It was very easy to make a mistake that rendered the entire system unusable. Our measurements were possible thanks to VMware's virtualization software (see Chapter 6). Whenever we made a mistake, we simply discarded all our changes to the file system and tried again.

Two things stand out in the table. First is that the graphical user interface surpasses in complexity the entire system that it runs on. The second thing that stands out is the large number of requests involving nonexistent pathnames. One source of nonexistent pathnames is sloppiness in the form of default command PATH searches. A second source is a different form of sloppiness: many start-up scripts probe the file system to find out what is installed. Finally, a major source of nonexistent pathname lookups is the backward-compatibility support for legacy pathnames that are built in to program and configuration files.

What the table does not show is the large number of attempts to access the same pathname repeatedly, regardless of whether the pathname exists. This is a symptom of inefficiency, and all the little inefficiencies together ensure that system start-up times do not improve, despite continual enhancements to hardware performance.

Our little study shows that there are literally hundreds, if not thousands, of opportunities to subvert the integrity of a system *without changing any file*. It is sufficient to add one extra file in an innocuous place so that it is accessed during, for example, system start-up. This kind of subversion can be prevented to some extent by requiring that files have valid digital signatures. At the time of writing, such features are still in an experimental stage (van Doorn et al. 2001, Williams 2002).

5.5 Kernel Configuration Mechanisms

After the overview of architecture and the system life cycle, we now take a closer look at the individual software layers of the system architecture. First, we focus on the kernel level. The purpose of the operating system kernel is to make computer hardware more useful to application programs, just as the purpose of application programs is to make computer systems more useful to human beings. Although the application program interfaces provided by UNIX kernels and system libraries are relatively standardized by organizations such as ISO, IEEE, and XOPEN, there can be large differences between kernel internals. We focus on the common elements in the architecture of typical UNIX kernels, as shown in Figure 5.3.

When a machine is turned on, built-in firmware configures the hardware and loads a boot program from disk or from a network server. Depending on how powerful this boot program is, one or more additional boot programs may be needed to get the kernel up and running. The general sequence of events is described in the system manual pages: Solaris `boot(1M)`, Linux `boot(7)`, and FreeBSD `boot(8)`. Boot programs are controlled by configuration parameters, and sometimes they configure initial kernel configuration parameter values; Table 5.2 gives some examples. Although the bootstrapping stage represents only a minuscule portion of the system life cycle, its integrity is critical for the integrity of the entire system. For an implementation of secure booting in the IBM PC environment, see Arbaugh et al. 1997.

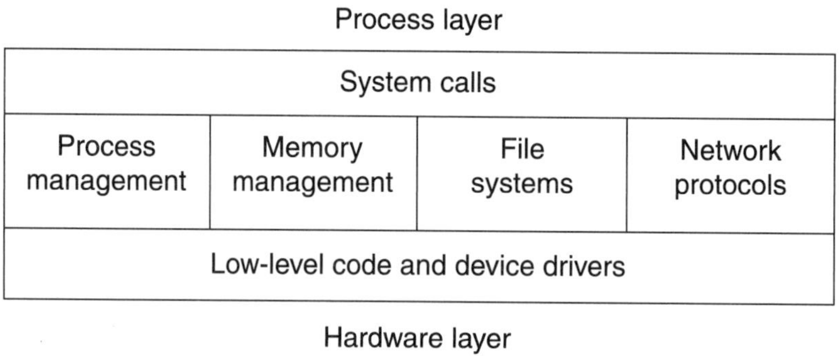

Process layer

System calls			
Process management	Memory management	File systems	Network protocols
Low-level code and device drivers			

Hardware layer

Figure 5.3 *The major subsystems of a typical UNIX kernel. The adjacent hardware and process architecture layers are shown for context.*

Table 5.2 *Typical boot loader and initial kernel configuration information*

System	Boot Loader Configuration	Kernel File Name	Kernel Configuration
Solaris	/etc/bootrc (x86 platform) firmware (SPARC platform)	/kernel/genunix	/etc/system
Linux	/boot/grub/grub.conf /boot/lilo.conf	/boot/vmlinuz	/etc/sysctl.conf
FreeBSD	/boot.config /boot/loader.conf /boot/loader.rc	/kernel /kernel/kernel	/boot/device.hints

As you might expect, there is great variation in the way kernels are configured. Linux and FreeBSD systems have a `sysctl` command, which gives read/write access to kernel configuration parameters and other data. The Linux `/proc` pseudo-file system also gives read/write access to a subset of those parameters and other data. Solaris has the `ndd` command for reading or writing parameters and other data that lives in the drivers that implement the IP protocol family; other Solaris kernel parameters may be set at run time with the `mdb` or `adb` commands. Listing 5.1 shows only a few of the more than 700 kernel configuration parameters of a FreeBSD kernel.

Loadable kernel modules are chunks of executable code and data that can be assimilated into a running kernel. Once a module is loaded, its code runs as part of the kernel. With monolithic kernels, this means the module's code has access to everything inside and outside the kernel. Kernel modules are used to implement functionality within all of the major kernel subsystems shown in Figure 5.3: from device drivers, file systems, and network protocols up to system calls that provide new features to

```
freebsd50% sysctl -a
kern.ostype: FreeBSD
kern.osrelease: 5.0-RELEASE
kern.osrevision: 199506
kern.version: FreeBSD 5.0-RELEASE #0: Thu Jan 16 22:16:53 GMT 2003
    root@hollin.btc.adaptec.com:/usr/obj/usr/src/sys/GENERIC

kern.maxvnodes: 4182
kern.maxproc: 532
kern.maxfiles: 1064
kern.argmax: 65536
kern.securelevel: 1
[. . . 728 more lines omitted . . .]
```

Listing 5.1 *Examples of FreeBSD kernel parameters*

processes. Modules are loaded while the kernel initializes and under the control of `init` start-up procedures. Table 5.3 shows typical commands to manipulate the status of loadable kernel modules.

Table 5.3 *Typical commands to load, unload, and query the status of loadable kernel modules*

System	Commands		
Solaris	`modload`	`modunload`	`modinfo`
Linux	`insmod`	`rmmod`	`lsmod`
FreeBSD	`kldload`	`kldunload`	`kldstat`

Many UNIX systems have relatively monolithic kernels: most of the code is permanently linked into the kernel file, and only a handful of modules are loaded dynamically. Solaris takes the opposite approach: more than a hundred modules are loaded dynamically. Even the process scheduler is loaded as a kernel module, as shown in Listing 5.2.

The convenience of loadable kernel modules also has a darker side. Because their code has access to everything inside and outside a monolithic kernel, they are also powerful tools in the hands of intruders. As we see later, kernel modules exist for hiding traces of intrusion (including the intruder's kernel modules) and for controlling nearly invisible back doors that give privileged access to intruders. We return to the issue of corruption and detection at the end of this chapter.

```
solaris9% modinfo
 Id Loadaddr   Size Info Rev Module Name
  5 fe925000   3e92   1   1  specfs (filesystem for specfs)
  7 fe92a275   2fda   1   1  TS (time sharing sched class)
  8 fe92cdcb    888   -   1  TS_DPTBL (Time sharing dispatch table)
 10 fe92ce43    208   -   1  pci_autoconfig (PCI BIOS interface 1.38)
 11 fe92cfc7  27d6e   2   1  ufs (filesystem for ufs)
[. . . 100 lines omitted . . .]
131 deeae12e    ae4  23   1  ptm (Master streams driver 'ptm' 1.4)
132 fe9610f1    be4  24   1  pts (Slave Stream Pseudo Terminal dr)
133 feaa37b7   12ae  17   1  ptem (pty hardware emulator)
```

Listing 5.2 *Examples of Solaris 9 kernel modules (ix86 platform)*

5.6 Protecting Forensic Information with Kernel Security Levels

Many kernel configuration parameter settings affect the security of a system. One kernel configuration parameter of particular interest is the kernel security level. This is a standard feature on 4.4 BSD-descendant systems, and it is available as an add-on feature for Linux. As the security level increases, functionality is reduced. The security level can be raised at any time with, for example, the `sysctl` command, but only the `init` process can lower the security level while the system is in single-user mode. Table 5.4 summarizes the semantics as defined with 4.4 BSD. Some systems support additional security levels or additional restrictions, or both. For precise details, see the `securelevel(7)` manual page or its equivalent.

These security features can be valuable for the protection of forensic information. An append-only flag protects log files against changes to already written contents, and an immutable flag protects a file against any change, including renaming (although such protection means little when a parent directory can still be renamed). Disallowing open-to-write of disk devices protects file systems against tampering that would otherwise be hard to detect. And none of these measures would be effective unless write access to the kernel memory or main memory devices is revoked, because then it would be trivial to turn off the protection offered by security levels.

Table 5.4 *Typical 4.4 BSD security level settings and restrictions*

Level	Restrictions
−1	Permanently insecure mode. Always run the system in level 0 mode, and do not raise the security level when changing from single-user mode to multi-user mode.
0	Insecure mode, normally used while booting the system. There are no additional restrictions beyond the usual file and system-call access controls.
1	Secure mode, normally used after the system switches to multi-user mode. Immutable and append-only file attributes may no longer be turned off; open-for-writing is no longer allowed with disk devices that contain mounted file systems, as well as memory devices; and kernel modules may no longer be loaded or unloaded.
2	Highly secure mode. Even unmounted disks may no longer be opened for writing.

The security level mechanism should not be confused with the discretionary or mandatory access control mechanisms that are built into many operating systems. The purpose of access control is to enforce a policy. The problem with policies is that they may be changed at any time by a suitably authorized process. The purpose of security levels, on the other hand, is to revoke access unconditionally. Once a system enters security level 1, there is no mechanism that grants permission to load kernel modules or to write to raw memory or mounted disk devices, except for returning the system to single-user mode with administrative access only via the system console. Thus, security levels are not impenetrable, but they add a barrier against compromise that cannot be implemented with access control alone.

5.7 Typical Process and System Status Tools

Each UNIX system comes with its own assortment of process and system status monitoring tools. Most tools look at one or two particular aspects of the system: process status, network status, input/output, and so on. Because of the large variation between tools and between systems, we introduce only a few representative tools and refer the reader to the system documentation for information about individual platforms. Process and system status tools can reveal signs of intruder activity, such as files, processes, or network connections. This makes the tools a prime target for subversion by intruders. We discuss subversion of status tools later in the chapter.

The `ps` command is the basic process status tool. Many systems provide multiple implementations or user interfaces; the Linux version even has more than a dozen personalities. In our examples, we use the BSD user interface because it provides information that is not available with some of the other user interfaces. Solaris has a BSD-compatible `ps` command in `/usr/ucb/ps`.

By default, the `ps` command tries to produce nice output, but that means a lot of information is suppressed or truncated. For example, to see the entire command line of a process, we need to specify one or more `w` options, and we need to specify the `e` option to display information in a process's environment. This is a list of *name=value* pairs that is inherited from the parent process. Linux and FreeBSD require super-user privileges in order to view environment information from other users' processes. Solaris currently does not impose this restriction.

A process environment may reveal whether the process was started in the regular manner or not. For example, system processes started at boot time tend to have few, if any, environment settings. If a system process such as `inetd` (the process that manages incoming connections for many common network services) was restarted by hand, then the environment could give away useful information, such as the remote user's origin, working directory information, and more, as shown with the following command:

```
$ ps -aewww
  PID  TT  STAT      TIME COMMAND
[. . .]
 6597 ??  Ss     0:00.01 PATH=/sbin:/bin:/usr/sbin:/usr/bin:/usr/game
s:/usr/local/sbin:/usr/local/bin:/usr/X11R6/bin:/root/bin MAIL=/var/ma
il/wietse BLOCKSIZE=K USER=wietse LOGNAME=wietse HOME=/root SHELL=/bin
/csh SSH_CLIENT=168.100.189.2 841 22 SSH_TTY=/dev/ttyp0 TERM=xterm PWD
=/home/wietse XNLSPATH=/usr/X11R6/lib/X11/nls XKEYSYMDB=/usr/X11R6/lib
/X11/XKeysymDB XAUTHORITY=/home/wietse/.Xauthority /usr/sbin/inetd -wW
[. . .]
```

The `lsof` (list open files) tool lists processes with all their open files, network ports, current directories, and other file system-related information (Abell 2004). This very useful program brings together information that is often scattered across several different tools. Because the output can reveal a lot about what a process is doing, many `lsof` implementations give little or no information about processes that are owned by other users. To examine those processes, `lsof` needs to be invoked by the super-user.

What follows is a typical sample of output for an OpenSSH server process that is waiting for connection requests. OpenSSH is an implementation of the SSH protocols for encrypted remote logins (OpenSSH 2004).

```
# ps ax | grep sshd
  186  ??  Is     0:01.17 /usr/sbin/sshd
39288 pb  R+     0:00.00 grep sshd
# lsof -p 186
COMMAND PID USER  FD TYPE      DEVICE SIZE/OFF  NODE NAME
sshd    186 root cwd VDIR  13,131072      512     2 /
sshd    186 root rtd VDIR  13,131072      512     2 /
sshd    186 root txt VREG  13,131072   198112 15795 /usr/sbin/sshd
[. . . 10 run-time library object files omitted . . .]
sshd    186 root  0u VCHR       2,2      0t0  7955 /dev/null
sshd    186 root  1u VCHR       2,2      0t0  7955 /dev/null
sshd    186 root  2u VCHR       2,2      0t0  7955 /dev/null
sshd    186 root  3u IPv6 0xd988e720      0t0  TCP *:ssh (LISTEN)
sshd    186 root  4u IPv4 0xd988e500      0t0  TCP *:ssh (LISTEN)
```

In the output, `cwd` is the current directory; `rtd` is the root directory, which in this case is the regular file system root; `txt` is the executable file; and `0..4` are open files and sockets. For each entry, `lsof` gives additional information, such as the type (for example, directory, regular file,

character special device, or socket for IP version 4 or 6) and other identi-
fying information, such as the device and inode number, or the address
of the socket control block.

Of particular interest is the lsof -i option, which shows all processes
with active network ports. The output can reveal processes that aren't
supposed to have open network connections, which could be a sign of
trouble. The next example shows a shell (command interpreter) process
that is attached to TCP port 21. Normally, this port is used by FTP server
processes to receive commands and report status results. In the example,
10.1.2.3 is the address of the local machine, and 192.168.3.2 is the address
of an attacking machine. Note: the -> arrow does not imply that the connection was initiated by the local machine; the lsof command has no
information about which end of a connection is the client or server.

```
# lsof -ni
COMMAND PID   USER FD TYPE     DEVICE NODE NAME
[. . .]
sh       39748 root 0u IPv4 0xd9892b60 TCP  10.1.2.3:21->192.168.3.2:1866
sh       39748 root 1u IPv4 0xd9892b60 TCP  10.1.2.3:21->192.168.3.2:1866
sh       39748 root 2u IPv4 0xd9892b60 TCP  10.1.2.3:21->192.168.3.2:1866
[. . .]
```

Output like this is a sure sign that someone exploited an FTP server vulnerability to spawn a shell process. These exploits are popular because
the shell process inherits full system privileges from the FTP server
process.

The findings of lsof can be checked against those of other tools that also
look at process or file/network information, such as the netstat command. The following command shows the status of all network ports and
all network connections. We omit everything but the connection that corresponds with the FTP server exploit.

```
# netstat -nf inet
Active Internet connections
Proto Recv-Q Send-Q Local Address Foreign Address (state)
[. . .]
tcp4      0      0 10.1.2.3.21    192.168.3.2.1866   ESTABLISHED
[. . .]
```

With Linux systems, one would specify netstat -n --inet for an
equivalent result. Speaking of Linux, its netstat command has the very
useful -p option to display process ID and process name information.

As you can see, there is significant overlap between tools. When only
some of the tools are compromised, the output from the other tools may
reveal the inconsistency. This is why intruders often replace multiple system utilities as part of their cover-up operation. However, system status

tools are not really independent. Ultimately, all tools rely on a common source of information, the kernel. When the kernel is compromised, all tools may fail; other techniques are then needed to expose the compromise. We return to this topic at the end of the chapter.

5.8 How Process and System Status Tools Work

All process and system status tools get their information from the running kernel. Historical UNIX systems made only a limited amount of process and system status information available through well-documented system calls. Most information was obtained by directly accessing poorly documented data structures in kernel memory via the `/dev/kmem` pseudo-device.

Modern UNIX systems make some process and system information accessible via the `/proc` pseudo-file system. Each process has a subdirectory `/proc/pid`, which is named after the numerical process ID. Each subdirectory contains an assortment of pseudo-files for different process attributes; Table 5.5 gives a few examples. Specific details of the `/proc` file system are described in the system manual: FreeBSD `procfs(4)`, Linux `proc(5)`, and Solaris `proc(4)`.

With the `/proc` pseudo-file system, process attributes are accessed by opening the corresponding pseudo-file. Process status reporting tools read status information, and programs such as debuggers manipulate processes by writing and reading control information. (Debuggers are discussed in Chapter 6.) Linux and FreeBSD `/proc` files are mostly text based and can be accessed in meaningful ways with the `cat` or `echo` commands; Solaris uses binary data structures that require specialized tools, as described in the `proc(1)` manual page.

Besides processes, Linux and FreeBSD make a limited amount of kernel status information available under `/proc`, while Solaris uses additional

Table 5.5 *Examples of per-process entries in the* `/proc` *file system. The Solaris* `psinfo` *pseudo-file contains most of the information needed by the* `ps` *(list processes) command.*

Process Attribute	Solaris	FreeBSD	Linux
Program file	/proc/*pid*/object/a.out	/proc/*pid*/file	/proc/*pid*/exe
Process memory	/proc/*pid*/as	/proc/*pid*/mem	/proc/*pid*/mem
Memory map	/proc/*pid*/map	/proc/*pid*/map	/proc/*pid*/maps
Command line	/proc/*pid*/psinfo	/proc/*pid*/cmdline	/proc/*pid*/cmdline

pseudo-devices, such as /dev/ip for network status and /dev/kstat for kernel statistics. This apparent chaos of lookup mechanisms is not a problem as long as you can depend on tools such as ps, netstat, or lsof, whose output is relatively system independent. It complicates life, however, when you need to write tools that attempt to bypass potentially compromised utilities.

5.9 Limitations of Process and System Status Tools

Unfortunately, the accuracy of information from system status tools is limited. Some limitations are unavoidable, because the tools look at information that is changing, such as memory usage or open files. Other limitations are less obvious, often accidental, and can complicate the interpretation of results. To illustrate this, we show some limitations in the way process status tools report process command-line information.

For example, process status tools may produce incomplete command-line information. Although UNIX systems have generous limits on the length of command lines, how much of this can be recovered depends on the UNIX system implementation and the tool being used. Table 5.6 shows typical limits for Solaris, Red Hat Linux, and FreeBSD systems on i386-type hardware. The NCARGS constant in the file <sys/param.h> defines the combined upper bound on the command line and process environment.

Table 5.6 *Command-line limitations in typical process status tools*

System	NCARGS	ps Command-Line Length Limit
FreeBSD 5.0	64 Kbytes	Length truncated to 0 if greater than 10,000 bytes
Red Hat 8.0	128 Kbytes	Length truncated to 0 if greater than 4 Kbytes
Solaris 9	1 Mbyte	/usr/ucb/ps: All information recoverable /usr/bin/ps: Length truncated to 80

Another oddity is that a process may modify its own command line as displayed by ps. This is possible on systems such as FreeBSD, Linux, and Solaris, but with Solaris, the changes are visible only if you invoke the BSD-style /usr/ucb/ps command with the w option; this is probably more an artifact of implementation than the result of a deliberate decision. For example, the Sendmail mail transfer agent routinely changes the command line to display the process state. Here is an example for Red Hat 8.0 Linux that displays all Sendmail-related processes:

```
redhat80% ps ax | egrep 'COMMAND|sendmail'
  PID TTY  STAT  TIME COMMAND
  604 ?    S     0:00 sendmail: accepting connections
  614 ?    S     0:00 sendmail: Queue runner@01:00:00 for
/var/spool/client
```

Finally, the process name (the first component of the command-line array) can be different from the executable file name. Some `ps` implementations will display the executable file name in parentheses when it differs from the process name. And even if the process name equals the file name, one UNIX file can have any number of names, as described in Chapter 3. A fine example of this is (again) Sendmail. This software is installed such that different hard links or symbolic links to the same program file have different names. Each name serves a different purpose, even though all names ultimately refer to the same executable file.

Having discussed how process and system status tools work, where they get their information, and the origins of some of their limitations, we now turn to popular methods to subvert the findings of these tools.

5.10 Subversion with Rootkit Software

As mentioned in the preceding sections, the results from process and system status tools are subject to subversion. In the sections that follow, we discuss how systems are subverted, how subversion is hidden, and how subversion may be detected. We limit the discussion to the upper three layers of the system architecture: executable file, library, and kernel. Detection of subversion at the hardware level is beyond the scope of this book.

In our discussion of software subversion, we look at a category of malware known as *rootkit*, which first became popular in the mid-1990s. The name stands for a combination of malicious software (such as a network sniffer or an attack tool), back-door software (which gives intruders access to a machine without having to break in), and a collection of modifications to system software that hide the rootkit and other traces of the intrusion.

Rootkits are popular because they automate the process of installation and hiding, making it quick and painless. Typically, a rootkit is installed after system security is breached with a procedure that is also highly automated. When a rootkit is found on a compromised machine, it's possible that the whole incident occurred without any human control. While the intruder was doing something else, the rootkit installed itself and announced the compromised machine as another victim via some IRC channel.

5.11 Command-Level Subversion

Command-level rootkits hide the presence of malware by making changes to system commands. This approach is based on a very simple principle: To suppress bad news, silence the messenger. Table 5.7 shows a list of typical command-level rootkit modifications. Depending on the specific type of malware involved, many rootkits make other modifications, in addition to those listed in the table.

Table 5.7 *Typical system utilities that are replaced by command-level rootkits, and the information that the replacements attempt to hide*

Replaced Commands	Hidden Information
du, find, ls	Malware configuration files and network sniffer logs
pidof, ps, top	Network sniffer or back-door process
netstat	Network ports associated with malware
ifconfig	Network sniffing "enabled" status

As intrusion technology has evolved, so have rootkits. The first rootkits came with network sniffers to collect user names and passwords (such as the esniff program); later versions came with remotely controlled agents for distributed denial-of-service attacks (such as the T0rn rootkit).

Typical back-door software takes the form of a modified login program, a nonstandard or modified network server for the finger or ssh service, or an inetd server that listens on a secret network port. The back door is usually enabled by entering a specific password or by connecting from a particular network source port or IP address. However, these are not the only types of back door in existence, as we will see later.

5.12 Command-Level Evasion and Detection

To evade detection, early rootkits not only replaced system utility software but also erased records in system log files. Some rootkits even gave modified system utilities the same file time stamps and cyclic redundancy check (CRC) values as the original files. Later command-level rootkits don't bother; they simply install modified programs that hide the presence of malware.

Regardless of these details, none of the changes compromises the integrity of the kernel. Detection of command-level rootkit modifications is therefore relatively easy, as long as one uses a trusted copy of the system utilities. Here are a number of ways in which command-level root-kits can be discovered:

- If a rootkit installs a back-door server process that listens for connections, the network port will be visible to an external network port scanner. To avoid detection in this manner, some rootkits come with a nonlistening back-door server that is triggered by a sequence of packets of specific type or with specific contents. For example, a "raw" ICMP socket bypasses the TCP/IP protocol stack and receives a copy of all ICMP datagrams, except those for which the local kernel generates its own responses (Stevens 1997).

- On many operating systems (but not Linux), the strings command will reveal the names of all directory entries, including hidden or deleted files. The fls command can do the same, with more accuracy, when applied to the disk device (fls is introduced in Chapter 3). In fact, any tool that bypasses the file system can reveal information that is hidden by file system utilities, including the ils tool (also introduced in Chapter 3). These techniques do not work with file systems that are mounted from a server.

- Commands such as strings may reveal the presence of nonstandard file names that are embedded in modified system utility programs. These files control the hiding of processes, network connections, or files, and they often have unusual names. We give an example later.

- Although corrupted versions of ps and other utilities hide malware processes, those processes can still be found using, for example, the /proc file system, as we show in an upcoming example.

- Deleted login/logout records in the wtmp file leave behind holes (actually, sequences of null bytes) that can be detected with a program that understands the binary format of the file.

- Although the ifconfig command might report that a network interface is not in network sniffer mode, it takes only a small C program to query the kernel directly for the interface status.

- Although the CRC checksums of malware executable files might match those of the original system utility executable files, as reported by the sum or cksum command, the modifications still show up unmistakably when one compares the outputs of a strong cryptographic hash such as MD5 or SHA-1.

- No files or modifications remain hidden when one examines (a low-level copy of) the file system on a trusted machine. All the hidden files and modifications will be visible in plain sight. Chapter 4 describes disk imaging and analysis in detail.

As an example of exposing a command-level rootkit, we examine two utilities that are part of the T0rn rootkit for Linux, which was in widespread use in 2001. First we search the /bin/ls executable file with the strings and grep commands for strings that look like file names:

```
$ strings /bin/ls | grep /
/lib/ld-linux.so.1
>/t[j/
/usr/local/share/locale
/usr/src/.puta/.1file
[. . . Five more lines omitted . . .]
```

The file name /usr/src/.puta/.1file looks very suspicious. If we try to list the /usr/src/.puta directory, the ls command hides the name, as we would expect:

```
$ cd /usr/src
$ ls -a
.                    ..           linux         linux-2.2.14   redhat
```

However, the directory name still shows up when we use the echo command, together with the .* wildcard expansion feature that is built into the command shell:

```
$ echo .* *
. .. .puta linux linux-2.2.14 redhat
```

In the .puta/.1file rootkit configuration file, we find a lengthy list of file and directory names that must remain hidden, because these contain the malware program files, configuration files, and data files:

```
$ cat .puta/.1file
.puta
.t0rn
.1proc
.1addr
xlogin
[. . . 29 more lines omitted . . .]
```

Just as we can detect modified file utilities by comparing their results against output from an unmodified tool, we can detect modified process status utilities by comparing their output against information from the /proc file system. Table 5.8 shows that the ps command is hiding a process with ID 153. (It also shows that /proc and ps disagree on whether "2" corresponds to a process, but that is a different issue.)

The system utilities that were replaced by the rootkit do a good job of hiding process 153. Not only is it censored by process status tools such as ps, but also it does not show up with network status tools such as netstat. However, for reasons that we may never know, this rootkit does not re-

Table 5.8 *A comparison of process information from the* /proc *file system and the* ps *command*

Entries in /proc	Output from ps ax
1	1 ? S 0:06 init [3]
2	
3	3 ? SW 0:00 (kupdate)
4	4 ? SW 0:00 (kpiod)
5	5 ? SW 0:00 (kswapd)
6	6 ? SW< 0:00 (mdrecoveryd)
153	
271	271 ? S 0:00 /sbin/pump -i eth0
341	341 ? S 0:00 portmap
356	356 ? SW 0:00 (lockd)

place the lsof command, which can therefore help reveal the purpose of process 153:

```
# lsof -p 153
COMMAND PID USER    FD    TYPE DEVICE   SIZE  NODE NAME
nscd    153 root    cwd    DIR   3,5    4096     2 /
nscd    153 root    rtd    DIR   3,5    4096     2 /
nscd    153 root    txt    REG   3,5 201552 35646 /usr/sbin/nscd
[. . .]
nscd    153 root     7u   IPv4    177           TCP *:47017 (LISTEN)
[. . .]
```

The file name /usr/sbin/nscd suggests that it is a system program, but comparison with uncompromised systems shows that this program is present only in later Linux versions. Connecting with telnet to TCP port 47017 on the local machine confirms that we are looking at a backdoor process. In this case, we are welcomed by the opening banner of what appears to be an SSH server. SSH is popular with legitimate and illegitimate users because it encrypts and protects network traffic, making it immune to inspection and manipulation.

```
# telnet localhost 47017
Trying 127.0.0.1...
Connected to localhost.
Escape character is '^]'.
SSH-1.5-1.2.27
```

Each rootkit differs slightly in its approach to hiding the presence of malware, and therefore each rootkit requires us to take a slightly different approach to detect it. An example of software that automates the search for known rootkits is the Chkrootkit toolkit (Murilo and Steding-Jessen 2003). It runs on a dozen different UNIX platforms and, at the time of writing, recognizes more than fifty different rootkits. Chkrootkit looks for deleted login/logout records, signatures of replaced system utilities, rootkit configuration files and directories, missing processes, and signs of kernel-level subversion. But that is a topic for a later section (namely, Section 5.14).

5.13 Library-Level Subversion

Instead of replacing system utilities, rootkits can hide their existence by making changes at the next level down in the system architecture, the system run-time library. A good example of this is redirecting the open() and stat() calls. The purpose of these modifications is to fool file-integrity-checking software that examines executable file contents and attributes. By redirecting the open() and stat() calls to the original file, the rootkit makes it appear as if the file is still intact, while the execve() call executes the subverted file. For example, Listing 5.3 shows how one could redirect the open() call in a typical Linux run-time library.

Would an MD5 or SHA-1 hash reveal the library modification? Not necessarily. While the run-time linker uses the low-level open() system call

```
#include <errno.h>
#include <syscall.h>
#include <real_syscall.h>

/*
 * Define a real_open() function to invoke the SYS_open system call.
 */
static  real_syscall3(int, open, const char *, path,
                    int, flags, int, mode)

/*
 * Intercept the open() library call and redirect attempts to open
 * the file /bin/ls to the unmodified file /dev/.hide/ls.
 */
int open(const char *path, int flags, int mode)
{
    if (strcmp(path, "/bin/ls") == 0)
        path = "/dev/.hide/ls";
    return (real_open(path, flags, mode));
}
```

Listing 5.3 *A library-level back door to redirect specific* open() *system calls. The* real_syscall3() *macro, whose definition is too ugly to be shown here, is a slightly modified copy of the standard Linux* _syscall3() *macro. We use it to define our own* real_open() *function that invokes the* SYS_open *system call.*

when it accesses the modified library file, commands such as `md5sum` use the `fopen()` library routine and can be still redirected to the unmodified library file.

To work around modifications at this level, rootkit detection tools need to carry their own trusted copy of the system library routines. However, such measures and countermeasures have become less relevant with the arrival of rootkits that make changes to the running kernel—making them much harder to circumvent or detect.

5.14 Kernel-Level Subversion

As we have seen in the previous section, rootkit modifications to system utilities are easy to circumvent. As long as we have a copy of the unmodified utilities, we can still find the malware files, processes, and network ports. In a similar manner, rootkit modifications to system library routines are easy to circumvent.

The game changes dramatically when modifications are moved from the process layer into the kernel layer. Compromised kernel code cannot be circumvented easily, because hardware memory protection prevents user processes from doing so. All accesses to kernel memory must be mediated by the kernel, whether it is compromised or not. And because the running kernel is the source of information for all file, process, and network status tools, those tools may produce inaccurate results when the kernel is compromised. Despite all these handicaps, kernel-level modifications may still be detectable, as we show at the end of the chapter.

5.15 Kernel Rootkit Installation

Just like command-level rootkits, kernel-level rootkits are installed after the security of a system has been breached. Over time, different methods have been developed to inject rootkit code into a kernel.

- **Loading a kernel module into a running kernel.** This technique uses officially documented interfaces and is therefore easier to use than other techniques. For the same reason, this technique is also easier to detect. Some rootkit implementations attempt to remove their module names from the external kernel symbol table (Solaris `/dev/ksyms` or Linux `/proc/ksyms`) and from internal kernel tables. They might also intercept system calls that report on the status of kernel modules (Plaguez 1998; Plasmoid 1999, Pragmatic 1999). We give an example at the end of this chapter.

- **Injecting code into the memory of a running kernel that has no support for module loading.** This involves writing new code to a piece of unused kernel memory via the /dev/kmem device and then activating the new code by redirecting, for example, a system call (ASR 1996, Cesare 1999, Sd and Devik 2001).

- **Injecting code into the kernel file or into a kernel module file.** These changes are persistent across reboot, but they require that the system be rebooted to activate the subverted code (Jbtzhm 2002, Truff 2003).

The exact details of these methods are highly system dependent. Even the methods that use officially documented interfaces are likely to break with different versions of the same operating system. For more information, see the references.

5.16 Kernel Rootkit Operation

As we've stated, the purpose of many kernel rootkits is to hide malware processes, files, and network ports—and of course to hide the rootkit itself. There are two sides to information hiding: output and input. On the output side, the kernel must censor the output from system calls that produce a list of processes, files, network ports, and so on. On the input side, any attempt to manipulate a hidden process, file, network port, and so on must fail as if the object did not exist. In addition, rootkits may redirect system calls such as open(), to subvert the operation of software that verifies the integrity of executable file contents and attributes. Figure 5.4 shows the typical architecture of early kernel rootkit implementations.

Early kernel rootkits subvert system calls close to the process-kernel boundary. To prevent access to a hidden file, process, and so on, they redirect specific system calls to wrapper code that inspects the parameters and decides whether the system call is allowed to happen. For example, code to subvert the open() system call goes like this:

```
evil_open(pathname, flags, mode)
    if (some_magical test succeeds)
        call real_open(pathname, flags, mode)
    else
        error: No such file or directory
```

To prevent rootkit disclosure, system calls that produce lists of files, processes, network ports, or kernel modules are intercepted to suppress information that must remain hidden. For example, the code that subverts the getdents() system call (list directory entries) goes like this:

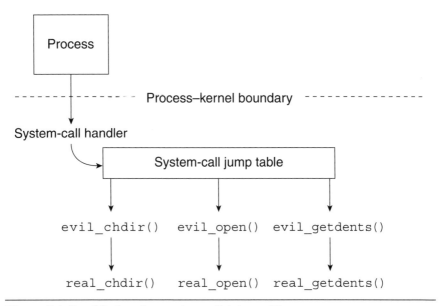

Figure 5.4 *Rootkits based on system-call interposition*

```
evil_getdents(handle, result)
    call real_getdents(handle, result)
    if (some_magical test fails)
        remove hidden objects from result
```

The advantage of system-call interposition is that the code is relatively easy to understand: the change is made at a point that is close to the user of those system calls. One drawback of this approach is that many system calls need to be intercepted. For example, to hide the existence of a file, one would have to intercept all system calls that have a file name argument: open(), chdir(), unlink(), and many others. That alone is some forty system calls on Linux, FreeBSD, and Solaris.

This drawback is addressed by subverting UNIX kernels at a level that is closer to the information being hidden. In the next example, we show how this approach can be used to hide files. Figure 5.5 depicts the typical architecture of such subversion.

UNIX systems support a variety of file system types. Besides file systems with a UNIX origin, such as UFS, Ext2fs, and Ext3fs, many systems support non-UNIX file systems, such as FAT16, FAT32, NTFS, and others. Typically, each file system implements a common virtual file system (VFS) interface, with operations to look up, open, or close a file; to read directory entries; and a dozen or so other operations (Kleiman 1986).

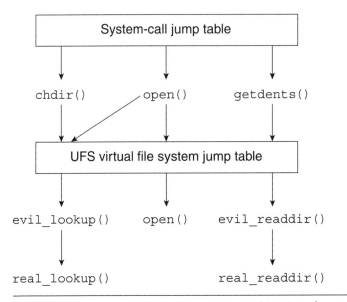

Figure 5.5 *Rootkits based on interposition at object interfaces, showing subversion of multiple UFS file system methods*

Of all the operations provided by the virtual file system interface, the lookup() operation is of particular interest. System calls that access an existing file or directory, and so on, by name use the lookup() operation to translate the pathname into the underlying file system object. By redirecting the lookup() call at the virtual file system layer, it is possible to hide a file from all system calls that access an existing file by name:

```
evil_lookup(parent_directory, pathname, . . . )
    if (some_magical test succeeds)
        call real_lookup(parent_directory, pathname, . . . )
    else
        error: No such file or directory
```

This modification is sufficient to hide an existing file from system calls that attempt to access it, such as chdir() or open(). However, it does not hide the file's existence from system calls that *create* a new directory entry, such as link(), mkdir(), socket(), mkfifo(), and others. Unless the malware is prepared to redirect names of new files that collide with names of hidden files, the system calls will fail with a "File exists" error. A rootkit detector that knows specific rootkit file names can exploit this property.

The kernel changes that we discussed so far are relatively easy to detect, because they change code addresses in kernel tables that normally never change. We can examine these tables from outside the kernel by accessing `/dev/kmem` or from inside the kernel with a forensic kernel module. An example follows in the next section.

Detection methods that look for changes in kernel tables can be defeated by leaving the tables alone and by patching an existing kernel function so that it calls the malware. For an example of patching live kernel code, see Cesare 1999. Such modifications can be found by inspecting all the running kernel code and verifying all instructions against all kernel files and all kernel module files. This a nontrivial task, because the contents of modules change while they are linked into the kernel, to update references to external functions and data.

5.17 Kernel Rootkit Detection and Evasion

Kernel rootkits, like their nonkernel predecessors, may be exposed because they introduce little inconsistencies into a system. Some inconsistencies may show up externally, in the results from system calls that manipulate processes, files, kernel modules, and other objects. Other inconsistencies show up only internally, in the contents of kernel data structures. Internal inconsistency is unavoidable, because every hidden process, file, or kernel module occupies some storage. That storage has to be claimed as "in use," and it has to be referenced by something in the kernel's path of execution, even though the storage does not appear in kernel symbol tables. We present examples of both types of inconsistency later in this section. Here is a list of inconsistencies that may reveal the presence of kernel rootkits:

- As with command-level subversion, output from tools that bypass the file system can reveal information that is hidden by compromised file system code. Examples are `ils` and `fls` from the Coroner's Toolkit and the Sleuth Kit, respectively, and even the good old `strings` command.

- Even perfectly invisible kernel rootkits may give themselves away due to an oversight. For example, the modification time of an important system directory is changed, but there is no obvious change to the contents of that directory.

- The results from process-manipulating system calls and from the `/proc` file system should be consistent. If a process is being hidden, then some system calls will report "not found" while other system calls may not. The Checkps rootkit detector relies, among others, on such discrepancies (Simpson 2001); Chkrootkit also has tests for invisible processes. In an upcoming example, we show a different approach to detect a hidden process.

- Some kernel-based rootkits are controlled by invoking a legitimate system call with a special parameter value. For example, when the Adore rootkit is installed, `setuid()` (change process privileges) will report success for some parameter values even though the user does not have sufficient privileges. When the Knark rootkit is installed, `settimeofday()` (set the system clock) will report success for some parameter values even though it should always fail when invoked by an unprivileged user. Magical numerical parameter values are easily detected by brute force: just try every possible value and then look at the system call result. Evasion of this detection method is easy, too: switch from a single call with a special parameter value to a sequence of calls with special parameter values, or use system calls with non-numerical parameter values.

- The hard link count of a directory, as reported by the `stat()` system call, should equal the number of subdirectories, as reported by the `getdents()` system call. If a directory is being hidden, then it may show up as a missing hard link. This test is implemented by the `chkdirs` utility, part of the Chkrootkit rootkit detector.

- Modifications to kernel tables such as the system call table or the virtual file system table may be detected after the fact by reading kernel memory via `/dev/kmem` or by examining kernel memory from inside with a forensic kernel module such as Carbonite (Mandia and Jones 2001). We show results from a tool based on `/dev/kmem` in an upcoming example.

- Modifications to kernel tables or kernel code may also be detected as they happen, using a kernel intrusion-detection module that samples critical data structures periodically or looks for undesirable event sequences. An example of this category is StJude (Saint Jude 2002).

- Modifications that hide files can show up as inconsistencies between information from the raw disk device and information returned by the kernel file system code. Likewise, modifications that hide network ports, processes, or kernel modules may be exposed by reading kernel memory and comparing the contents of kernel data structures with results from system calls.

As an example of externally visible inconsistency, we present a simple technique that detects hidden processes. The idea is to create a long sequence of processes. On UNIX systems that allocate process ID (PID) values sequentially, the sequence will show a hole where a PID is in use or where a PID falls within a reserved range. For example, UNIX systems consider a PID to be "in use" when it belongs to a running process or to a group of processes (either as a process group ID or as its politically correct version, a POSIX session ID). As examples of reserved ranges,

FreeBSD and Linux skip over the first 100 and 300 PID values, respectively, when the PID counter wraps around at its maximal value.

The hidden-process search can be implemented with the somewhat slow Perl program shown in Listing 5.4, which creates a sequence of child processes using the `fork()` system call. Whenever a hole appears in the sequence of child PID numbers, the program attempts to fill the hole with information about existing processes in `/proc`. To avoid false alarms due to short-lived processes that terminate before `/proc` can be searched, the program cycles twice through the entire PID range, which makes the program even slower.

The implementation of the `check_existing_processes()` function is system dependent and is omitted to save space; the complete script is

```perl
#!/usr/bin/perl

# checkpid - find hidden processes

$last_pid = $PROCESS_ID;
$first_pid = $last_pid + 1;

for (;;) {

    # Fork a child process and wait until the child terminates.
    if (($pid = fork()) < 0) { die "cannot fork: $!\n"; }
    if ($pid == 0) { exit; }
    wait;

    # Update the visible process list. Fill gaps in the PID sequence
    # with information from the /proc file system.
    $proc_seen[$pid] = 1;
    if ($last_pid + 1 < $pid - 1) { check_existing_processes(); }

    # Update the maximal process ID, and how many times we reached it.
    if ($pid > $max_pid) { $max_pid = $pid; }
    if ($last_pid > $pid) { $wrapped_around++; }
    $last_pid = $pid;

    # Report findings when we complete two passes over the PID range.
    if ($wrapped_around > 1 && $pid >= $first_pid) {
      print "Maximal PID: $max_pid\n";
      for $pid (0..$max_pid) {
          report_missing($pid) if !$proc_seen[$pid]; }
      exit 0;
    }
}
```

Listing 5.4 *A program that cycles through the process ID space and recognizes hidden processes by the holes they leave behind* available at the book's Web site. When this program is run on a rootkit-infested Solaris system, it produces output such as the following:

```
Maximal PID: 29999
Missing PID: 10257
```

The first line reports the highest process ID observed, and the second line reports a PID that was never observed as a process ID or as the ID of a process group or a POSIX session. Indeed, ID 10257 corresponds to a hidden process that was set up in a lab environment to test this tool.

Due to the way the hidden-process-finding tool works, a positive signal should definitely be taken seriously. A negative result, on the other hand, does not mean that a system is clean. The rootkit might be too sophisticated for detection in this manner. Another limitation of the tool is that it cannot explore the reserved PID range (0–99 on BSD, 0–299 on Linux) and consequently will report those ranges as possibly hidden processes.

The Findrootkit tool works in a very different manner. It examines kernel memory and can therefore give specific answers.[1] Findrootkit is written in Perl and uses the `mdb` low-level debugger to examine the running Solaris kernel via the `/dev/kmem` interface. The tool checks the consistency of information from multiple sources inside and outside the kernel:

- The `/dev/ksyms` symbol table, with kernel function and data addresses and sizes
- The in-kernel module list, with executable code and data segment addresses and sizes of loaded kernel modules
- The in-kernel "text arena" table, with executable code segment addresses and sizes
- The function addresses in the system call jump tables and in file system operation jump tables
- The executable code and data segment sizes, as specified in the symbol tables of kernel module files

These consistency checks can reveal the presence of hidden kernel modules and other code that hides in the kernel. Additionally, the tool knows that specific kernel modules implement specific functions. For example, Findrootkit knows the kernel modules that implement specific file systems or specific system calls. Table 5.9 shows an example of a kernel modification report.

The report in Table 5.9 shows the Findrootkit results for a Solaris kernel with a hidden kernel module. A number of file system operations and sys-

---

1. From a private communication with Casper H. S. Dik.

Table 5.9 *A Solaris rootkit kernel modification report, showing changes to (a) the file system operations table and (b) the system-call jump table*

Interposed Vnode Operation	Interposing Function	Interposed System Call	Interposing Function
specfs:ioctl	0xfe9f23c8	fork	0xfe9f2fb4
procfs:lookup	0xfe9f2080	fork1	0xfe9f3058
procfs:readdir	0xfe9f22fc	kill	0xfe9f30fc
ufs:setattr	0xfe9f1420	sigqueue	0xfe9f31a4
ufs:getattr	0xfe9f174c	exec	0xfe9f324c
ufs:lookup	0xfe9f1a08	exece	0xfe9f3264
ufs:readdir	0xfe9f1d50		(b)
ufs:remove	0xfe9f1e30		
ufs:rename	0xfe9f1eec		
(a)			

tem calls are interposed and are shown with the hexadecimal address of each interposing function. The kernel module name and interposing function names are unavailable, because those names were removed by the kernel module. The replacements in the /proc file system are what one would expect for process hiding: the procfs:lookup() operation reports that a hidden process does not exist, and the procfs:readdir() operation removes hidden processes from process listings. Numerous operations for the Solaris UFS file system have been modified for presumably nefarious purposes, as well as the specfs:ioctl() operation for the SPECFS file system, which provides access to device special files, network sockets, and other objects that exist outside the Solaris file system.

As with the previous tool, a sufficiently sophisticated rootkit can evade detection. In particular, tools like the last one, which examine a kernel from outside, can be fooled by subverting the /dev/ksyms or /dev/kmem drivers—or both—so that they lie about the contents of kernel memory. Even running the consistency checker inside the kernel would not make it immune to such tampering.

5.18 Conclusion

Writing this chapter has produced at least one good result: it has convinced its author to raise the BSD security level on critical machines. Although such protection can be subverted, it buys additional time, and it forces an intruder to raise alarms.

The rootkits discussed in this chapter expend a lot of effort to hide processes or files, but there is no good reason why a rootkit should need to use processes or files in the first place. With some loss of convenience, back-door software can run entirely within the kernel, or at least the part of the back door that is memory resident. If storage space is needed, there is plenty available in the mostly unused swap space, and the back door can be controlled via any number of local or networked covert channels. A rootkit that makes no persistent changes to the machine can be practically undetectable by software that runs within or above a compromised kernel. Finding it requires direct hardware access or software that runs between the kernel and the hardware, such as a virtual machine monitor or so-called hypervisor (virtualization is discussed in the next chapter). At the time of writing, monitors and hypervisors are rarely used. And they are not the ultimate solution, either. Such programs will have bugs and therefore will be prone to subversion.

Although this chapter did not cover the possibilities for subversion at the hardware level, that does not mean we are ignorant of its potential. Any writable storage presents an opportunity for subversion, especially when that storage is associated with, or is even part of, a processor of some kind. Hoglund and McGraw (2004) discuss this topic in the context of PC hardware.

CHAPTER 6

Malware Analysis Basics

6.1 Introduction

There are many ways to study a program's behavior. With static analysis, we study a program without actually executing it. Tools of the trade are disassemblers, decompilers, source code analyzers, and even such basic utilities as `strings` and `grep`. The advantage of static analysis is completeness: it can reveal parts of a program that normally do not execute. In real life, static analysis gives an approximate picture at best. It is impossible to fully predict the behavior of any but the smallest programs. We illustrate static analysis with a real-life example at the end of the chapter.

With dynamic analysis, we study a program as it executes. Here, tools of the trade are debuggers, function call tracers, machine emulators, logic analyzers, and network sniffers. Dynamic analysis has the advantage of speed. However, it has the disadvantage that "what you see is all you get." For the same reason that it is not possible to predict the behavior of a nontrivial program, it is also not possible to make a nontrivial program traverse all paths through its code. We delve into dynamic analysis early in this chapter.

A special case is "black-box" dynamic analysis, in which a system is studied without knowledge of its internals. The only observables are the external inputs, outputs, and their timing relationships. In some cases, the inputs and outputs include power consumption and electromagnetic radiation as well. As we show in an example, software black-box analysis can yield remarkably useful results despite its apparent limitations.

Finally, there is post-mortem analysis, the study of program behavior by looking at the aftereffects of execution. Examples include local or remote logs, changes to file contents or to file access time patterns, deleted file information, data that was written to swap space, data that still lingers in memory, and information that was recorded outside the machine. Post-mortem analysis is often the only tool available after an incident. Its disadvantage is that information disappears over time, as normal system behavior erodes the evidence. However, memory-based aftereffects can persist for hours to days, and disk-based aftereffects can persist for days to weeks, as discussed in Chapters 7 and 8. We don't cover post-mortem analysis in this chapter, because it comes up in so many other places in this book; we mention it here only for completeness.

After an introduction of the major safety measures, we look at several techniques to run an unknown program in a controlled environment. Using examples from real intrusions, we show that simple techniques can often be sufficient to determine the purpose of malicious code. Program disassembly and decompilation are only for the dedicated, as we show at the end of the chapter.

6.2 The Dangers of Dynamic Program Analysis

One way to find out the purpose of an unknown program is to run it and see what happens. There are lots of potential problems with this approach. The program could run amok and destroy all information on the machine. Or the program could send threatening e-mail to other people you don't want to upset. All this would not make a good impression.

Rather than run an unknown program in an environment where it can do damage, it is safer to run the program in a sandbox. The term *sandbox* is stolen from ballistics, where people test weapons by shooting bullets into a box filled with sand, so that the bullets can do no harm. A software sandbox is a controlled environment for running software.

Sandboxes for software can be implemented in several ways. The most straightforward approach is the sacrificial lamb: a real, but disposable, machine with limited network access or with no network access at all. This is the most realistic approach, but it can be inconvenient if you want to make reproducible measurements.

Instead of giving the unknown program an entire sacrificial machine, you can use more subtle techniques. These range from passively monitoring a program as it executes to making the program run like a marionette, hanging off wires that are entirely under the investigator's control.

In the next few sections, we review techniques to implement a controlled environment for execution of untrusted software, as well as techniques to monitor or manipulate software while it executes.

6.3 Program Confinement with Hard Virtual Machines

Many techniques exist to split a computer system into multiple more-or-less independent compartments. They range from methods that are implemented entirely in hardware to methods that implement resource sharing entirely in software. As we will see, they differ not only in functionality and performance, but also in the degree of separation between compartments.

Higher-end multiprocessor systems have hardware support for splitting one machine into a small number of hardware-level partitions, as shown in Figure 6.1. When each partition runs its own operating system and its own processes on top of its own CPU(s) and disk(s), hardware-level partitions can be equivalent to having multiple independent computer systems in the same physical enclosure.

Because of the specialized hardware involved, systems that support hardware-level partitions are currently outside the budget of the typical malware analyst. We mention hard virtual machines for completeness, so that we can avoid confusion with the software-based techniques that we discuss in the next sections.

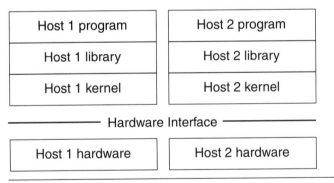

Figure 6.1 *Typical architecture of a hard virtual machine*

6.4 Program Confinement with Soft Virtual Machines

Virtual machines implemented in software provide a flexible way to share hardware among multiple simultaneously running operating systems. As illustrated in Figure 6.2, one or more guest operating systems run on top of a virtual hardware interface, while a virtual machine monitor program (sometimes called a hypervisor) mediates access to the real hardware. Each guest executes at normal speed, except when it attempts to access hardware or execute certain CPU instructions. These operations are handled by the virtual machine monitor, in a manner that is meant to be invisible to the guest.

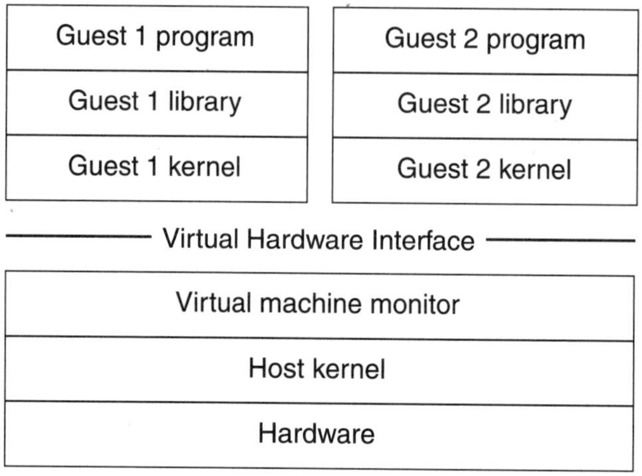

Guest 1 program	Guest 2 program
Guest 1 library	Guest 2 library
Guest 1 kernel	Guest 2 kernel

———————— Virtual Hardware Interface ————————

Virtual machine monitor
Host kernel
Hardware

Figure 6.2 *Typical architecture of a soft virtual machine. Some implementations of virtual machine monitors run on bare hardware (Karger et al. 1991); some run as an application on top of a host operating system (VMware 2004); and many use a protocol between guests and the virtual machine monitor to mediate access to the underlying hardware or to improve performance (Dunlap et al. 2002).*

The flexibility of soft virtual machines comes at the cost of some software overhead in the virtual machine monitor. In return, they can offer features that are not available in real hardware or in guest operating systems. For example, virtual machine monitors can implement support for "undoable" file system changes, by redirecting disk write operations to a log file outside the virtual machine. This feature makes it easy to repeat an experiment multiple times with the exact same initial conditions. We relied on this ability for some experiments described elsewhere in this book when we used the VMware system for the i386-processor family (VMware 2004).

As another example of enhanced functionality, the ReVirt system (Dunlap et al. 2002) allows an investigator to replay an "incident" and to rewind, pause, or fast-forward the virtual machine at any point in time. This is possible because the ReVirt virtual monitor records all interrupts and external inputs, including keystrokes and network packet contents. This information, combined with a complete record of the initial file system state, allows an investigator to replay every machine instruction and to view data before, during, and after modification. It is even possible to log in to a virtual machine while it is replaying an "incident," although from that point on, the reconstruction is of course no longer accurate. ReVirt is based on user-mode Linux and is therefore specific to Linux applications. Although it can reconstruct every CPU cycle of past program execution, the amount of storage needed is limited, because ReVirt stores only the interrupts and the external inputs.

6.5 The Dangers of Confinement with Soft Virtual Machines

When a virtual machine is used for hostile code analysis, it must not allow untrusted software to escape. Keeping malware confined with a soft virtual machine requires not only the correct implementation of the protection features of the processor hardware. It also requires the correct implementation of the virtual machine monitor, the software that mediates all access requests to real hardware from software running inside a virtual machine. If hostile software can recognize its virtual environment, then it may be able to exploit bugs in the implementation of the virtual monitor and escape confinement.

In some cases, subtle details may give away the fact that software is running in a virtual machine. For example, a guest with access to accurate time may notice that some machine instructions are comparatively slow. And when one virtual disk track spans multiple physical disk tracks, disk blocks that are adjacent on the virtual media can be nonadjacent on the physical media, resulting in unusual access time properties.

On the other hand, the VMware virtual hardware environment is really easy to recognize; Listing 6.1 shows an example. Some details, such as device identification strings, can be recognized by any process that runs in the virtual machine; other details can even be recognized remotely. In particular, the hardware Ethernet address prefix 00:50:56, which is reserved for VMware, may be recognized remotely in IP version 6 (IPv6) network addresses, according to RFC 2373 (Hinden and Deering 1998).

```
$ dmesg
[. . .]
lnc0: PCnet-PCI II address 00:50:56:10:bd:03
ad0: 1999MB <VMware Virtual IDE Hard Drive> [4334/15/63] at ata0-
master UDMA33
acd0: CDROM <VMware Virtual IDE CDROM Drive> at ata1-master PIO4
[. . .]

$ ifconfig lnc0
lnc0: flags=8843<UP,BROADCAST,RUNNING,SIMPLEX,MULTICAST> mtu 1500
        address: 00:50:56:10:bd:03
        [. . .]
        inet6 fe80::250:56ff:fe10:bd03%le0 prefixlen 64 scopeid 0x1
        inet6 2001:240:587:0:250:56ff:fe10:bd03 prefixlen 64
```

Listing 6.1 *Signs of a VMware environment in system boot messages and in IPv6 network addresses. The Ethernet address information in the IPv6 addresses is indicated in bold. The first Ethernet address octet is transformed per RFC 2373 (Hinden and Deering 1998).*

In the case of VMware, note that there is an undocumented channel that allows the guest operating system to send requests to the virtual machine monitor. These include requests to get the virtual machine monitor version, to connect or disconnect virtual devices, and to get or set user preferences (Kato 2004).

Implementing a secure virtual machine monitor program is a nontrivial exercise, but it is possible to combine a high level of security with good performance (Karger et al. 1991). Additional complications arise in the case of the i386-processor family, because some CPU instructions lack virtual machine support. It is the job of the virtual machine monitor to correctly identify, intercept, and emulate all those instructions in software (Robin and Irvine 2000), so that software inside the virtual machine sees the correct result.

Because of their extended flexibility and complexity, soft virtual machines provide no more separation than hard virtual machines, let alone physically separate machines. We advise the reader to exercise caution, and to conduct virtual machine experiments on a dedicated host machine that contains no sensitive information.

6.6 Program Confinement with Jails and `chroot()`

While virtual machines separate instances of entire operating systems, a number of solutions provide separation at the process level. Under the hood is only one kernel instance. The approaches differ in suitability for malware confinement.

A traditional UNIX security feature is the `chroot()` system call. This feature restricts access to the file system by changing the root directory of a process. It limits a system's exposure, and it is often used to harden FTP and Web servers against compromise.

One obvious drawback of `chroot()` is that it limits file system access only. In particular, it provides no isolation from processes or from other nonfile objects that exist on the same system. Because of these limitations, a privileged intruder can escape relatively easily via any number of system calls. We definitely do not recommend `chroot()` for confinement of untrusted processes that must run in a complete UNIX system environment.

Over time, people have expanded the ideas of `chroot()` to cover the scope of other system calls. These features are known as *jails* in FreeBSD version 4, *zones* or *containers* in Solaris 10 (Sun Microsystems 2004), and as the VServer patch for Linux (VServer 2004). We use the term *jail* in the remainder of this discussion. Jails change not only a process's idea of its file system root directory, but also what its neighbor processes are, what the system's IP address is, and so on. With this architecture, shown in Figure 6.3, a process that runs inside a software jail has no access to processes, files, and other objects outside its jail. To maintain this separation, a super-user process inside a jail is not allowed to execute operations that could interfere with the operation of other jails or with the nonjail environment. For example, the jail environment has no /dev/mem or /dev/kmem memory devices, and a jailed process is not allowed to update kernel configuration parameters or to manipulate kernel modules.

These properties make jails suitable for hosting complete system environments, with their own users, processes, and files. They contain everything except the operating system kernel, which is shared among jails and the nonjail environment. The advantage of jails over virtual machines is cost: they suffer neither the software overhead of a virtual machine monitor nor the expense of specialized hardware. The drawback of jails is that everything runs on the same kernel and that this kernel must consistently enforce jail separation across a very complex kernel-process interface. For this reason, jails are no more secure than soft virtual machines.

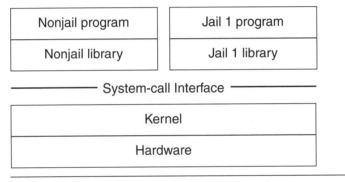

Figure 6.3 *Typical architecture of a software jail*

6.7 Dynamic Analysis with System-Call Monitors

Having introduced virtual machine and jail techniques that allow us to encapsulate a complete system environment for hostile code analysis, we now turn to methods that target individual processes. We proceed from passive observation techniques to more powerful techniques for active manipulation.

With system calls, we look at information that crosses the process-to-kernel boundary: function call names, arguments, and result values. In between system calls, we completely ignore what happens within a process. Effectively, the entire process is treated as a black box. This approach makes sense in operating environments where every file access, every network access, and even something as simple as getting the time of day requires a system call for assistance by the operating system kernel.

In many programs, system calls happen at a relatively low frequency, and watching them produces more useful information than watching individual machine instructions. System-call information is particularly suitable for filtering on the function call name, argument values, or result values. This can help narrow down the search before going down to the machine-instruction level for finer detail.

Modern UNIX systems provide tools for monitoring system calls in real time. The commands are called `strace` (Linux, FreeBSD, Solaris, and others) or `truss` (Solaris). As shown in Figure 6.4, these tools run as a monitoring process that actively controls a monitored process. The underlying mechanism is based on the `/proc` file system or the `ptrace()` system call. The 4.4BSD `ktrace` command is somewhat different. Instead of actively controlling a monitored process, it uses the `ktrace()` system call, which appends system-call information to a regular file. Because the mechanism behind `ktrace` is limited to passive monitoring, we do not discuss it further in this chapter.

The following summarizes how typical applications for monitoring system calls work.

1. The monitored process invokes a system call.
2. The operating system kernel gives control to the monitoring process so that it can inspect the monitored process. This includes process memory, processor registers, the system-call number that identifies the requested operation, and the system-call arguments.

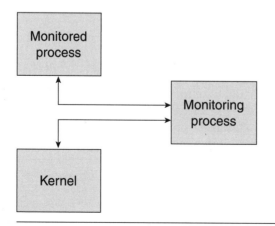

Figure 6.4 *Control flow with a typical application that monitors system calls*

3. The operating system kernel executes the system call.

4. Upon completion of the system call, the monitoring process can inspect the monitored process again, including the memory, processor registers, and the system-call results.

5. The kernel passes control back to the monitored process.

Usually, system-call tracing programs produce one line of output per call, with the system-call name, its arguments, and its result value. For example, here are all the I/O-related system calls that are made by the Solaris `date` command, after process initialization is completed:

```
$ truss -t open,read,write,close date >/dev/null
[. . . process initialization system calls skipped . . .]
open("/usr/share/lib/zoneinfo/US/Eastern", O_RDONLY) = 3
read(3, "\0\0\0\0\0\0\0\0\0\0\0\0".., 8192)     = 1250
close(3)                                        = 0
write(1, " M o n   A p r   2 4   1".., 29)      = 29
```

In this example, we skip the process initialization system calls that bind several system libraries into the process address space. Once process initialization is complete, the process opens, reads, and closes the file that describes the time conversion rules for the U.S. Eastern time zone, which corresponds to the location of the system. The program uses the time zone information to convert the system time (UNIX systems keep time in Universal Time Coordinates, or UTC) to the local representation, taking account of daylight saving time where applicable, and finally it writes the result. In the example, the output from the `date` command itself was discarded to avoid interference with the system-call trace output.

Besides starting a process under control of a system-call tracer as just shown, it is also possible to attach a system-call tracer to an already running process. As an illustration of the power of system-call tracing, the following command puts software crocodile clamps on an `ssh` server process with ID 3733 and reveals the cleartext contents of login sessions; Figure 6.5 shows the information flows in more detail.

```
# strace -f -p 3733 -e trace=read,write -e write=3 -e read=5
```

The `strace` command attaches to the process with ID 3733 and to any child process that is born after the `strace` command starts. The command displays all data written to file descriptor 3 and read to file descriptor 5. These file descriptors are connected to the processes that run on behalf of the remote user. The actual file descriptor numbers are system and version specific, and they are likely to differ for your environment.

Thus, the `strace` command displays the cleartext of everything that a remote user types on the keyboard, including passwords that are used for logging in to other systems, and including everything that is sent back

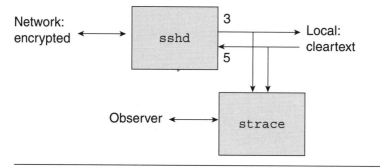

Figure 6.5 *Wiretapping an* `ssh` *server process*

to the remote user. However, `strace` is unable to show the information that is sent while a user authenticates to the `ssh` server itself, because that information is never sent across the monitored file descriptors.

The `strace` command is a generic system-call tracer. When it is used for wiretapping read and write system calls, the output still contains a lot of noise that needs to be filtered away. If you plan to take this approach, it pays off to prepare a modified `strace` command that produces less noise. If you don't have time to plan, then you simply take whatever tool is available.

Of course, login sessions can be wiretapped more conveniently with utilities that attach directly to a user's terminal port, such as `ttywatch` (Linux), `watch` (4.4BSD), TTY-Watcher (Solaris), and Sebek (Linux, OpenBSD, Solaris, and Win32). (For more on the TTY-Watcher program, see Neuman 2000; for more on the Sebek program, see Balas et al. 2004.) Finally, login sessions can be wiretapped by making small changes to the `ssh` server code itself.

There is one major downside to system-call tracing: there can be only one tracing process per traced process. It is therefore possible for a determined attacker to make a process untraceable by attaching to the process before someone else gets a chance to do so. The mere existence of such an untraceable process can, of course, raise extreme suspicion.

6.8 Program Confinement with System-Call Censors

Besides passive monitoring, system-call monitoring hooks can be deployed to restrict the actions of a monitored process. System-call censoring tools can help run unknown software through its paces without allowing it to inflict damage on its environment. The restrictions are enforced either by a user-level process that censors unwanted system calls or by kernel-level code that does the same. We present an example of each approach.

The Janus system is an example of a user-level system-call censor (Goldberg et al. 1996). Figure 6.6 shows the general architecture. The purpose of Janus is to limit the damage that buggy applications can do when run by normal users. Janus intercepts system calls by a monitored process and examines their argument values. Acceptable system calls are allowed to proceed without interference; unacceptable calls are aborted so that the monitored process receives an error result. An alternative to aborting a call is to terminate a monitored process, but this is reserved for problematic cases; users would object to trigger-happy security software. Janus uses static policies that must be defined in advance. The following are examples of entries in a Janus policy file:

```
# The initial directory
starting_dir /some/where
# Allow password file read access
path allow read /etc/passwd
# Allow connections to host 128.36.31.50 port 80
net allow connect tcp 128.36.31.50 80
```

The original Janus sandbox was implemented with a user-level censoring process. Because of this architecture, Janus was subject to race conditions and could fail to keep track of monitored process state (Garfinkel 2003). The current Janus system uses a different architecture: it is implemented as a Linux kernel module that talks to a user-level monitor process, much like Systrace, which we will describe next.

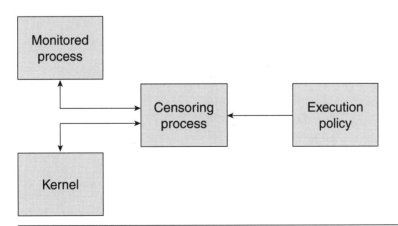

Figure 6.6 *The initial implementation of the Janus system-call sandbox, with a user-level monitoring process*

An example of a kernel-based system-call censor is Systrace (Provos 2003). Systrace intercepts the system calls made by a monitored process and communicates with a user-level process that makes policy decisions. Figure 6.7 shows the general architecture. Systrace currently runs on several flavors of BSD, on Linux, and on Mac OS X. Policies are expressed as rules, with the system-call name (for example, `linux-connect` for the Linux emulation mode of the `connect()` system call), the arguments (such as the remote IP address and network port), and the action (`permit`, `deny`, or `ask`). These rules are kept in policy files that are named after the executable program file. By default, Systrace looks for policy files under the user's home directory and in a shared system directory. The following are examples of Systrace policy rules:

```
# Allow stat(), lstat(), readlink(), access(), open() for reading.
native-fsread: filename eq "$HOME" then permit
native-fsread: filename match "$HOME/*" then permit
# Allow connections to any WWW server.
native-connect: sockaddr match "inet-*:80" then permit
```

Systrace can be run in three major modes: policy-generating mode, policy-enforcing mode, and interactive mode.

- Policy-generating mode, "`systrace -A command`", executes the specified command, examines the system calls that the program executes during that particular run, and generates a policy file with rules that allow only those specific system calls. This mode is used to generate a baseline policy file with allowed program behavior.

- Policy-enforcing mode, "`systrace -a command`", executes the specified command, applies the rules in the policy file for the command, and denies and logs each system call that isn't matched by an existing rule. This mode is used for routine confinement of untrusted software or users.

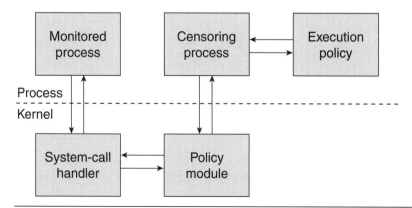

Figure 6.7 *A Systrace system-call sandbox implemented with a policy kernel module*

- Interactive mode, "`systrace` *command*", executes the specified command, applies the rules in the policy file for the command if that file exists, and asks permission to execute each system call that isn't matched by an existing rule. User interaction can occur through a graphical pop-up window or in plain-text mode. The user can then decide to permit or fail the call, to terminate the process, or to enter a permanent Systrace rule that automatically handles future occurrences of that system call. Interactive mode gives maximal control to the user and can be used to run both known and unknown software with extreme prejudice.

As an example of large-scale deployment, OpenBSD has adopted Systrace policy enforcement for building software from external origin (in the so-called ports collection). This happened after an incident in which a subverted build procedure connected a local shell process to a remote intruder (Song 2002). When the same build procedure executes under control of Systrace, the attempt to connect to the intruder is denied and a record is logged to the `messages` file:

```
Sep  4 18:50:58 openbsd34 systrace: deny user: wietse, [ . . . ]
syscall: native-connect(98), sockaddr: inet-[204.120.36.206]:6667
```

System-call censors that run inside the kernel have a major advantage over user-level implementations: they have access to the complete state of the monitored process and can therefore be more accurate. However, even kernel-based system-call censors can have limitations, as we discuss in Section 6.10.

6.9 Program Confinement with System-Call Spoofing

Although running a program under the control of a system-call censor prevents damage, it also prevents us from learning about that damage. The alternative is to allow damage to happen, but without permanent effects. One approach is to use a soft virtual machine with undoable file system support, as discussed earlier. In this section, we explore a different method.

Let's review how system-call monitors work. There are two points in time when a monitoring process can easily access the memory and processor registers of a monitored process: upon system-call entry and upon system-call return. On many systems, these same opportunities can also be used to redirect system calls or modify arguments and results, as shown in Figure 6.8.

Here is a small example. While monitoring a possibly hostile piece of software, we want to prevent the process from creating another copy of itself with the `fork()` system call. That would allow the new process to

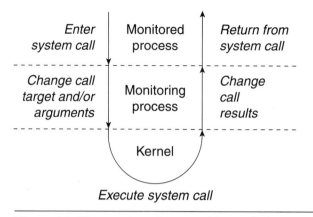

Figure 6.8 *The sequence of events with a typical system-call-spoofing application*

run as a background process and thereby escape our control. Allowing hostile code to multiply itself is something that we should probably disallow in any case. With the example in Listing 6.2, we intercept the process when it enters the `fork()` system call. We change the call from `fork()` to the harmless `getpid()` system call. The `getpid()` call takes no arguments, which is very convenient; we could also have specified the number of a nonexistent system call. Upon completion of the system call, we set the result value to zero, so that the monitored process believes that it is now running as the newly created background process.

```
/* Run the untrusted program in a child process. */
child = spawn_child(command);
spoof_return = 0;

/* Intercept each fork() system call by the child process. */
for (;;) {
    wait_for_child(child);
    if (spoof_return == 0) {
      syscall_number = read_register(child, ORIG_EAX);
      if (syscall_number == SYS_fork) {
          write_register(child, ORIG_EAX, SYS_getpid);
          spoof_return = 1;
      }
    } else {
      write_register(child, EAX, 0);
      spoof_return = 0;
    }
}
```

Listing 6.2 *A program fragment that runs an untrusted program in a controlled process and that changes the target and the result of the* `fork()` *system call. The* ORIG_EAX *and* EAX *register names are specific to Linux on the i386-processor family.*

Thus, we have the beginning of a system-call-spoofing sandbox. The monitored process makes system calls, but those calls don't really happen. The monitored process stays isolated from the world, and the monitoring process provides only an illusion.

The Alcatraz system, shown in Figure 6.9, uses system-call interception to isolate an untrusted process from other processes that are running on the same system (Liang 2003). A monitored process is allowed to make changes to the file system (subject to access permissions), but those changes are redirected by Alcatraz so that they are visible only to the monitored process. After the process terminates, the user can decide whether or not the changes are to be made permanent.

Alcatraz runs as a user-level process that keeps track of what files are opened and makes copies of all the files that are changed. Because these copies are owned by the user who runs the monitoring process, this introduces some interesting puzzles with respect to the handling of file-access permissions. Alcatraz also has to keep track of the current directory of the monitored process, in order to resolve relative pathnames. Although the Alcatraz system is already useful, it would probably benefit from a kernel-based implementation, which would avoid these and other complications inherent in a process-level implementation.

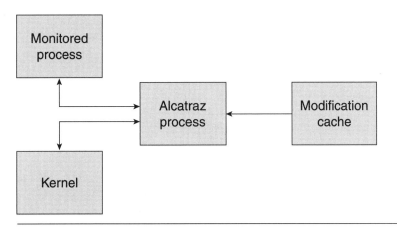

Figure 6.9 *System-call redirection with Alcatraz*

6.10 The Dangers of Confinement with System Calls

As we have seen in the previous sections, system-call interception is attractive because it covers all interactions between a process and its environment, and because it manipulates information at a useful level of aggregation. There are potential pitfalls, however.

- When system-call censoring is implemented by a user-level process, that process has to keep track of the monitored process's current directory, open files, open network sockets, and so on. That information is maintained by the kernel, and trying to track its evolution in a user-level process introduces opportunities for errors, race conditions, and other problems. Tal Garfinkel (2003) documents several problems that were found in the original user-level Janus implementation.

- System-call censors have problems with multi-threaded processes, in which multiple threads of execution share the same address space. When one thread makes a system call, only that thread is blocked. At any time after the censor has inspected the arguments, a different thread in the same process can still change the system-call argument values or change their meaning—for example, by changing the current directory. This makes system-call censors vulnerable to race conditions, whether they run as a user-level process or as a kernel module. At the time of writing, neither Janus nor Systrace supports multi-threaded processes.

6.11 Dynamic Analysis with Library-Call Monitors

While system-call monitoring treats a program as a black box and looks at inputs and outputs only, library-call monitoring gives more insight into a program's internal structure. First, we introduce passive monitoring and compare it with system-call monitoring.

Examples of library-call monitoring programs are ltrace (Linux and some 4.4BSD descendants) and sotruss (Solaris). These programs can typically show both system calls and library calls, although they show library calls only by default. Not surprisingly, the user interface of library-call monitoring programs is very similar to that of system-call monitoring programs. Here is an example that shows a fragment of a library-call trace of the Linux date command:

```
$ ltrace date >/dev/null
[. . . process initialization omitted . . .]
time(0xbffffa64)                                    = 1001919960
localtime(0xbffffa3c)                               = 0x40150ee0
realloc(NULL, 200)                                  = 0x08050d68
strftime("Mon Oct  1 11:06:00 EDT 2001", 200,
        "%a %b %e %H:%M:%S %Z %Y", 0x40150ee0) = 28
printf("%s\n", "Mon Oct  1 11:06:00 EDT 2001")    = 29
[. . . process cleanup omitted . . .]
```

In the example, the Linux date command looks up the UNIX system time with the time() call, converts from system time to local time with the localtime() call, and formats the result with strftime(), after allocating 200 bytes of memory for the result. The result is then printed with the `printf()` call. Again, output from the `date` command itself was discarded in the listing, to avoid interference with the trace output.

If we compare this example with the earlier system-call trace of the Solaris `date` command, then we see that the library trace reveals some of the internal workings that are not visible with system calls. In particular, the `localtime()` call in the Linux library-call trace corresponds to the `open()`, `read()`, and `close()` system calls in the Solaris system-call trace. After this brief introduction to passive monitoring, we now turn to a more invasive example.

6.12 Program Confinement with Library Calls

Library-call spoofing is a technique that intercepts calls from some program into system libraries. In a simple application, one monitors system library routine calls and perhaps modifies some arguments or results. In a more extreme application, the system libraries are never invoked at all.

We illustrate the principles with a small program that an Internet provider found on one of its FreeBSD systems. A quick disassembly into Intel machine language with the `gdb` debugger gives us an idea of the general nature of the program. The output, fragments of which are shown in Listing 6.3, contains all the signatures of a classic back-door program. A complete machine-language dump and analysis follow at the end of the chapter, in Section 6.15.

```
$ gdb unknown-program-file
[. . .]
(gdb) disassemble main
[. . .]
0x8048616 <main+54>:    call   0x80484a4 <scanf>
[. . .]
0x8048629 <main+73>:    call   0x8048484 <strcmp>
[. . .]
0x804863f <main+95>:    call   0x8048464 <puts>
[. . .]
0x804864a <main+106>:   push   $0x0
0x804864c <main+108>:   call   0x80484c4 <setuid>
[. . .]
0x8048657 <main+119>:   push   $0x0
0x8048659 <main+121>:   call   0x8048474 <setgid>
[. . .]
0x8048664 <main+132>:   push   $0x0
0x8048666 <main+134>:   push   $0x80486bc
0x804866b <main+139>:   push   $0x80486bf
0x8048670 <main+144>:   call   0x8048454 <execl>
```

Listing 6.3 *Fragments of machine-language disassembly of an unknown program, revealing system library routine calls and some of their arguments*

The calling pattern of system library routines suggests the purpose of the program: (1) read some input string with `scanf()`, (2) compare that input string against some other string with `strcmp()`, (3) print some third string with `puts()`, (4) request super-user privileges by calling `setuid(0)` and `setgid(0)`, and finally (5) call `execl()` to execute a program by its full pathname. The program executes without any command-line arguments, which simplifies the analysis.

A more systematic way to find out what system library routines a program invokes is to examine the symbol tables in the program file. If a program plays by the rules, then it has a table with the names of all the system library routines that it invokes. A somewhat-portable command to display the names of those system library routines is `objdump`. For the back-door program presented in this section, the following is the output for "undefined" symbols—that is, symbols that are resolved by system libraries:

```
$ objdump --dynamic-syms program-file | grep UND
08048454        DF *UND*   0000007d execl
08048464        DF *UND*   000000bf puts
00000000   w   D  *UND*   00000000 __deregister_frame_info
08048474        DF *UND*   00000000 setgid
08048484        DF *UND*   00000000 strcmp
08048494        DF *UND*   00000070 atexit
080484a4        DF *UND*   0000006a scanf
080484b4        DF *UND*   0000005b exit
080484c4        DF *UND*   00000000 setuid
00000000   w   D  *UND*   00000000 __register_frame_info
```

On systems without the `objdump` command, one can try the following command instead:

```
$ nm -op program-file | grep ' U '
```

Two major unknowns need to be determined: (1) the back-door password that must be entered to use the program and (2) the command that the back door executes with super-user privileges when the correct password is given. The `strings` command reveals a `/bin/sh` string in the back-door program file. This is likely to be the target command. As for the password, `strings` does not reveal an obvious candidate.

To discover the back-door password, we run the program in a software sandbox. We use a modified `strcmp()` (compare strings) routine. Unlike the system library routine, our version prints its arguments, the real password and our input, and then terminates the program before it can do harm.

```
$ cat strcmp.c
int strcmp(const char *a1, const char *a2)
{
    printf("strcmp call arguments: \"%s\" and \"%s\"\n", a1, a2);
    exit(0);
}
```

To force the back-door program to use our `strcmp()` routine instead of the one in the system library, we specify our code through the `LD_PRELOAD` environment variable. This directs the run-time linker to look at our code first when it needs to find a `strcmp()` routine. The following shows how we compile our `strcmp()` routine and how we run the back-door program, with a test password of `asdasd`.

```
$ cc -shared -o strcmp.so strcmp.c
$ LD_PRELOAD=`pwd`/strcmp.so ./backdoor-program-file
asdasd
strcmp call arguments: "socket11" and "asdasd"
```

So there is the back-door password: `socket11`, right next to the test password that we gave as input. Note: The example does not show the real back-door password, which was the name of an existing site whose identity we prefer to keep confidential. The replacement password, `socket11`, features in intrusions that are linked to the Berferd episode (Cheswick 1992, Venema 1992).

The library-level sandboxing method as discussed here works on Solaris, FreeBSD, Linux, and other systems that have a similar software architecture.

6.13 The Dangers of Confinement with Library Calls

Although system-call and library-call interception appear to be very similar techniques, there are major differences as far as security is concerned. System calls have to cross a hard barrier (the process-kernel interface) and cannot go undetected, nor can a process lie about the system-call name (although a multi-threaded process can lie about its argument values, as discussed previously).

Library-call monitors, on the other hand, depend entirely on information that exists within the address space of the monitored process. If a program does not play by the rules and if the monitoring program isn't designed to control hostile code, then that code can bypass library-call monitoring mechanisms with relative ease.

For example, a malicious program can invoke system calls or system library routines without involving the normal run-time linker mechanisms, and thus escape from the library-level sandbox. Examples of such code can be found in buffer-overflow exploits. A self-inflicted buffer-overflow exploit would be problematic not only for dynamic analysis. It would likely defeat detection by static analysis, too, because buffer-overflow code starts its life as data, not code.

6.14 Dynamic Analysis at the Machine-Instruction Level

This brings us to the last topic on malware analysis. We looked at controlled execution of virtual machines, system calls, and library calls. The next step is controlled execution of individual machine instructions with software debuggers or machine emulators. These tools give total control over the contents of memory locations and processor registers, and they can change the program flow arbitrarily, jumping over function calls and changing the branch taken after a decision. Using such tools is also incredibly time-consuming. We recommend first using the higher-level tools to zoom in on the code of interest and then proceeding to study the finer details using the material covered in the next section.

6.15 Static Analysis and Reverse Engineering

In this section, we cover the techniques that we consider suitable only for the highly motivated: program disassembly (converting a program file into a listing of machine-language instructions), program decompilation (converting machine-language instructions into the equivalent source code in a higher-level language), and static analysis (examining a program without actually executing it).

Program disassembly is a standard feature of every self-respecting debugger program. However, tools that decompile programs back into a higher-level language such as C exist only for limited environments (Cifuentes 1994). Concerns about intellectual property theft may have a lot to do with the limited availability of decompilers. The threat of reverse engineering also presents an interesting problem to programmers of Java applications. Compiled Java code contains so much additional information that very good decompilers already exist (Kouznetsov 2001).

Recovering C source code by reverse engineering is not as difficult as it may appear. The typical C compiler produces machine code by filling in standard instruction templates. The resulting code contains a lot of redundant instructions that are eliminated by the compiler optimizer (which is disabled by default on UNIX). In the case study that follows, the redundancy was still present in all its glory, and it is relatively easy to recognize the individual templates for each C language statement.

In the text that follows, we present the machine-language listing of the previous section's back-door program, as well as the C source code that was recovered by reverse engineering. Blocks of machine language are followed by the corresponding C language statements.

Note that we make a few simplifications in our analysis. The back-door program file contains more instructions than those produced by compiling the intruder's C program source code. The back-door program also contains a block of code that runs when the program starts up. On many UNIX systems, there is also a block of code that runs when the program terminates. Those code blocks are the same for every program file. A proper analysis would require that this so-called preamble and postamble code be verified as authentic. A program that breaks the rules could be hiding evil code in these code sections.

```
0x80485e0 <main>:       push   %ebp
0x80485e1 <main+1>:     mov    %esp,%ebp
0x80485e3 <main+3>:     sub    $0x68,%esp
```

```
main()
{
    char    buffer[80];
    char    password[12];
```

This code block enters the main program, saves the stack frame pointer, and reserves some space on the memory stack for local variables. The actual sizes of the two character array buffers were deduced by looking at the code that follows next. The names of the local variables could not be recovered from the program file, either. The names used here are not part of the program but are the result of an educated guess.

```
0x80485e6 <main+6>:     movb   $0x73,0xfffffa4(%ebp) ; %ebp-0x5c
0x80485ea <main+10>:    movb   $0x6f,0xfffffa5(%ebp) ; %ebp-0x5b
0x80485ee <main+14>:    movb   $0x63,0xfffffa6(%ebp) ; %ebp-0x5a
0x80485f2 <main+18>:    movb   $0x6b,0xfffffa7(%ebp) ; %ebp-0x59
0x80485f6 <main+22>:    movb   $0x65,0xfffffa8(%ebp) ; %ebp-0x58
0x80485fa <main+26>:    movb   $0x74,0xfffffa9(%ebp) ; %ebp-0x57
0x80485fe <main+30>:    movb   $0x31,0xfffffaa(%ebp) ; %ebp-0x56
0x8048602 <main+34>:    movb   $0x31,0xfffffab(%ebp) ; %ebp-0x55
0x8048606 <main+38>:    movb   $0x0,0xfffffac(%ebp)  ; %ebp-0x54
```

```
        password[0] = 's';
        password[1] = 'o';
        password[2] = 'c';
        password[3] = 'k';
        password[4] = 'e'
        password[5] = 't';
        password[6] = '1';
        password[7] = '1';
        password[8] = 0;
```

Aha! This explains why it was not possible to find the back-door password with the `strings` command. The password string is built one character at a time, a crude form of password obfuscation. To change the password, one has to actually change the program source code.

```
0x804860a <main+42>:    add    $0xfffffff8,%esp     ; space for 8 bytes
0x804860d <main+45>:    lea    0xffffffb0(%ebp),%eax; %ebp-0x50
0x8048610 <main+48>:    push   %eax                 ; buffer
0x8048611 <main+49>:    push   $0x80486b7           ; "%s"
0x8048616 <main+54>:    call   0x80484a4 <scanf>
0x804861b <main+59>:    add    $0x10,%esp           ; restore stack
```

```
        scanf("%s", buffer);
```

The program makes space on the memory stack for two `scanf()` function arguments (four bytes per argument). The arguments are the address of a string buffer for the result and the address of the `"%s"` format string, which requests string input. The `scanf()` routine reads a string from the default input stream. Note the absence of any result buffer-length specification; functions such as `scanf()` are extremely vulnerable to buffer-overflow problems and should never be used. After the `scanf()` call completes, the program restores the old stack pointer value.

```
0x804861e <main+62>:    add    $0xfffffff8,%esp     ; space for 8 bytes
0x8048621 <main+65>:    lea    0xffffffb0(%ebp),%eax; %ebp-0x50
0x8048624 <main+68>:    push   %eax                 ; buffer
0x8048625 <main+69>:    lea    0xffffffa4(%ebp),%eax; %ebp-0x5c
0x8048628 <main+72>:    push   %eax                 ; password
0x8048629 <main+73>:    call   0x8048484 <strcmp>
0x804862e <main+78>:    add    $0x10,%esp           ; restore stack
```

```
        strcmp(password, buffer);
```

The program makes space on the memory stack for two `strcmp()` function arguments (four bytes per argument). The arguments are the address of the string buffer with the input that was read with `scanf()` and the address of the password string buffer that was initialized one character at a time. The `strcmp()` call compares the two strings and returns a value less than zero, zero, or greater than zero, depending on the result of alphabetical comparison. After the `strcmp()` call completes, the program restores the old stack pointer value.

```
0x8048631 <main+81>:    mov    %eax,%eax
0x8048633 <main+83>:    test   %eax,%eax
0x8048635 <main+85>:    jne    0x8048678 <main+152>
```

This is a conditional jump. If the result from `strcmp()` is nonzero, the program jumps to the end of the main program. We must therefore read this code block together with the previous code block as:

```
        if (strcmp(password, buffer) == 0) {
```

What follows are blocks of code that execute only when the user enters the correct password (or that is what the program believes when the `strcmp()` routine returns a zero result).

```
0x8048637 <main+87>:    add   $0xfffffff4,%esp    ; space for 4 bytes
0x804863a <main+90>:    push  $0x80486ba          ; "."
0x804863f <main+95>:    call  0x8048464 <puts>
0x8048644 <main+100>:   add   $0x10,%esp          ; restore stack

          puts(".");
```

The program makes space on the memory stack for one puts() function
argument (four bytes per argument). The argument is the address of a
string consisting of a sole "." (period) character. The puts() routine
prints the string on the default output stream and automatically appends
an end-of-line character. After the puts() call completes, the program
restores the old stack pointer value.

```
0x8048647 <main+103>:   add   $0xfffffff4,%esp    ; space for 4 bytes
0x804864a <main+106>:   push  $0x0
0x804864c <main+108>:   call  0x80484c4 <setuid>
0x8048651 <main+113>:   add   $0x10,%esp          ; restore stack

          setuid(0);


0x8048654 <main+116>:   add   $0xfffffff4,%esp    ; space for 4 bytes
0x8048657 <main+119>:   push  $0x0
0x8048659 <main+121>:   call  0x8048474 <setgid>
0x804865e <main+126>:   add   $0x10,%esp          ; restore stack

          setgid(0);
```

The program makes space on the memory stack for one setuid() function argument. The argument is a null integer value, the user ID of the
super-user. The setuid() routine sets the process user ID to zero.[1] After
the setuid() call completes, the program restores the old stack pointer
value. The setuid() call is followed by similar code, which calls the
setgid() function to set the process group ID to zero.

```
0x8048661 <main+129>:   add   $0xfffffffc,%esp    ; space for 12 bytes
0x8048664 <main+132>:   push  $0x0                ; NULL
0x8048666 <main+134>:   push  $0x80486bc          ; "sh"
0x804866b <main+139>:   push  $0x80486bf          ; "/bin/sh"
0x8048670 <main+144>:   call  0x8048454 <execl>
0x8048675 <main+149>:   add   $0x10,%esp          ; restore stack

          execl("/bin/sh", "sh", (char *) 0);
```

---

1. setuid(0) sets the real and effective user IDs and the saved set-userid to the
   specified value. setgid(0) sets the real and effective group ID and the saved
   set-groupid to the specified value. These two calls are necessary only after
   exploiting a vulnerability in a set-userid root program. With other programs,
   the three user IDs are already the same, as are the three group IDs.

The program makes space on the memory stack for three `execl()` arguments (four bytes per argument). The arguments are the full pathname of the standard UNIX command interpreter (`/bin/sh`), the process name for the command to be executed (`sh`, almost always the last component of the program file pathname), and a null terminator. The `execl()` call executes the named command. In this case, the command has no command-line parameters.

At this point we are right before the last statement of the main program, the place to which the program jumps when the user enters an incorrect password.

```
0x8048678 <main+152>:   xor    %eax,%eax              ; zero result
0x804867a <main+154>:   jmp    0x804867c <main+156>
0x804867c <main+156>:   leave
0x804867d <main+157>:   ret


        }
        return (0);
```

The program returns the null result code and terminates. This completes the decompilation of the back-door program.

6.16 Small Programs Can Have Many Problems

Now that we have recovered the C source code, it is worthwhile to take one last look. The main portion of interest of the back-door program is only a few statements long, but it is simply amazing to see how many problems that code has.

```
scanf("%s", buffer);
if (strcmp(password, buffer) == 0) {
    puts(".");
    setuid(0);
    setgid(0);
    execl("/bin/sh", "sh", (char *) 0);
}
return (0);
```

With the exception of the `strcmp()` string comparison function call, none of the function calls is tested for error returns. If an operation fails, the program simply marches on. Input read error from `scanf()`? Never mind. Unable to set super-user privileges with `setuid()` and `setgid()`? Who cares. Can't execute the standard UNIX command interpreter with `execl()`? The program terminates silently without any sort of explanation of what and why.

6.17 Malware Analysis Countermeasures

In the preceding sections, we mentioned that some malware does not play by the rules in order to complicate program analysis. Many of these techniques also have legitimate uses, either to protect the intellectual property of the software itself or to protect the data handled by that software.

- A program file won't decompile into high-level source code if that program was not generated by a high-level language compiler or if the compiler output was run through a code obfuscator.

- An encrypted executable file can be examined only by those who know the decryption key. For example, Burneye encrypts executables and wraps them with a decrypting bootstrap program (Grugq and Scut 2001). However, when the program is run, the bootstrap code decrypts the entire program, so that it can still be captured in the clear with a utility such as `pcat` or the equivalent. This loophole could have been avoided with just-in-time decryption and deletion of code after it is used.

- Analysis is complicated by self-modifying code (which is especially popular with writers of computer viruses), code that jumps into data (including buffer-overflow code), code that actually is data for a private interpreter, and other tricks that fuzz the boundary between code and data.

As malware evolves, we can expect to see the adoption of increasingly sophisticated techniques to frustrate attempts to reverse engineer suspect programs.

6.18 Conclusion

In this chapter, we have touched upon many topics, introducing the basics of passive monitoring, execution in controlled or isolated environments, static machine-code analysis, and reverse engineering. Each technique has its domain of applicability. The disassembly and decompilation example at the end illustrates that static analysis is feasible with only very small programs. With larger programs, a combination of dynamic analysis and static analysis has more promise: dynamic analysis shows where execution goes, and static analysis shows why the program goes there. However, dynamic analysis is not recommended without safeguards, as described at the beginning of the chapter: dedicated hosts, virtual hosts, or at the very least, jails, to confine suspect software in where it can go and what permanent damage it can do.

PART III

Beyond the Abstractions

In this final part of the book, we move beyond abstractions, leaving behind the notions of files and processes while delving into the longevity and decay of data in the file system and in memory.

Users certainly contribute to the decline of deleted data, by running programs and by saving and creating files. But computers also have the power to destroy. In the background, processes are steadily eating away at the prior state of the computer. Despite this reality, we found that deleted information can be surprisingly resilient against destruction: Everyone knows it's easy to lose data you want to keep, but few people know that data can be hard to destroy completely. Behind the scenes, systems produce multiple copies as they move information through a variety of locations.

In Chapter 7, "The Persistence of Deleted File Information," we show that large amounts of deleted file content and metadata can survive intact for extended periods of time, and we provide a roughly estimated half-life for deleted data on file systems.

Chapter 8, "Beyond Processes," shows examples of the persistence of information in main memory. Different classes of data survive in very different ways, including the decrypted content of encrypted files. Hardware platforms and operating systems can have major effects on persistence. We finish the book discussing the tenacity of memory and the difficulty of clearing it through software.

This is perhaps the most challenging and unusual part of the book. The experiments often took several months before we had enough data to draw any conclusions. In particular, the experiments with main memory might be the most impractical, if not challenging, to use in investigations. The results, however, are of general importance, for they provide a deeper insight into the complexity that is inherent in what might seem like a simple investigative situation.

## CHAPTER 7

The Persistence of Deleted File Information

7.1 Introduction

Computers delete files frequently. Sometimes this happens on explicit request by a user. Often, information is deleted implicitly when an application discards some temporary file for its own internal use. Examples of such implicit file-deletion activity are text editor temporary files, files with intermediate results from program compilers, and files in Web browser caches. As you use a computer system, you unwittingly leave behind a trail of deleted information.

Computer systems have minds of their own, too, leaving their own trails of deletion as a side effect of activity that happens in the background. Examples of background deletion activity are temporary files in mail system queues or in printer queues. Such files exist for only a few seconds or minutes. If your machine provides network services to other systems, information from systems you aren't even aware of may hit your disk. Log files are another example of background file-creation and file-deletion activity.

With many computer systems, deleted file information remains intact on the disk, in unallocated data blocks and in unallocated file attribute blocks, until it is overwritten in the course of other activity. This can result in unexpected disclosure of information when a machine (or its disk) is retired and resold as secondhand equipment. For a study on how much information can be found on secondhand disk drives after the owners thought they had deleted all their files, see Garfinkel and Shelat 2003.

In this chapter, we study how deleted file information can escape destruction intact for months or even years, and how deleted file attribute information can provide insight into past system activity. We examine several systems and discover how well past activity can be preserved in unallocated disk space. At the end of the chapter, we explain why deleted file information can be more persistent than ordinary file information.

Although our results are based on UNIX file systems, we expect that they will be applicable to any modern file system that maintains a low degree of file fragmentation.

7.2 Examples of Deleted Information Persistence

In 1996, Peter Gutmann presented a paper on the problem of data destruction (Gutmann 1996), and in 2001, he delivered a follow-up paper (Gutmann 2001). Peter's concern is with the security of sensitive information such as cryptographic keys and unencrypted data. The best encryption in the world is no good when keys or unencrypted contents can be recovered.

Destroying information turns out to be difficult. Memory chips can be read even after a machine is turned off. Data on a magnetic disk can be recovered even after it has been overwritten multiple times.

Although memory chips and magnetic disks are designed to store digital information, the underlying technology is analog. With analog storage of digital information, the value of a bit is a complex combination of past stored values. Memory chips have undocumented diagnostic modes that allow access to values smaller than a bit. With modified electronic circuitry, signals from disk read heads can reveal older data as modulations on the analog signal.

Another way to examine disks is by scanning the surface. Figure 7.1 gives a spectacular example of old magnetic patterns that persist on the side of a disk track. You can find other images of semiconductors and magnetic patterns on the Veeco Web site (Veeco 2004).

However, lots of deleted information can be recovered without ever scanning the surface of magnetic disks, even when that information was deleted long ago. We examined the disk from a machine that began its life as a Windows PC, had a second life as a Solaris firewall, and finally was converted into a Linux system. After one operating system was installed over another, the deleted Solaris and Windows files were still clearly present as the contents of unallocated disk blocks. For example, we found intact copies of many deleted Solaris firewall configuration files. They could have been sitting on the machine for many more years without ever being overwritten.

Figure 7.1 *Residuals of overwritten information on the sides of magnetic disk tracks. Reproduced with permission of Veeco.*

7.3 Measuring the Persistence of Deleted File Contents

The previous Windows PC example is unusual. We were able to estimate the age of deleted information simply because the Windows files were installed before Solaris, and because the Solaris files were installed before Linux. Although files often contain clues about when information was created, the contents of a deleted file rarely provide obvious clues about when that file was deleted.

To find out how long deleted file contents survive, we ran a 20-week experiment on a few machines on our own networks. We followed the history of each data block from day to day, from the time it was deleted to the time it was overwritten. Every night, an automated script examined each 1-Kbyte disk block and recorded a hash of the disk block's contents as well as the disk block's status: allocated, unallocated, or overhead such as inode (file attribute) or bitmap block.

Figure 7.2 shows the distribution of surviving file contents versus time of deletion for a small server file system. Despite significant fluctuation, the trend is clear. We found about 100 Mbytes of contents that were deleted less than a week ago, while about 10 Mbytes were left over from contents that were deleted 20 weeks ago. At the time of the measurement, this machine handled about 1,500 e-mail messages daily (about 10 Mbytes of data) and did limited amounts of WWW, FTP, and DNS service. Logging by the mail system amounted to about 1.5 Mbytes of data each day. The file system of 8.0 Gbytes was about 50 percent full, and most of the e-mail contents and logging were automatically deleted after a short time.

With this particular machine, half the deleted file contents were overwritten after about 35 days. Table 7.1 summarizes the results for a variety of file systems. There is some variation, but differences less than a

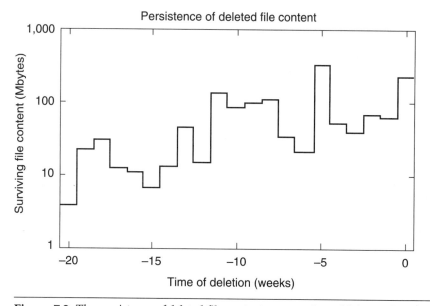

Figure 7.2 *The persistence of deleted file contents versus time of deletion for a small server file system. Time 0 corresponds to the present, and negative times represent the past. The data in the graph represent one-third of all unallocated disk blocks in the file system. The machine, spike.porcupine.org, is Wietse's FreeBSD server.*

factor of two are not significant. The lesson is that deleted data can stay around for weeks or more.

What the graph and the table do not show is how information survives. Does a deleted file slowly erode away, or does it stay mostly intact until it is finally destroyed? With file systems that suffer from fragmentation problems, we expect that a deleted file is destroyed gradually, one fragment at a time. With file systems that avoid fragmentation, we expect that a deleted file stays mostly intact until it is destroyed, in a relatively short time. We return to this topic at the end of this chapter.

Table 7.1 *The half-life of deleted file contents for three systems: spike.porcupine.org (Wietse's FreeBSD server), flying.fish.com (Dan's Linux workstation and server), and www.porcupine.org (Wietse's FreeBSD WWW and FTP server)*

Machine	File System	Half-Life
spike.porcupine.org	Entire disk	35 days
flying.fish.com	/	17 days
flying.fish.com	/usr	19 days
www.porcupine.org	Entire disk	12 days

7.4 Measuring the Persistence of Deleted File MACtimes

We recall from Chapter 2 that MACtimes, the time attributes of files, can give great insight into past activity on a machine. In this chapter, we apply the same technique to deleted file attribute information.

Furthermore, we recall from Chapter 3 that UNIX file systems store file attributes separately from file contents, and from Chapter 4 that some MACtime information survives when a file is deleted:

- The last modification time attribute (mtime) does not change (in Linux) or is set to the time of deletion (in BSD and Solaris).

- The last read access time attribute (atime) does not change.

- The last status change time attribute (ctime) is set to the time of deletion.

- Some Linux file systems have a fourth time attribute (dtime) that records when a file was deleted, but the attribute doesn't add much value; we do not discuss it further.

As we show in the next sections, deleted file attribute information can survive for months or even years, just like deleted file contents. Sometimes the reasons for survival are rather subtle, involving a combination of dumb luck and the existence of pockets of low activity in the file system. Sometimes the reasons for survival are not subtle, involving mainly the application of brute force.

7.5 The Brute-Force Persistence of Deleted File MACtimes

To find out how robust deleted file attribute information can be, we set up a disposable Linux machine and downloaded version 4 of the Linux rootkit source code, `lrk4.tgz`, from one of many malware download sites. The rootkit installs a network password sniffer program and replaces a dozen system programs with modified versions. The rootkit installation procedure uses stealth techniques to ensure that the modified program files have the same MACtimes, file sizes, and file cyclic redundancy check (CRC) values as the files being replaced. See Section 5.10 for more information about subversion with rootkit software.

We compiled the rootkit software, ran the procedure that installs the modified system utilities, and removed the rootkit source code, just as an intruder would do. Then we did just about the worst possible thing imaginable: We downloaded the Coroner's Toolkit source code distribution, unpacked the archive in the exact same directory where the "intruder" unpacked the rootkit archive, compiled our toolkit, and then ran the software in order to collect "evidence." Note: To avoid the kind of data destruction described here, the authors recommend the use of CD-ROM images with ready-to-run software. For examples, see FIRE 2004 and KNOPPIX 2004a, 2004b.

By using the Coroner's Toolkit in this manner, we knowingly destroyed large amounts of information. We overwrote data blocks that belonged to deleted rootkit files, we overwrote file attribute blocks (MACtimes!) that belonged to deleted rootkit files, and we destroyed last file access time information for compiler-related files. Kids, don't do this at home! Even after all that destruction, the Coroner's Toolkit still found the attributes of 476 deleted files and directories that existed during the rootkit incident.

In Figure 7.3, the ctime graph at the top shows the approximate times at which files were deleted. Notice the large peak on the right-hand side of the graph; this shows when the rootkit directory was removed, along with the source code and the compiler output files.

The atime graph in the middle shows when deleted files were accessed in order to compile the rootkit source code. The large atime peak on the left-hand side corresponds to rootkit files that were unpacked but not used. This is an artifact of many UNIX file systems: they set the atime of a file to the time when it is created.

The mtime graph at the bottom shows the last time that file contents were modified before they were deleted. Only 165 of the 476 deleted file residuals had mtimes in the incident time window; the data points correspond to files that were produced while compiling the rootkit source code. The remaining 311 deleted file residuals had nearly identical last file modification times in the distant past. Presumably, that was the time when the rootkit source code was packaged for distribution on some other machine.

The signal of surviving deleted file MACtimes was so strong that it should be hard to miss for anyone who knows what to look for, even days after the event. The reason for the strong signal is that rootkit software, just like other software, suffers from bloat and feature creep. Linux rootkit version 4 has a rather large total footprint of approximately 780 files and directories, including the compiler output files that are produced when the software is compiled. The Coroner's Toolkit, on the other hand, has a footprint of "only" 300 files. The number is not large enough to wipe out all the rootkit's deleted file MACtime information.

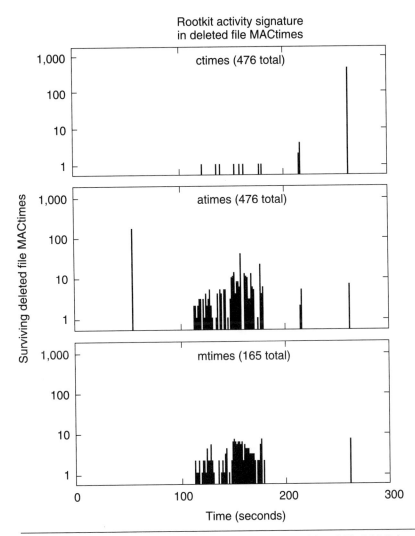

Figure 7.3 *The signature of Linux rootkit activity in deleted file MACtimes after downloading, compiling, and running the Coroner's Toolkit software. The ctime graph shows the time a file was deleted, atime shows the last read operation before a file was deleted, and mtime shows the last time the file contents were modified. See the text for a discussion of specific graph features.*

Using MACtimes for Malware Detection

MACtimes of deleted or existing files can reveal that someone may have brought specific malware into a system. Malware, like any software, is usually distributed in the form of archives that contain multiple files. The software that maintains archives carefully preserves the last modification time stamps of the original files and carefully restores those time stamps upon extraction. Even after the files are deleted, the malware's last modification time stamps can persist in the unallocated file attribute blocks.

This rootkit incident has an especially revealing signature, as shown in Figure 7.4. Of the 311 deleted file last modification times not in the incident time window, 296 were identical to within 15 seconds. Whether or not the time in the time stamps is forged does not matter. A peak with hundreds of deleted mtimes in this particular time interval should raise suspicion.

A MACtime malware signature analysis can be done relatively quickly. For example, the Coroner's Toolkit `ils` (list inodes) command can read all the 2 million file attribute blocks within an 8-Gbyte FreeBSD file system in less than half a minute, much less time than would be needed to examine gigabytes of data blocks.

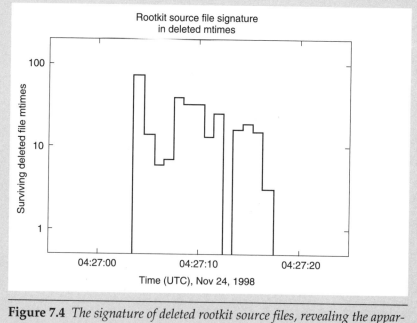

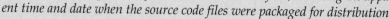

Figure 7.4 *The signature of deleted rootkit source files, revealing the apparent time and date when the source code files were packaged for distribution*

7.6 The Long-Term Persistence of Deleted File MACtimes

The brute-force persistence of deleted file MACtimes, as shown in the previous section, relies on massive file system activity in a relatively short time. This produces a strong signal that stands out well above the noise. The signal survives even when the event is followed by a significant file system activity.

The brute-force example does not tell us how long deleted file MACtime information can survive. To explore that question, we analyzed the file systems of several machines. We were surprised to find deleted file MACtime information going back an entire year or more, typically back to the time the file system was created on the disk.

Figure 7.5 shows deleted file MACtime attributes for a FreeBSD server machine that spends most of its time doing routine work: sending and receiving e-mail; providing network services such as DNS, FTP, and WWW; and maintaining log files. There is one exception to the routine. The system owner is the author of an open source mail server, and he is the "first user" of every release. "First use" involves unpacking, compiling, and removing the source code. At the time of the measurement, releases happened roughly in monthly bursts.

On the right-hand side of the figure, deleted file MACtime information decays gradually as one goes back in time. On this particular machine, 90 percent of the deleted file MACtime information is overwritten in about 60 days, as the result of routine machine activity. This corresponds with a half-life of about 20 days. This is less than the 35-day half-life found earlier for deleted file contents, but the difference is not meaningful given the accuracy of the measurements. On the left-hand side of the figure, the deleted file MACtime distributions are relatively sparse, but the patterns go back until the time that FreeBSD was installed on the machine.

The top graph, with the distribution of the ctime attribute, shows the approximate time that a file was deleted. Any deleted file ctime attributes that survive beyond the first 100 days of history are likely to be the result of nonroutine activity on the machine. For this particular machine, the most likely candidate is the compiling and installing of new mail software on the machine, and the subsequent removal of the source code.

The atime graph in the middle shows the last time that a file was accessed before it was deleted. The atime information goes back by hundreds of days, just like the graph of ctimes (file deletion times). This is not at all what one would find with ordinary file MACtimes: with ordinary files,

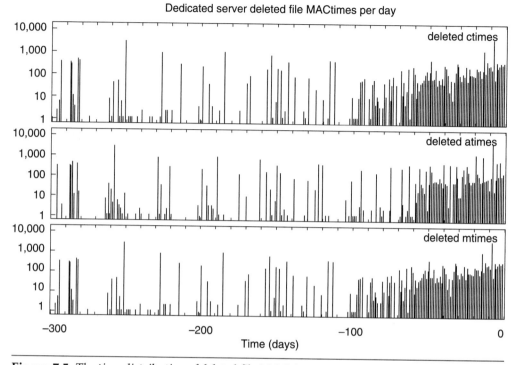

Figure 7.5 *The time distribution of deleted file MACtime attributes for a small server file system. Time 0 corresponds to the present, and negative times represent the past. The machine, spike.porcupine.org, is Wietse's FreeBSD server.*

atimes are the most volatile MACtime component. With deleted information, the rules are different: deleted file last access times are as persistent as any deleted file attribute, because they are no longer updated. We return to this phenomenon of fossilization in Section 7.10.

The bottom graph shows the distribution of the mtime attribute (file modification time). The FreeBSD file system sets the mtime to the time of deletion, and therefore its graph is identical to the ctime graph.

7.7 The Impact of User Activity on Deleted File MACtimes

Just like regular MACtimes, deleted file MACtimes are sensitive to system usage patterns. The data in the previous section are typical of a dedicated machine that spends most of its time doing routine work. The analysis of a personal workstation is more complex, because system behavior is dominated by less predictable user activity.

Figure 7.6 shows the time distribution of deleted file MACtimes for a personal workstation. This machine is the user's primary work environment for sending and receiving e-mail, surfing the Web, and developing software. In addition, it also does a limited amount of routine WWW and DNS service. The MACtime patterns for this machine are dramatically different from those of the dedicated server in Figure 7.5.

On the right-hand side, the graphs of deleted file ctimes (times of deletion) and atimes (last read access times) show decay of recent history. The decay is not nearly as smooth as in Figure 7.5. On the left-hand side, the ctime and atime graphs show residuals from significant activity in the more distant past. As with the dedicated server, the residuals go back in time until the file system was created.

The graph of the workstation's deleted file mtimes (last modification times) is unlike all the other graphs we have discussed. The workstation's distribution actually comprises two components. One component correlates with the ctime and atime graphs and corresponds to relatively

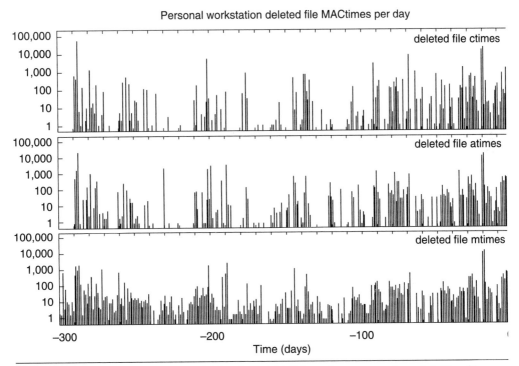

Figure 7.6 *The time distribution of deleted file MACtimes for a personal workstation file system. Time 0 corresponds to the present, and negative times represent the past. The machine flying.fish.com is Dan's Red Hat Linux workstation.*

short-lived files; the other component shows up as a more or less time-independent background of about ten deleted file residuals a day.

The existence of the time-independent component means that some files have no correlation between the time of last update and the time of deletion. This is consistent with the primary user's behavior. According to the user, files accumulate over time at a steady rate. Every few months, the user deletes a large number of files to free up some space.

7.8 The Trustworthiness of Deleted File Information

Deleted file MACtimes or contents present the investigator with great opportunities. Because deleted information is less visible than ordinary information, an opponent is less likely to be aware that the information exists, and therefore is less likely to tamper with it. For example, if a log file was modified, it is possible that portions of the unmodified file can still be recovered from unallocated file system space.

Deleted file MACtimes inherit only some of the limitations of existing file MACtimes. Prior to deletion, a file is relatively easy to access. Its MACtime information is volatile and is easily forged, as described in Chapter 2. After deletion, it is relatively easy to nonselectively overwrite deleted file MACtimes by creating a large number of small files. Changing specific deleted attributes becomes more difficult, at least on systems that can permanently revoke write access to kernel memory and disk devices (see, for example, the discussion of kernel security levels in Section 5.6).

A similar argument can be made for deleted file contents. Prior to deletion, information is relatively easy to access, and therefore relatively easy to modify. After deletion, it is relatively easy to nonselectively overwrite deleted file contents by creating a small number of large files. Changing specific deleted data blocks becomes more difficult, at least on systems that can permanently revoke write access to kernel memory and disk devices.

After deletion, forging file MACtimes or contents can be risky. The straightforward approach is to bypass the file system and write to the raw disk. There is a definite possibility of file system corruption when a mala fide opponent competes with a bona fide file system for access to the same file system block. A more reliable approach would involve a kernel module that performs the cleansing while cooperating with the file system, rather than competing against it.

Completeness is an obvious issue with deleted information. Contrary to existing file MACtimes or file contents, deleted information can be overwritten at any time, and therefore it is more likely to be incomplete. As discussed in Chapter 1, the absence of specific information must not be used as evidence that the information was never stored. With unallocated storage, this is even truer than with ordinary file information.

7.9 Why Deleted File Information Can Survive Intact

In the previous sections, we have shown that deleted information can escape destruction for months or even years. In this section, we illustrate how the design of high-performance file systems can influence the long-term survival of deleted file information.

High-performance file systems avoid disk head movements by keeping related information close together. This not only reduces the fragmentation of individual file contents, it also reduces delays while traversing directories to access a file. Although the details that follow are specific to popular UNIX systems, we expect that similar persistence effects happen with any file system that has good locality properties.

The typical UFS or Ext3fs file system is organized into equal-size zones, as shown in Figure 7.7. These file systems descend from the Berkeley Fast File System (McKusick et al. 1984) and are found on Solaris, FreeBSD, and Linux (Card et al. 1994). Typical zone sizes are 32,768 blocks; the actual block size depends on the file system type; for some systems, it also

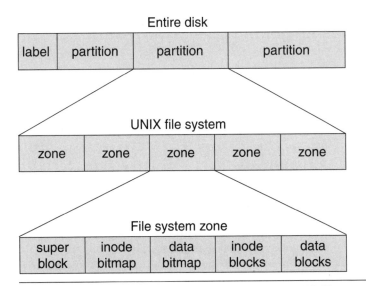

Figure 7.7 *The on-disk layout of a typical UFS or Ext3fs file system. Storage space is divided into multiple zones. Each zone contains its own allocation bitmaps, file data blocks, and file attribute (inode) blocks. Normally, information about a small file is stored entirely within one zone. The figure is not drawn to scale.*

depends on the file system size. New files are created preferably in the same file system zone as their parent directory; this improves the clustering of related information. New directories are created in zones that have few directories and lots of unused space.

By keeping related information within the same file system zone, typical UFS or Ext3fs file systems tend to cluster the files from different users or applications according to different file system zones. Because of this, the survival time of deleted information depends strongly on the amount of file write activity within its zone. As shown in Figure 7.8, write activity can be highly focused within specific file system zones.

When a file is deleted in a high-activity zone, its data blocks and file attribute information will be overwritten relatively quickly by new files. We saw an example of this in Chapter 4, when we failed to recover files that were deleted from the /tmp directory.

On the other hand, when a file is deleted in a low-activity zone, its data blocks and file attribute information can escape destruction as long as file system activity stays within other file system zones. As the disk fills up over time, write activity will unavoidably migrate into the quiet neighborhoods of low-activity zones, turning them into destructive, high-activity zones. Until that time, deleted file information in low-activity zones can survive intact and in copious amounts.

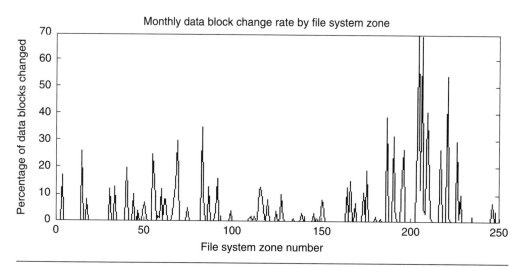

Figure 7.8 *The percentage of data blocks per file system zone that were overwritten in one month's time, for a small FreeBSD server with an 8-Gbyte file system that was filled to 50 percent capacity. The figure shows that disk write activity is focused within specific zones. Less than 4 percent of all data blocks were changed during this one-month interval.*

In Chapter 1, we observed that computer systems tend to spend most of their time running around performing routine activity. In terms of file system zones, this means that write activity tends to be focused in a limited number of zones where information is created and destroyed relatively quickly. The rest of the file system is relatively static, and any file deleted there is likely to survive for a relatively long time.

Thus, what we observed in Chapters 1 and 2 for ordinary files turns out to be true for deleted files as well: traces from routine activity erode quickly, while unusual activity stands out because its traces survive longer.

7.10 Conclusion

This chapter shows that deleted file information can survive intact for months or even years, and that deleted file attribute information can give insights about past system activity that you can't get from ordinary file attribute information.

In Chapter 1, we found that MACtime file access times for existing files can provide great insight into past system behavior. We also found that they suffer from a major drawback: MACtime information is destroyed anytime a file is accessed. Existing file MACtime information is volatile, like a footstep in sand. The next time you look, it has changed.

Deleted file MACtime information is different. When a file is deleted, its MACtime information does not change until it is overwritten. In other words, deleted file MACtime information becomes frozen in time.

The same is true for deleted file contents. Once deleted, file content does not change until it is overwritten. On file systems with good clustering properties, deleted files can remain intact for years. Deleted file information is like a fossil: a skeleton may be missing a bone here or there, but the fossil does not change until it is destroyed.

This phenomenon of deletion and persistence can happen at any abstraction level. At the abstraction level of file systems, deleted information persists as unallocated disk blocks until it is overwritten. At the abstraction level of magnetic-disk-reading heads, overwritten information persists as analog modulations on the newer information. And at the abstraction level of magnetic domains, overwritten information persists as magnetic patterns on the sides of magnetic tracks, as we saw in Figure 7.1.

At each layer in the hierarchy of abstractions that make up computer systems, information becomes frozen when it is deleted. Although deleted information becomes more and more ambiguous as we descend to lower and lower levels of abstraction, we also find that deleted information becomes ever more persistent. Volatility is an artifact of the abstractions that make computer systems useful.

All this has major consequences not only for intruders whose activity is reconstructed with post-mortem intrusion analysis, but also for the privacy of legitimate users of computer systems. For a discussion that covers much more than just computer systems, we refer the reader to Michael Caloyannides's book on privacy versus forensics (Caloyannides 2004).

## CHAPTER 8

Beyond Processes

8.1 Introduction

Thus far, we've covered only the elementary aspects of memory and the basic analysis of processes. However, the tools we've seen so far give access to the memory of running processes only; they're useless once a process terminates. Now we move beyond the process abstraction and start investigating a computer's virtual memory (VM) subsystem.

In this chapter, we find and recognize contents and files in raw memory, explore how long information can be expected to survive in main memory on a running computer, and investigate what factors contribute to a computer's amnesia. The main problem faced here is the great variation in the internals of how memory is implemented, not only from one operating system to the next, but also among even minor releases of the same memory manager. This means that system-specific techniques will have high development costs, high learning costs, and a short shelf life.

To make the problem less quixotic, we restrict our discussion to the architecture of a general-purpose machine, where programs and data are stored in permanent files and must be copied from the file store into main memory to be executed or processed. This is unlike various special-purpose architectures (such as those found in many PDAs, cell phones, and the like) that store programs and data in directly addressable memory locations so they never need to be copied into main memory.

First, we introduce the basics of virtual memory and memory-capturing techniques. Next, we show how information in memory may be identified using digital hashes, and we describe how the decay of memory contents is influenced by properties of the computer system architecture (including decrypted contents from the Windows encrypted file system). Finally, we conclude by looking at memory's resilience to destructive forces.

8.2 The Basics of Virtual Memory

All modern operating systems use virtual memory as an abstraction to handle combinations of RAM (or what we call main memory), swap space, ROM, NVRAM, and other memory resources. The memory manager, which runs in the kernel, handles the allocation and deallocation of the memory on a computer (the kernel has its own special-purpose memory manager). The file system has always been cached to some degree, but over the years, all the operating systems we discuss in this book have adopted a unified caching scheme that marries the file system cache with the rest of the virtual memory system. As a result, not only do they share the same memory pool, but the performance of the file system (one of the major drains on system performance) is also greatly enhanced. Figure 8.1 illustrates the layers between an application and the actual data on the disk.

The virtual memory system is organized into fixed-size blocks of data called *pages*, which in turn are mapped to actual physical addresses of memory. This scheme yields a simple and consistent virtual address space, irrespective of the underlying setup of physical memory. It also dynamically loads only the portions of a program file that are required for execution, instead of the entire executable file, and supports the sharing of memory between processes that use the same data or program code.

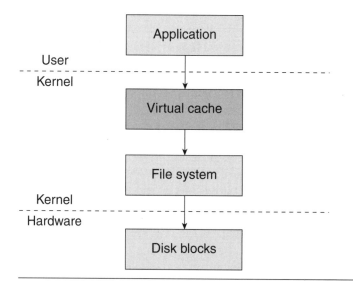

Figure 8.1 *Contemporary file system caching*

In this chapter, we focus on three classes of memory: kernel, process, and buffer. The UNIX virtual memory system unifies the allocation of memory for these areas; nearly all free memory (memory not used for processes or the kernel) is allocated for caching or buffering files. Thus, initial operations using the file system take a significant amount of time because information is not cached, but subsequent usage of the same data may be much faster, as the I/O takes place in memory rather than on disk. It's also crucial to note that these file system buffers are owned by the operating system, not by user-level applications that access files. Consequently, file contents remain cached in main memory even after any requesting application has terminated.

If a piece of memory is not directly associated with a file or the kernel, it is called *anonymous*; when the virtual memory manager runs low on main memory, it may use swap space as a secondary location for anonymous memory. Swap is nearly always stored on disk, and it has significantly poorer performance and slower access speeds than main memory. We have found in our measurements, however, that modern computers swap less and less often as memory has gotten larger and cheaper. This is both bad and good news for forensic analysts. The bad news is that because swap is more persistent than main memory and is used less frequently, the odds of the swap space having useful information are lower. But the good news is that once data has been placed into swap, it can stay there for some time.

Demand paging is an efficiency measure that allocates memory pages as they are referenced (that is, as they are actually used). This technique significantly reduces the memory footprint and lowers the start-up time of processes. Consider this output from ps:

```
linux % ps ux
USER       PID %CPU %MEM   VSZ  RSS TTY       STAT START    TIME COMMAND
zen       6201  0.0  0.1  2140 1336 pts/0     S    Dec22    0:00 -bash
zen      12837  0.5  0.1  2096 1268 pts/1     S    15:04    0:00 -bash
zen      12855  0.0  0.0  2668  952 pts/0     R    15:04    0:00 ps ux
```

VSZ is the virtual size of the processes, that is, how many kilobytes the virtual memory system has allocated for it. RSS stands for the resident set size of a process, or how many kilobytes of the process are actually in memory. Notice how even identical programs (in this case the bash login shell) may have different sizes of virtual and resident memory. This is because as they run, identical programs may dynamically allocate anonymous memory, use demand paging when executing different parts of the program, or swap in different ways and at different times.

8.3 The Basics of Memory Pages

Computer systems organize memory into fixed-size pages just as they organize file systems into fixed-size disk blocks. A page is the smallest unit of data that may be allocated by a system's virtual memory manager and is generally 4096 or 8192 bytes long. (Some architectures support memory pages of 4 Mbytes or more, but this won't affect our discussion; the concepts are the same. The `getpagesize()` library function will return the size of a memory page. Solaris and FreeBSD systems can also print out the memory page size with the `pagesize` command.)

To learn how to find information in memory, we need first to understand what data sits in memory pages and how. There are two basic types of data outside the kernel: data read from files and data in anonymous pages. The latter contain state information from processes (whether alive or dead). The virtual memory manager decides if a page is backed by a file, by physical memory, or by swap, depending on its needs and the type of data involved.

8.4 Files and Memory Pages

Any memory page that originates from a file has special status within memory because of the aggressive file-caching strategies used by the virtual memory manager. Files may also be memory mapped, which means that changes to a page in main memory also change the corresponding bytes of a file. In any case once a file has been read into main memory, its data remains for some time, depending on how busy the computer is after the event.

A process consists of a set of executable statements, usually from a file. A process is allocated a certain amount of memory that it sees as a seamless virtual address space, whether or not it's contiguous in the pages of actual memory. To recapitulate, Figure 8.2 shows the virtual view, as seen by the process.

The parts labeled private are swappable, but shared bits are taken from the file system and don't need to be swapped. All of our example systems have reasonably nice methods of displaying how individual processes rest in memory. FreeBSD has the `/proc/[pid]/map` file, Linux has `/proc/[pid]/maps`, and Solaris has the `pmap` command.

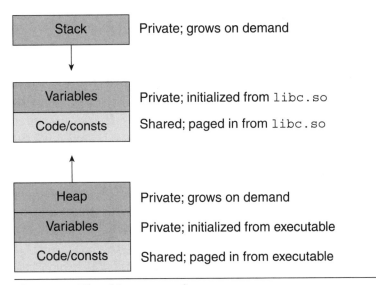

Figure 8.2 *The address space of a process*

8.5 Anonymous Memory Pages

Pages that aren't associated with a file compose the electronic flotsam and jetsam of memory. These include process state data: the heap, the stack, and so on. Most such anonymous data is in no discernible format whatsoever, unless you know the data structures that the individual programs use to save arbitrary data in memory.

Anonymous data can be long lasting, but it tends to be much more volatile than file data because, unlike file data, it isn't cached. We discuss anonymous pages in more detail in Section 8.14.

8.6 Capturing Memory

Before we can begin analyzing memory, we need to capture it—or at least capture what we can. In addition to the `savecore` command, we look at the three primary locations where UNIX systems interface with memory: the `/dev/mem` and `/dev/kmem` special devices, swap, and the various peripherals and hardware that have memory capacity (such as NVRAM and PROMs).

Determining the available amount of main memory and swap space is easy with the `top` command. If `top` isn't available, there are a variety of alternatives on any given operating system.

Solaris has the `prtconf` (print system configuration) utility and the `swap` command:

```
solaris # prtconf |grep -i 'memory size'
Memory size: 768 Megabytes
solaris # swap -l
swapfile              dev   swaplo blocks    free
/dev/dsk/c0t0d0s1     32,1       16 304544 298144
```

FreeBSD has `sysctl`, which can print and configure the kernel, and `pstat`, which displays system swap characteristics:

```
freebsd # sysctl hw.physmem
hw.physmem: 532013056
freebsd # pstat -s
Device         1K-blocks    Used    Avail Capacity Type
/dev/rad0s4b     1048448       0  1048448      0%   Interleaved
```

Linux can use the `/proc` memory file system and `kcore` to get memory and swap size information:

```
linux   # ls -l /proc/kcore
-r--------   1 root      root      1006637056 Mar 22 12:24 /proc/kcore
linux   # swapon -s
Filename                         Type          Size     Used
Priority
/foo/swapfile                    file          1999992 4092     -1
```

(The result returned by `kcore` is actually 4 Kbytes larger than the actual physical memory.)

As the Heisenberg property of computing reminds us (see Section 1.4), when we use software to capture memory, we're also disturbing the current memory image by executing a program and reading data. Writing the results of the memory capture presents another problem. The unification of file buffers into virtual memory means that any file output will be cached in memory, replacing the very information that you are trying to capture! Using a remote computer may be the best way to save data with minimal memory mutilation; we talk more about this when we look at device files, in the next section.

All this means that anytime you want to save memory, you face a conundrum: you want to preserve this very volatile data early on in a forensic investigation, but saving it can destroy additional evidence. What to do? Although there is no guarantee, here is our rule of thumb: If you suspect something of interest is on the computer, try to capture as much memory as you can, even if it means risking some damage to other evidence.

Many computers (especially laptops) have a hibernation mode that will store varying amounts of main memory and computer state on disk. Hibernation mode sounds promising: simply copy the data from the disk, restore the computer to its previous state, and go on with your analysis. Unfortunately, unallocated memory (which is important for our analytic methods) isn't usually saved. To make matters worse, hibernation mode frequently stores memory in some compressed or ill-documented format. In a real investigation, you should use any available method to capture memory, but in this chapter, we focus only on pure software methods.

8.7 The `savecore` Command

Most flavors of UNIX feature the `savecore` command, which saves a dump of some, if not all, of the computer's main memory. (As of this writing, Linux doesn't have this capability, although there are some distributions and patches that allow this.) This command is one of the more attractive options for saving memory, as it bypasses the file system and should disturb memory the least. The `savecore` command instructs the kernel to write memory directly to swap or to a designated raw disk partition, after which (usually upon reboot) `savecore` may be called to recover the core dump and store it in a regular file system. The core dump contains the kernel's memory and either the process memory or all of main memory.

The computer must also be set up properly for dumping before `savecore` may be used. To manage the `savecore` process, FreeBSD uses the `dumpon` command; Solaris has `dumpadm`. As far as we know, only Solaris can execute `savecore` on a running system without requiring a reboot, as shown in Listing 8.1.

Crash dumps of memory on Solaris and FreeBSD may also be forced with the `-d` flag to the `reboot` command.[1] Obviously this option can be damaging to other types of forensic evidence, but it might still be useful.

FreeBSD systems and older versions of Solaris can use options to commands such as `ps`, `netstat`, and `ipcs` to directly query a saved memory image, allowing you to see what was running at the time of the dump. Solaris tools have been constantly evolving. Currently, Solaris has

---

1. Microsoft's Windows XP and Windows 2000 operating systems may set a registry variable that allows a computer to dump up to 2 Gbytes of RAM by using a Ctrl–Scroll Lock keyboard sequence (Microsoft Knowledge Base Article 244139: "Windows 2000 Memory Dump Options Overview"). This is similar to FreeBSD's `reboot` command, but it has the added disadvantage of requiring an additional reboot of the system in advance in order to enable this. (Some other UNIX computers allow you to dump memory in a similarly destructive manner, such as typing `Stop-A` or `L1-A` on a Sun console, followed by the `sync` command.

```
solaris # dumpadm
      Dump content: all pages
        Dump device: /dev/dsk/c0t4d0s1 (dedicated)
Savecore directory: /foo/savecore
  Savecore enabled: yes
solaris # savecore -v -L
dumping to /dev/dsk/c0t4d0s1, offset 65536
100% done: 16384 pages dumped, compression ratio 2.29, dump succeeded
System dump time: Mon Dec 30 14:57:30 2002
Constructing namelist /foo/savecore/unix.1
Constructing corefile /foo/savecore/vmcore.1
100% done: 16384 of 16384 pages saved
solaris # ls -asl /foo/savecore/
total 264354
     2 drwxr-xr-x   2 root      other         512 Dec 30 14:57 ./
     2 drwxr-xr-x   4 root      root          512 Oct 22 22:44 ../
     2 -rwxr-xr-x   1 root      sys             2 Dec 30 14:58 bounds*
   704 -rw-------   1 root      sys        349164 Dec 30 14:57 unix.1
263472 -rw-------   1 root      sys     134905856 Dec 30 14:58 vmcore.1
```

Listing 8.1 *Saving the kernel memory core dump via* savecore. *The kernel's symbol table was stored in* unix.1, *main memory in* vmcore.1.

the mdb command, which improves on the functionality of older tools; the more ambitious MemTool and Solaris Crash Analysis Tool are available online (MemTool 2004, SCAT 2004). In the right hands, a saved crash dump paired with appropriate tools can reveal volumes. However, retrieving such things is outside the scope of this book. (For a good, albeit dated, discussion of this subject, see Drake and Brown 1995.)

Memory Device Files: /dev/mem and /dev/kmem

If savecore isn't practical, there are other methods for capturing memory. Accessing the memory of a system is easy if you have sufficient user privileges. UNIX systems permit you to read or write to memory via the /dev/mem or /dev/kmem device files. The /dev/mem device file is a special file that mirrors main memory; byte offsets in the device file are interpreted as memory addresses by the kernel. The /dev/kmem file represents the *virtual* (rather than physical) address space of the kernel, presenting a more uniform view of the memory in question.

Merely trying (say) cat or dd on memory device files to capture memory won't work very well on many systems, however. For instance, the FreeBSD /dev/mem implementation currently doesn't return an EOF when it reaches the end of physical memory. Solaris, on the other hand, might not start at address 0 or might have holes in the memory mapping if it isn't using maximum-size memory chips—in which case you'll get either nothing or an incomplete version of the system's memory.[2]

The memdump program was written to avoid such problems (it can be found at the book's Web site). It was designed to disturb memory as little as possible and use a minimum of memory when running.

Whatever method you choose—memdump, Solaris commands that save memory without rebooting, or some other technique—saving memory to disk is not without forensic flaws. Writing the data to any device—whether it's swap space, unused space, or anything containing a file system—can potentially compromise forensic data. Perhaps the best solution, and the one we recommend, is to use the network as a storage facility. Although there will be some memory agitation, you can try to minimize it. Red Hat, for instance, has introduced a network version of a Linux crash-dump facility that runs on its advanced server; the program sends the memory dump over the network rather than saving it to the local disk. Simply using a good capture method with a tool such as Netcat can provide a reasonable way of saving the memory of a running computer:

```
solaris # memdump | nc receiver 666
```

Remember that the memory dump could contain sensitive information. So unless you are working on a trusted LAN, the results of this command should be piped through a program that encrypts the data or sent through an encrypted tunnel (for example, using ssh). See Chapter 4 for more details.

Swap Space

We've already seen how to find the swap devices of a system (in Section 8.6). Swap space is the easiest type of memory to copy: simply cat or dd the device or file in question. Again, writing the results to the network (via Netcat or other means) is the preferred method of saving what you capture.

Other Memory Locations

System peripherals (such as graphics boards, disk drives, and others) often contain memory, sometimes in large quantities. If a peripheral shows up as a device in the file system (most often in the /dev directory),

---

2. Microsoft Windows users can try George Garner's port of dd to capture physical memory (Garner 2003).

The Quick and Dirty Way to Capture Memory

Although we advocate using a special-purpose program such as mem-dump, in some situations you may have turned off your Internet access after an incident. Or you might not want to risk disturbing the system by downloading a program and compiling it. You possibly don't even have a working compiler installed. In such cases, you may capture a goodly amount of a system's raw memory by using a simple program that cycles over the memory address space one memory page at a time.

Although Perl and other scripting languages don't have particularly small memory footprints (and thus destroy some memory when run), this Perl program shows how a few lines of code can capture most of a computer's memory.

```
#!/usr/local/bin/perl -s
#
# Open /dev/mem or /dev/kmem and read page-size chunks.
# Ignore errors; just seek and read one page at a time.
#
#       Usage: $0 [-k] N
#
# Where "N" is the number of pages to read. The -k flag tells
# it to read from kmem (dangerous!); else it reads /dev/mem.
#

$page_length = 4096;            # some pages are longer . . .
$ARGV[0] = "262144" unless $#ARGV >= 0;   # get 1 Gbyte of memory
if ($k) { $MEMORY = "/dev/kmem"; }
else    { $MEMORY = "/dev/mem"; }

die "Can't open $MEMORY\n" unless open(MEMORY, $MEMORY);

# for this many megabytes of data
for $n (0..($ARGV[0]-1)) {
        $position = $n * $page_length;
        seek(MEMORY,$position,0);
        if (($bytes_read = sysread(MEMORY, $page, $page_length))) {
          print $page;
          $total_bytes_read += $bytes_read;
          }
        }
warn "successfully read $total_bytes_read bytes from $MEMORY\n";
```

This program can then be used with Netcat to send the memory to a waiting remote system (in this case, "receiver"):

```
freebsd # ./dump-mem.pl 512 | nc -w 5 receiver
successfully read 536870912 bytes
freebsd #
```

then using `cat` can often be enough to capture the memory. Unfortunately, this isn't the norm; almost every device uses a different method to access and store memory. Alas, retrieving such device memory is outside the scope of this book.

It's fairly simple to use peripheral memory to stash data or programs. Michal Schulz (2002) has shown how to use a video card's unused memory to create a UNIX file system as a RAM disk.

Finally, in a literal, outside-the-box way of thinking, virtual machines (such as VMware and Virtual PC) can be quite useful as tools to capture a system's memory, especially in laboratory or testing situations. Often a virtual machine runs as a regular process, and its entire memory space can be captured with a command such as `pcat`. However, for efficiency, some programs will map only a slice of the entire memory space at any one time.

8.8 Static Analysis: Recognizing Memory from Files

Data from files gets into memory either by being executed or by otherwise being read by the operating system. Perhaps the simplest way to find useful data in captured memory is to use either a directed search of known contents (such as `grep`), to brute-force recognized text (for example, using `strings`), or to use a combination of the two. If you're trying this out on a running system, you must exercise a tiny bit of care to ensure that you don't find the string you're searching for as the search string gets loaded into memory itself:

```
freebsd # ./dump-mem.pl > giga-mem-img-1
successfully read 1073741824 bytes
freebsd # strings giga-mem-img-1 | fgrep "Supercalif"
freebsd # cat helloworld
Supercalifragilisticexpialidocious
freebsd # ./dump-mem.pl > giga-mem-img-2
successfully read 1073741824 bytes
freebsd # strings giga-mem-img-2 | fgrep "Supercalifr"
Supercalifragilisticexpialidocious
Supercalifragilisticexpialidocious
freebsd #
```

This command sequence demonstrates that the entire file containing the string "Supercalifragilisticexpialidocious" is small enough that it is unlikely to be broken across page boundaries and is therefore easily found.

8.9 Recovering Encrypted File Contents Without Keys

Several file systems can encrypt all or part of their contents. Windows XP Professional, for example, has a fairly user-friendly file system encryption feature that may be turned on for each file or directory. This may be set using the Windows Explorer Properties dialog.

When a directory has the encryption feature turned on, any file created in that directory will be stored encrypted. This is very different from encrypting a file after it is created as cleartext. The main difference is that no cleartext data is written to the file system, so that the data cannot be recovered by reading the raw disk.

Creating an Encrypted File

For testing purposes, we used a Windows XP Professional system with 160 Mbytes of memory that runs inside VMware. We created a folder with the pathname `C:\temp\encrypted` and set its properties so that any files created there would be encrypted. Then we downloaded a file into this directory via FTP. The file contents consisted of lines starting with a number followed by text:

```
00001   this is the cleartext
00002   this is the cleartext
00003   this is the cleartext
[. . . 11930 lines omitted . . .]
11934   this is the cleartext
11935   this is the cleartext
11936   this is the cleartext
```

In all, there were 11,936 lines of text, for a total of 358,080 bytes.

The file system encryption appeared to do its job. After downloading this file into the encrypting directory, we did a quick search of the raw disk. There were no traces of the original cleartext. This search for plaintext data was relatively easy because the Windows disk was accessible as an ordinary file from the UNIX operating system on which VMware was running.

Recovering the Encrypted File from Main Memory

As we've seen in this chapter, the disk is not the only place where file contents are found. To access a file, its contents are copied into main memory. To improve system performance, recently or frequently accessed file contents stay cached in main memory for some amount of time, depending on system usage patterns.

All this applies to encrypted files, too: at some point, the contents of our target file had to be decrypted and copied into main memory. The unencrypted contents remain cached for some amount of time, which depends on system usage patterns. We wanted to know just how long they remained in cache, and if the data persisted once the user logged off.

There are several ways to access the main memory of a Windows system. We used the previously mentioned Ctrl–Scroll Lock keyboard sequence (from Microsoft Knowledge Base article 254649). Once this feature is enabled, anyone with access to the keyboard can request a memory dump, even without logging in to the machine. The resulting dump file was transferred to a UNIX computer for simple string analysis:

```
freebsd # strings memory.dmp | grep 'this is the cleartext' | wc
 (lines) (words) (bytes)
  20091  120547  582564
```

Obviously, 20,091 lines is a lot more than the 11,936 that were in the original file, so some information was present more than once. Elimination of the duplicates showed that practically all the unencrypted contents could be recovered from the memory dump:

```
freebsd # strings memory.dmp | grep 'this is the cleartext' | sort -u | wc
 (lines) (words) (bytes)
  11927   71567  345848
```

Of the 11,936 lines of cleartext, 11,927 were recovered from main memory.

Windows file encryption provides privacy by encrypting file contents before they are written to disk. This is good, because the unencrypted contents cannot then be recovered from the raw disk. However, unencrypted contents stay cached in main memory, even after the user has logged off. This is bad, because the unencrypted contents can still be recovered from raw memory. The cached data will decay over time, according to the usage patterns of the system, but the multiple copies of the data present in memory will only lengthen its persistence.

This is presumably contrary to expectation, and hopefully to design. At a minimum, once the user logs off, not only should any decrypting key information be purged from main memory, but the cleartext contents of encrypted files should also be purged from main memory.

8.10 File System Blocks vs. Memory Page Technique

Because a significant portion of what is loaded into memory comes from the file system, we can identify portions of memory by comparing them with what is in the file system. The structure of memory makes this easier.

We know where the data starts, where the data boundaries are, and how big the page-size chunks of data are. So we can simply break the raw blocks of a file system into similar-size chunks and do a brute-force comparison against all the pages in memory. Although a match—or a miss—doesn't absolutely prove whether the memory page actually came from a given file system, it does *identify* the memory page with certainty, which for our purposes is equally important. Executable files in memory might be somewhat problematic to spot, because they can be broken into pieces in memory; we examine that problem in the next section.

Table 8.1 shows a slightly more efficient method of comparing the MD5 hashes of all the pages in memory against the MD5 hashes of the raw disk. We used VMware to manipulate the available memory of the test systems, and we took the measurements immediately after the starting the system.

We found a large number of null memory pages because the systems had just started, so they hadn't yet written any data to most of the memory

Table 8.1 *Recognizing contents in memory using MD5 hashes of 4096-byte blocks and memory pages (with Intel x86 versions of each OS)*

Available Memory (Mbytes)	Page Matches		Null Pages		Unrecognized	
	%	Mbytes	%	Mbytes	%	Mbytes
FreeBSD 5.0 and KDE 2.1						
128	20.6	26.4	44.3	56.7	35.1	44.9
192	19.9	38.2	53.0	101.8	27.1	52.0
256	11.7	30.0	73.3	187.6	15.0	38.4
384	8.6	33.0	79.9	306.8	11.5	44.2
SuSe 7.1 and KDE 2.1						
128	31.2	39.9	32.3	41.3	36.5	46.7
192	20.7	39.7	56.0	107.5	23.3	44.7
256	15.9	40.7	65.8	168.4	18.3	46.8
384	12.9	49.5	74.4	285.7	12.7	48.8
Solaris 2.51 and OpenWindows						
128	39.3	50.3	15.3	19.6	45.4	58.1
192	37.6	72.2	15.0	28.8	47.4	91.0
256	37.3	95.5	13.1	33.5	49.6	127.0
384	38.4	147.5	16.3	62.6	45.3	174.0

pages. The number of actual memory page matches generally rises as the system usage time increases, because the file system is cached according to how much memory is available. By itself, this page-block-matching technique has limited use, but it's helpful in a variety of situations for obtaining measurements and observations, as we'll see throughout the rest of the chapter.

The percentage of identified files varies significantly depending on what the computer does and what it has been doing lately. For instance, using large portions of memory for calculations or database manipulation can easily fill main memory with data that isn't from files and is hard to recognize. Still, when measuring live or production computers, we routinely identified 60 to 70 percent of the memory space; in one system with 1 Gbyte of memory, we identified more than 97 percent of the memory pages.

8.11 Recognizing Files in Memory

Because files are placed into memory pages, another way to find a specific file containing the aforementioned word "Supercalifragilisticexpialidocious" would be to take the MD5 hash of the file (null-padding it, when needed, to correspond to the size of a memory page) and compare it to all the MD5 hashes of all the pages in memory. The memory page that contained the word would have the same MD5 hash as the file. This method would find only small files, however—those that fit into a page of memory. And it might well fail to find executables associated with even very small processes, because the image associated with the file isn't always stored in a contiguous space in memory.

Of course we can break files into page-size pieces in the same manner that we did with the raw disk. If we take the MD5 hashes of every page-size chunk of every file on a computer's file system and compare them to the MD5 hashes of every page of memory, then a match means that that file— or one with a block of identical data—has been loaded into memory.

The result of such a brute-force approach is something like a `ps` command that finds the executable and library files, directory entries, and any other files that are currently in main memory. They may be in use or simply in memory after being used in the past; there is no way of finding out using this method. Some files or portions of files may not currently be in memory even while they are being used by the system: a sleeping process, a file that is open but has not been accessed in some time, and so on. So this might be a modestly unreliable way of reporting memory usage, but it can yield information that is difficult to get using traditional methods.

Here we use this method to see files accessed during a compiler run, served up by the Web server, opened by the mail program, and the like. The results in Listing 8.2 are something akin to what we might get from an ephemeral MACtime tool (a program that is part of the Coroner's Toolkit software package; see Appendix A for more information). In this case, however, our tool shows only that a file has been read or written to.

You'll often see only parts of larger files in memory, because the data is loaded only as it is accessed.

In our measurements, collisions—two or more page-size disk chunks that have the same contents and therefore the same MD5 hash—occur roughly 10 percent of the time when comparing file blocks. Though this might sound rather high, in practice collisions are fairly rare and tend to concentrate over certain popular values (a block containing all nulls, for instance, is rather popular). Most of the uninteresting results can be removed by listing all the files that could possibly match or by using a threshold scheme, in which a file has to have a certain percentage of blocks in memory before it is identified.

When such methods are used in adversarial situations where intruders might modify data, the MD5 hash databases must be kept off the systems from which the measurements are taken. If the hashes are saved as text and the page size is 4096 bytes, the size of such a database will be a bit less than 1 percent of the original data. Add a few percentage points if file names are also stored, but this could obviously be improved.

Though not particularly effective, this method may also achieve some crude level of malware detection: rootkit files, program files, exploits,

```
/kernel                    (80.7% found, 3814504 bytes)
/modules/ng_socket.ko      (84.6%,          12747)
/modules/ng_ether.ko       (81.8%,          10899)
/modules/ng_bridge.ko      (84.6%,          13074)
/modules/netgraph.ko       (94.7%,          38556)
/modules/linprocfs.ko      (92.8%,          27843)
/var/run/ppp               (100%,             512)
/var/run/syslog.pid        (100%,               3)
/var/run/dev.db            (25.0%,          65536)
/var/run/ld-elf.so.hints   (100%,             203)
/var/log/sendmail.st       (100%,             628)
/var/log/auth.log          (66.7%,          15345)
[. . . 500 more lines omitted . . .]
```

Listing 8.2 *A snippet of user files currently in memory, this time found by comparing MD5 hashes of 1024-byte pieces of files against the memory pages in a computer running 4.6 FreeBSD*

and other suspect code might be spotted in memory, even if they no longer exist on the computer's disks. This topic raises a question: How long do the echoes of files remain in memory?

8.12 Dynamic Analysis: The Persistence of Data in Memory

Now that we know how to recognize data and files in memory, we can measure how long they stay there. Note that unless you look at more than raw memory or make measurements over time, you can't tell how long data has been there. And because every kernel implements things differently, there is no easily obtainable time-associated metadata about memory (unlike the file system's MACtimes, for instance).

We used two primary methods to measure this persistence. In the first we captured all the individual pages in memory and measured their change over time. In the second we used a program that first fills memory with a unique but repeating pattern. The program would then deallocate the memory and repeatedly scan /dev/mem for any signs of the previously filled memory. The former was used for some of the longer experiments; the latter was more helpful for spotting rapidly decaying memory.

We first examined fish.com, a moderately busy Red Hat server with 1 Gbyte of main memory. Over our two-and-a-half-week observation period, it handled some 65,000 Web requests and e-mail messages per day. At any given time, about 40 to 45 percent of the server's main memory is consumed by the kernel and by running processes; the rest is devoted to the file cache and a free memory pool. Every hour memory measurements were sent to a remote computer; the results are shown in Figure 8.3.

Obviously some pages changed many more times than we recorded in between our hourly measurements. But we saw one page changing 76 times over this 402-hour period, or about every five hours. Almost 2,350 memory pages (out of 256,000) didn't change at all (or changed and then changed back); some 1,400 changed with every reading.

In our second case we looked at a very lightly used Solaris 8 computer with 768 Mbytes of main memory (98,304 memory pages of 8192 bytes), of which more than 600 Mbytes was marked as free. Almost all of the free memory was used for file caching. Other than handling a few administrative logins, the machine was a secondary DNS server that ran standard system programs over a 46-day period. Its memory was captured once per day, as shown in Figure 8.4.

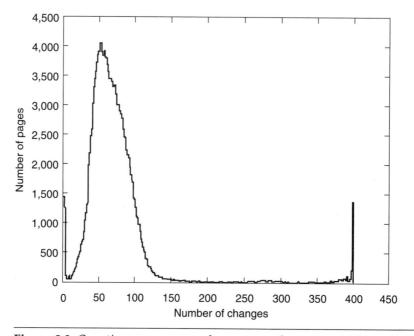

Figure 8.3 *Counting memory page changes every hour over 402 hours (16.75 days), using MD5 hashes of memory pages (Red Hat Linux 6.1)*

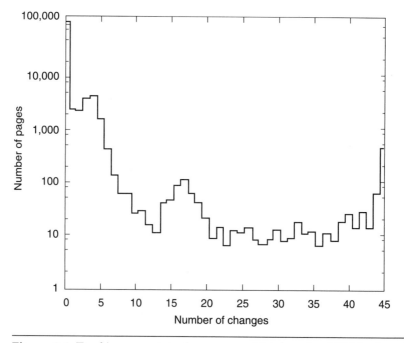

Figure 8.4 *Tracking page state changes over 46 days using MD5 hashes of memory pages (Solaris 8 on SPARC architecture)*

This graph shows that very few memory pages changed at all in a month and a half of recording data. The average time between observed memory page changes is 41.2 days; fully 86 percent of the memory pages never changed during the experiment, and only 0.4 percent changed every day.

Unsurprisingly there are great differences in how long memory pages stay around, depending on the activity of the computer in question. For seldom-used computers, data can persist for a long time. There is more to the story, however: we now explore the differences between anonymous memory and file-backed memory pages.

8.13 File Persistence in Memory

How long files persist in memory strongly depends on the demands placed on the resources of the computer involved, the amount of memory in the computer, and many other factors. We can easily determine if a given file is in memory by using our MD5-hash-matching method, as discussed in previous sections. The experimental results from fish.com show that about 37,500 pages that corresponded to files were recognized over two and a half weeks. Of these pages, the average page remained unchanged in memory for 13 hours—a considerable boost over the previously measured five hours for pages of all types. Although only 8.5 percent of the files recognized were executable in nature, they were seen in memory for longer periods of time: 20 hours, versus 12 hours for a nonexecutable file.

Other than the tools that were used to do the measurements, 84 files were found in every reading, indicating that they were running either continuously or repeatedly during this time. Of those 84 files, 13 were from executable files (mostly system utilities, with a couple of user programs):

```
/bin/hostname
/bin/rm
/bin/su
/bin/uname
/sbin/syslogd
/usr/bin/perl
/usr/bin/procmail
/usr/sbin/atd
/usr/sbin/crond
/usr/sbin/inetd
/usr/sbin/tcpd
/usr/local/bin/mutt
/usr/local/bin/spamassassin
```

Of the remaining pages, 53 were taken from libraries (29 of those were associated with the Apache Web server), 18 were from Perl modules or support files (8 of those were associated with the SpamAssassin antispam package), and only 2 were nonexecutable files: `/usr/lib/powerchute/powerchute.ini` and `/etc/ld.so.cache`. At any given time, traces of considerable numbers of files were found in fish.com's memory. The average count was 1,220, but this varied considerably, going from a low of 135 files to a high of 10,200.

Figure 8.5 illustrates files being pulled into memory (in this case, by a FreeBSD 4 Web server). A file gets loaded, stays for a few hours, and, unless it gets requested again, goes away as new data is loaded into the cache.

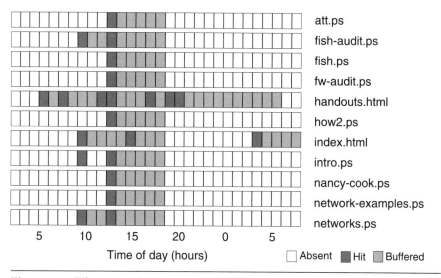

Figure 8.5 *File-system-backed Web pages moving in and out of the memory cache*

8.14 The Persistence of Nonfile, or Anonymous, Data

After a file is deleted, the persistence of memory backed by that file is similar to that of anonymous memory. We've already seen that file data lives longer than what was observed for memory pages, so it's obvious that data not associated with files has a shorter life span. How short, however?

Here we used moderately busy FreeBSD 4.1 and Red Hat 6.2 Linux computers. We wrote a program to measure the decay of 1 Mbyte of private memory after a process exits, repeating the experiment many times and then taking the average of the readings. Unlike some of the other measurements taken in this chapter, we did not use MD5 hashes, and we allowed partial matches of memory pages to capture fragments of memory still remaining. We did this because we suspected some virtual memory systems might change pages to store status info. As shown in Figure 8.6, we placed one measurement above the other on the same scale, or else they would have been almost indistinguishable.

Don't think that anonymous data deteriorates slowly and regularly; this graph aggregates many measurements and displays an artificial smoothness. Instead, the data remains intact for some time—depending on the activity of the system in question—and then it is quickly reclaimed by other processes. In any case, after some ten minutes, about 90 percent of the monitored memory was changed. What's most remarkable is how closely the measurements align, despite entirely different operating systems, memory size, and kernels. Under normal use computers experience a fairly rapid and inevitable degradation of anonymous memory pages. This volatility depends greatly on the computer in question, however: when a computer isn't doing anything, anonymous memory can persist for long periods of time. For instance, in some computers, passwords and other precalculated data were easily recovered many days after they were typed or loaded into memory. In other computers, even though they were idle, the same data was lost within minutes or hours.

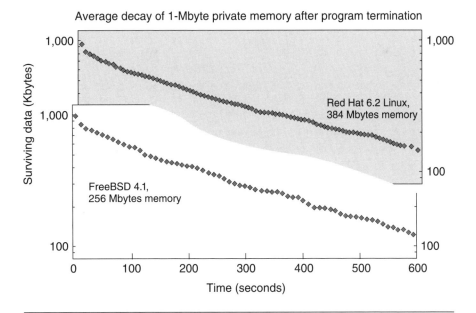

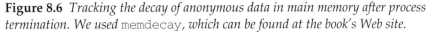

Figure 8.6 *Tracking the decay of anonymous data in main memory after process termination. We used* `memdecay`*, which can be found at the book's Web site.*

For investigators this pattern of decay can be unfortunate, because often the entire point of capturing memory is to retrieve the transient data. The aggressive file-caching schemes now universally present mean that much of memory is used to store already persistent data for performance reasons. Passwords, text documents, and other interesting pieces of data are often the first to be lost after their associated processes terminate.

8.15 Swap Persistence

Swap consists of anonymous data that was once in memory but has been saved to disk because of a shortage of system resources. Because systems swap rarely, information written to swap becomes preserved, or fossilized. Files do not appear in swap (although parts of any file might, if the file has been used as data) because they are already backed by the file system, so there is no reason to save them again.

Memory is so inexpensive that modern computers often have more RAM than they need for general operations; therefore the system swaps only when it is under heavy stress. Such unusual behavior is likely to leave footprints for some time.

8.16 The Persistence of Memory Through the Boot Process

Although most computers automatically zero main memory upon rebooting, many do not. This difference is generally independent of the operating system. For instance, motherboards fueled by Intel CPUs tend to have BIOS settings that clear main memory upon restart, but there is no requirement for this to happen.

Normally this distinction is of little concern, but it can be important when capturing forensic data, considering the potential longevity of data in main memory. Sun SPARC systems, Apple G4 computers, and others don't regularly clear memory upon reboot (although most may be configured to do so via BIOS, EEPROM, or other settings).

8.17 The Trustworthiness and Tenacity of Memory Data

The contents of main memory can be perverted and subverted, but it would be very difficult to compromise all the potential sources of information. Any hardware-assisted memory dump is nearly impossible to fool without physical access to the computer. This makes hardware-assisted memory dumps the most trustworthy of all, but unfortunately, they aren't supported by many systems. We've seen several special-purpose methods for dumping memory: running `savecore` or using keystroke sequences (such as Sun's L1–A and Microsoft's Ctrl–Scroll Lock) are two examples. These techniques have perhaps a slightly higher veracity than those that rely on a more general source, such as `/dev/mem`—if only because it would take so much work to subvert all such special-purpose avenues. It's comparatively easy to modify the kernel's interface to a single file so that it gives out false readings. Swap is usually the most easily modified, because it is stored as a disk partition or even as a file.

You might think that because memory is fragile, it would be relatively easy to clear all memory or fill it with arbitrary data, thereby frustrating many of the methods discussed in this chapter. This is almost true. For example, the following tiny Perl program allocates and fills memory with nulls until it runs out of memory:

```
# Fill as much memory as possible with null bytes, one page at a time.

for (;;) {
        $buffer[$n++] = '\000' x 4096;
        }
```

As the size of the memory-filling process grows, so does the rate of memory decay of cached files and of terminated anonymous process memory. Eventually, the system starts to cannibalize memory from running processes, moving their writable pages to the swap space. That is what we expected, at least. Unfortunately, even repeat runs of this program as root changed only about three-fourths of the main memory of various computers we tested. Not only did the program not consume all anonymous memory, but it didn't even have much of an effect on the kernel and file caches.

Overwriting most of memory, even just the cached and temporarily saved data, turns out to be slightly challenging. Attempts to use higher-level abstractions to change low-level data fail. Efforts to read and write either large files or large numbers of files also had limited success. In this case, it turned out (ironically?) that running the Coroner's Toolkit in a full forensic data-gathering effort is a pretty good—though slow—way to clear memory. The Coroner's Toolkit destroys the contents of the file cache and main memory by reading many different files and performing lots of calculations, including an MD5 hash of every file on the entire machine. Even kernel memory is affected, as shown in Table 8.2.

If you're concerned with preserving evidence from memory, making a file system backup is the last thing you want to do, for it not only destroys all the file access times but also thrashes all the volatile memory. On the bright side, however, perhaps intruders will start to back up your data after breaking in.

Table 8.2 *The effects of activity on memory pages (the average amount of memory changed over three trials)*

Action	Solaris 8, 768 Mbytes Memory		SuSe Linux 7.1, 256 Mbytes Memory		FreeBSD 5.0RC2, 192 Mbytes Memory	
	% Changed	Mbytes Changed	% Changed	Mbytes Changed	% Changed	Mbytes Changed
Running memdump	0.7	5.4	1.2	3.2	0.8	1.6
Unpacking, configuring, and compiling the Coroner's Toolkit	24	185	7.6	19	17	33
Writing nulls to memory once	75	576	76	194	82	157
Writing nulls to memory again	76	580	77	196	84	161
Running the Coroner's Toolkit	98	749	95	244	91	174

Filling main memory with data from actual files has the added benefit of making analysis and detection more difficult than if someone were to use a fixed pattern to wipe memory. In our testing, however, we couldn't totally eradicate evidence that we planted in memory (such as passwords, pieces of files, and the like). In the end, rebooting the computers was the only effective way to clear memory for most of our computers that reset memory upon reboot. The SPARC and Apple G4 systems had to be physically turned off and then turned back on, because they don't reset memory when rebooted, as mentioned earlier.

Whatever method used, it can be very difficult to wipe out all traces of activity in main memory. Any program that runs, anything typed by a user, and any data that lives on a computer will at some point end up in main memory. While we demonstrate this with a very simple model, Jim Chow and his coauthors discuss this topic in significantly more depth in "Understanding Data Lifetime via Whole System Simulation" (Chow et al. 2004). In this paper, they discuss how they eliminate much of the guesswork concerning how information flows by essentially tagging data with virtual colored dyes, so that it can be followed in its migration through the kernel, application buffers, network transmissions, and elsewhere.

But complex subsystems such as memory management will behave quite differently under the hood of every type of computer and operating system, adding to the difficulty of tricking even our basic techniques, let alone more sophisticated methods. As one of the authors of Chow et al. 2004 admitted, significant analysis of even a single memory system can take "a group of Stanford systems Ph.D. students more than a few weeks" of time and effort to begin to understand.[3]

Certainly, success at masking or hiding behavior will vary substantially in accordance with the functionality and load of the computer, and of course, no single point of forensic data should be trusted absolutely. Even in isolation, memory analysis can tell quite a bit about the state of a computer. But when data taken from memory is correlated with data gleaned from other sources, such as log files, the file system, and the like, we can arrive at stronger conclusions.

8.18 Conclusion

Because of the page-based virtual memory allocation and file-caching schemes used to enhance the performance of computers, digital signature analysis of memory pages can find and identify significant portions of memory. String-based searches can also be valuable, despite the relatively unstructured and fragmented nature of main memory, as exemplified by our case study of the encrypted file system.

As in many other types of analysis, recognizing or eliminating the known can help clarify what's going on in a system. Certainly, wading through lots of data looking for clues can be a very dull adventure, and anything that can cut down on the work required is a big bonus. And though it can be difficult to find less-structured data in memory *somewhere*, if you know what needle you're looking for, even a few bytes of data may be located in a massive haystack.

The persistence of data in memory varies widely, not only because of the activity performed on a computer, but also because of how the memory was stored. File-backed data lasts significantly longer than anonymous data, due to the caching of file data. So what most people consider interesting data is more ephemeral than what is already saved on disk. If you want to capture such data, you need to move quickly.

The analysis of memory can reveal significant details about a computer's properties and activities—details that are nearly impossible to discover using other methods. When investigating a system, you should attempt to save as much memory as possible—or at a minimum, save a hash of the memory pages involved. Although the latter won't allow you to analyze the unknown contents in memory, knowing what was in memory can still be a big advantage.

---

3. Ben Pfaff, private communication, July 2004.

The Coroner's Toolkit and Related Software

A.1 Introduction

The Coroner's Toolkit (TCT) is a collection of forensic utilities written by Wietse Venema and Dan Farmer (Farmer and Venema 2004). The software was first presented in 1999, in a one-day forensic analysis class at the IBM T. J. Watson Research Center. The first general release was in 2000, via the authors' Web sites. The software was extended in various ways by Brian Carrier, who makes his version available as the Sleuth Kit (Carrier 2004a). This appendix presents an overview of TCT and some of its extensions.

A.2 Data Gathering with `grave-robber`

The `grave-robber` command collects forensic information. This tool can be used either on a "live" victim machine or on a disk image from a victim's file system. In "live" collection mode, `grave-robber` aims to respect the order of volatility (see Appendix B). It uses many of the utilities that are part of TCT to collect information in the following order:

- The attributes of all the commands and files that TCT accesses while it gathers information. These are collected first to preserve their MACtime attributes.

- Process status information and, optionally, the memory of all running processes.

- Deleted files that are still active.

- The executable files of all processes.

- All attributes from deleted files.

- Network status information.

- Host status information, via system-dependent commands that provide system configuration information.

- Attributes of existing files; this produces the `body` file that is used by the `mactime` tool, as described later.

- Optionally, security-sensitive information that is under the control of users of the system, such as files that grant remote access to a user's account, and `cron` jobs for unattended command execution on behalf of users.

- Copies of configuration files and other critical files.

All this information is stored in a "vault," a protected directory structure that is named after the host and the time of the start of data collection. For each file placed into the vault, `grave-robber` also computes the MD5 hash. At the end, as the vault is closed, `grave-robber` computes the MD5 hash over all individual file hashes.

By definition, `grave-robber` is exposed to information that comes from the untrusted victim machine. It frequently uses this information while executing TCT commands and system commands. While doing so, it takes great care never to expose that untrusted information to a shell command interpreter. For more about the philosophical issues behind `grave-robber`, see Appendix B.

A.3 Time Analysis with `mactime`

The `mactime` command takes file attribute information from a `body` file that was produced by `grave-robber` and produces a chronological report of all file access methods by file name. Alternatively, `mactime` can generate a `body` file on the fly while it scans a file system. This tool was written several years before the authors started work on TCT, and it was adapted to fit into the `grave-robber` framework. The `mactime` tool is introduced in Chapter 2, and a larger example can be found in Chapter 4.

As an example of the kind of insight that `mactime` can give, Listings A.1 and A.2 present different views of the same remote login session. The first shows what the remote user sees, and the second shows the corresponding MACtime report. For educational reasons, the example uses a very old machine, so that the MACtimes are spread out over time. This allows us to see a clear separation between the start-up of the telnet server and login software, the access of system files while the user logs in, and the start-up of the user's login shell process.

```
$ telnet sunos.fish.com
Trying 216.240.49.177...
Connected to sunos.fish.com.
Escape character is '^]'.

SunOS UNIX (sunos)

login: zen
Password:
Last login: Thu Dec 25 09:30:21 from flying.fish.com
Welcome to ancient history!
$
```

Listing A.1 *User view of a remote login session*

```
Time        Size MAC Permission Owner Group File name
19:47:04   49152 .a. -rwsr-xr-x root  staff /usr/bin/login
           32768 .a. -rwxr-xr-x root  staff /usr/etc/in.telnetd
19:47:08     272 .a. -rw-r--r-- root  staff /etc/group
             108 .a. -r--r--r-- root  staff /etc/motd
            8234 .a. -rw-r--r-- root  staff /etc/ttytab
            3636 m.c -rw-rw-rw- root  staff /etc/utmp
           28056 m.c -rw-r--r-- root  staff /var/adm/lastlog
         1250496 m.c -rw-r--r-- root  staff /var/adm/wtmp
19:47:09    1041 .a. -rw-r--r-- root  staff /etc/passwd
19:47:10  147456 .a. -rwxr-xr-x root  staff /bin/csh
```

Listing A.2 *MACtime view of the remote login session shown in Listing A.1. The* MAC *column indicates the file access method (**m**odify, read **a**ccess, or status **c**hange). File names with the same time stamp are sorted alphabetically.*

A.4 File Reconstruction with `lazarus`

As discussed in Chapters 3 and 7, modern file systems minimize file access times by keeping related information close together. Among other things, this reduces the fragmentation of individual files. The TCT program `lazarus` takes advantage of this property when attempting to reconstitute the structure of deleted file content.

`lazarus` is a simple program whose goal is to give unstructured data some form that is both viewable and manipulatable by users. It relies on a few simple principles and heuristics:

- All popular file systems divide their storage space into equal-size blocks. Typical block sizes are 1024 bytes and 4096 bytes. As long as `lazarus` uses an input block size that is consistent with this, it will never miss an opportunity for dividing up a file appropriately.

- File systems like to avoid file fragmentation for performance reasons. In particular, UNIX file systems tend to be relatively free of fragmentation even after years of use.

- Files often have a distinct signature at the beginning. The venerable UNIX `file` utility uses a database with patterns to recognize files by the signature of their contents. `lazarus` uses this database, in addition to a built-in pattern matcher, to recognize file headers and classify other file contents.

- If a disk block looks similar to the previous disk block, then `lazarus` assumes that both blocks are part of the same file.

With these principles in mind, `lazarus` implements a sort of primitive digital X-ray device. It creates a map of the disk that essentially makes the drive transparent: you can peer into the disk and see the data by content type, but the highly useful file system abstraction is lost. Figure A.1 shows an example of the interface and a once-deleted image file.

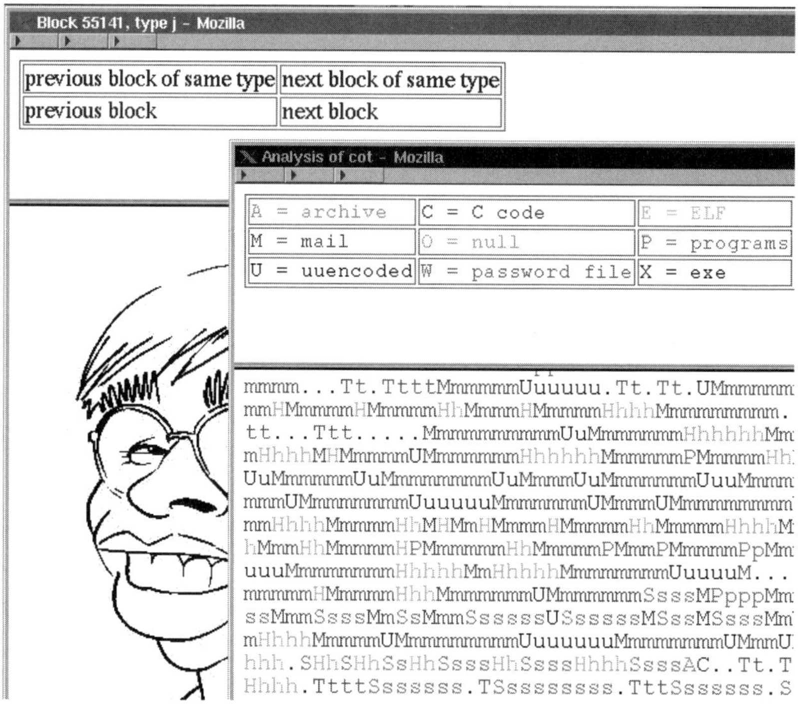

Figure A.1 `lazarus` *uncovering a deleted image*

In the map of a disk, `lazarus` uses simple text characters to represent data chunks. A capital letter is used for the first block of a chunk, while lowercase is used for its remainder. For example, *C* represents C source code, *H* stands for hypertext, *L* is a log file, *M* is mail, *U* is uuencoded content, and a period (.) is unrecognized binary data.

To keep the map manageable, `lazarus` compresses large chunks using a logarithmic (base 2) scale. This means a single character is one block of data, the second character is two blocks, the third is four blocks, and so on. This allows large files to be visually significant but not overwhelming: with a 1024-byte block size, a 1-Mbyte file would only take up ten times the space of a single block file.

`lazarus` demonstrates that UNIX file systems like to keep related information within the same file system zone. For example, Figure A.1 shows that e-mail files (indicated by "Mmmm") tend to be clustered together. The figure also shows that e-mail with lots of hypertext or uuencoded content is likely to be misidentified. The clustering of files and file activity has important consequences for the persistence of deleted information, as we see in Chapter 7.

Software such as `lazarus` presents a problem of nontrivial scope. Although `lazarus` takes care to neutralize active content in hypertext and other formats by rendering it as plain text, it does no sanity checks on other data, such as images. Thus, it may trip up bugs in a very large and complex Web browser program.

`lazarus` has not evolved since its initial release. People who want to browse disks should consider using Brian Carrier's Autopsy tool (Carrier 2004b).

A.5 Low-Level File System Utilities

TCT comes with a number of utilities that bypass the file system layer. This allows the software to access information from existing files as well as deleted files. Instead of file names, these programs use the lower-level abstractions of inode numbers and bitmap allocation blocks, or the even lower level abstraction of disk block numbers. These concepts are introduced in Chapter 3.

TCT supports popular UNIX file systems such as UFS (BSD and Solaris), Ext2fs, and Ext3fs (Linux). The Sleuth Kit also adds support for non-UNIX file systems such as NTFS, FAT16, and FAT32 (Microsoft Windows).

Utilities that are part of the original TCT distribution include the following:

- ils—Access file attributes by their inode number. By default, this lists all unallocated file attributes.

- icat—Access file contents by their inode number. This is used primarily to look up deleted file content.

- unrm—Access disk blocks by their disk block number. By default, this reads all unallocated file content and produces output that can be used by programs such as lazarus. In the Sleuth Kit distribution, unrm is renamed to dls.

The Sleuth Kit adds a number of other low-level utilities, such as these:

- ffind—Map an inode number to the directory entry that references the inode.

- fls—List directory entries, including deleted ones. Section 4.14 shows how to use this utility.

- ifind—Map a data block number to the inode that references the data block.

The success rate of low-level file system tools with deleted file information depends greatly on the file system type and even on the version of the operating system software. In Section 4.11, we discuss how much information is lost and what is preserved when a file is deleted.

A.6 Low-Level Memory Utilities

The tools described in this section are intended more for exploratory use than rock-solid analysis. Because their output contains little or no structural meta-information, it is suitable only for processing with tools that don't take advantage of such information.

- pcat—Dump the memory of a running process. This program is used in Section 2.6; other examples of its use can be found on the book's Web site.

- memdump—Dump system memory while disturbing it as little as possible. The output should be sent across the network, to avoid interaction with the contents of the file system cache. This program is used for some of the measurements in Chapter 8.

Data Gathering and the Order of Volatility

B.1 Introduction

In 1999, we defined forensic computing as "gathering and analyzing data in a manner as free from distortion or bias as possible to reconstruct data or what has happened in the past on a system." Trusting your tools and data once you have them is problematic enough (we talk about this at length in Chapter 5), but there is an even greater problem. Due to the Heisenberg principle of data gathering and system analysis (see Section 1.4), even with appropriate and trusted tools, you cannot retrieve all the data on a computer. So where should you start? In this appendix, we give an overview of how to gather data on a computer, and we look at some of the problems that can arise—most of which are caused by the order of volatility (OOV).

B.2 The Basics of Volatility

As we have demonstrated throughout the book, computers store a great amount of information in a significant number of locations and layers. Disk storage and RAM are the two most obvious data repositories, but useful data can hide in a great number of places—even outside the system if it is connected to a network.

All data is volatile, however. As time passes, the veracity of the information decreases, as does the ability to recall or validate the data. When looking at stored information, it is extremely difficult to verify that it has not been subverted or changed.

That said, certain types of data are generally more persistent, or long lasting, than others. Backup tapes, for instance, will typically remain unchanged longer than data in RAM; we say that backup tapes are less volatile than RAM. These are just two members of a hierarchy called *the order of volatility*. At the top of the hierarchy are pieces of information that are virtually impossible to recover within a very short time—sometimes nanoseconds (or less) from their inception date—such as data in CPU registers, frame buffers, and others. At the bottom of the hierarchy are forms that are very persistent and hard to change, such as stone tablets, printouts, and other ways of imprinting data on a semipermanent medium.

So in most cases, you try to capture data with this order in mind: the more rapidly changing information should almost always be preserved first. Table B.1, also shown in the first chapter, gives a rough guide to the life expectancy of data.

Information lost from one layer may still be found in a lower layer (see Sections 1.5 and 1.7 for more about this). But the point of the OOV is the opposite: doing something in one layer destroys information in all layers above it. Simply executing a command to retrieve information destroys the contents of registers, memory management units, physical memory, and time stamps in the file system.

Starting up a program to read or capture memory can destroy existing data in memory, because the kernel allocates memory to run the program that performs the examination. So what can you do?

Table B.1 *The expected life span of data*

Type of Data	Life Span
Registers, peripheral memory, caches, etc.	Nanoseconds
Main memory	Ten nanoseconds
Network state	Milliseconds
Running processes	Seconds
Disk	Minutes
Floppies, backup media, etc.	Years
CD-ROMs, printouts, etc.	Tens of years

B.3 The State of the Art

Since 1999, we have come to remove the phrase "in a manner as free from distortion or bias as possible" from our definition of forensic computing. We believe that by risking digital evidence, investigators are more likely to retrieve additional data and have a better chance of addressing and understanding the problem at hand.

Our approach goes against the traditional wisdom in forensic computing, which relies on very conservative methods—rarely more than turning off a computer and making a copy of a system's disk (U.S. DOJ 2004). Certainly if you need to ensure that the data being collected is optimized for admissibility in a court of law and you've got only one shot at capturing it, then a very cautious methodology can be the best approach in some cases.

Unfortunately, such conservative techniques miss a wealth of potentially useful information about the situation, such as running processes and kernels, network state, data in RAM, and more. Only a limited understanding can arise from looking at a dead disk. And although dynamic information is perhaps a bit more volatile and therefore suspect, any convictions based on a single set of data readings are suspect as well. Certainly, as we've seen throughout the book, no single data point should be trusted. Only by correlating data from many points can you begin to get a good understanding of what happened, and there is a lot of data to look at out there. It would be a pity to throw it away.

In general, gathering data according to the OOV helps preserve rather than destroy, but unless computer architectures change significantly, there is no single best way to capture digital evidence. For instance, RAM might be the first thing you'd like to save. But if you're at a remote site and you have no local disk, it could take hours to transfer the contents of RAM to a safe disk somewhere else. By the time you're done, much of the anonymous memory (the most ephemeral type, as discussed in Chapter 8) could be long gone.

Certainly the current set of software tools for capturing evidence is not terribly compelling. Our own Coroner's Toolkit, while at times useful, could be much improved upon. Other packages—most notably the Sleuth Kit (Carrier 2004a) and EnCase (Guidance Software 2004)—are worthy efforts, but they still have far to go. It's too bad that we have not progressed much further than the erstwhile dd copying program, but automated capture and analysis are very difficult.

B.4 How to Freeze a Computer

The spirit of Darryl Zero (see Section 1.1) infuses our mind-set: If you're looking for anything in particular, you're lost. But if you keep your mind and eyes open, you can go far.

Ensuring the reproducibility and provability of results is difficult when dealing with the capture of very complex systems that are constantly in motion. The starting states of computers will always be different, often with significant changes in operating system, kernel, and software versions that are too complex for anyone to understand fully.

Ideally, you want both raw and cooked (that is, processed) data. Having the process table from a FreeBSD computer is of limited worth if you don't have native programs for analysis, so the output from ps is still important. You also want to gather data on the system both while it is still running and while it is at rest, in case the two states return different results. Volume also becomes problematic. Where do you store all this data? It's one thing to store all the data from a personal workstation, but what happens when you need to analyze a petabyte-class or exabyte-class server?

A thorough discussion of how to gather and store digital evidence would perhaps warrant a book of its own, but here we try to give some basic guidelines.

Richard Saferstein (2003) writes that when processing a crime scene, investigators should follow a basic methodology, one that we espouse when dealing with a computer incident, as well. Here are his first steps to an investigation:

- Secure and isolate.
- Record the scene.
- Conduct a systematic search for evidence.
- Collect and package evidence.
- Maintain a chain of custody.

It doesn't take much imagination to see how all of these apply to computers.

Before You Start

First, you should consider how much time you plan to spend analyzing the data, because collecting and processing all the information is time-consuming. We offer Table B.2 as a slightly tongue-in-cheek guide.

You can consume a tremendous amount of time taking care of the problem at hand, but as a rule of thumb, if you don't expend at least a day or two, you're probably doing yourself and your system a disservice. One of the more difficult things to judge is how much effort to put into the analysis. Often the more analytical sweat you exude, the more clarity and understanding you gain. But some situations are harder than others, and some intruders are more careful and more skilled than others. Unfortunately, you never know before the break-in what to expect. The truth is

Table B.2 *A rough estimate of the range of costs of an investigation*

Level of Effort	Expertise Required	Time Consumed
None (Just go back to work.)	None	Almost none
Minimal effort	Normal user, with ability to install system software	Less than 1 day
Minimum recommended effort	Junior system administrator	1 to 2 days
Serious effort	Senior system administrator	2 days to several weeks
Fanatical effort	Expert system administrator	Several days to several months

that you'll never absolutely, positively know that you've found all you can. Experience will be your only guide.

Next, you'll need at least a pad of paper, something to write with, and a secure, preferably off-line location to store information that you collect. A second computer that can talk to the network would be a welcome, but not necessary, aid. You can use a laptop to store results, notes, and data, but be cautious about who can access it.

Even though downloading and installing programs will damage evidence, it is sometimes necessary to process a computer. The negative effects of this can be mitigated by having a personal collection of forensic tools at the ready. But you should use automation at all costs, unless doing so is completely unworkable.

If commercial packages are not an option, such open-source projects as FIRE (2004), PLAC (2004), and others based on the impressive KNOPPIX Linux distribution (KNOPPIX 2004a) may be placed on CDs or other portable media and used when an emergency occurs.

Actually Collecting Data

We apologize for our UNIX-centric advice, but the same roughly holds for any operating system. The computer(s) in question should be taken off-line. There are some potential problems with this, because the system might expect to be online. Thus, taking the machine off-line could destroy evidence as the system generates errors, repeatedly retries connections, or in general changes its state. Alternatively, you might try cutting the machine off the router and keeping it on a LAN, but DNS and network services, as well as other systems in the same network area, can still cause problems.

As you proceed, you need to keep track of everything you type or do. In general, it's a "grab first, analyze later" situation, however. Note the hardware, software, system, and network configurations that are in place.

If you're serious about collecting the data, however, we suggest that you capture it in the following order, which mirrors the OOV:

- Capture device memory, if possible. Alas, few tools exist to do this.

- Capture main memory. Using the guidelines described in Chapter 8, capture RAM and store it off-line.

- Get the journal, if you're dealing with a journaling file system. In Section 2.8, we show how this can be done for Ext3fs file systems with the Coroner's Toolkit's `icat` command.

- Get all the transient state that you can. The `grave-robber` program from the Coroner's Toolkit can help you with this. See Appendix A for more.

- Capture information from and about the disk. If possible, get the entire disk. We cover this step in Chapter 4. Again, `grave-robber` can help here, at least to get the important parts of the disk.

There you go. You now have all the data that is fit to save. Now all that remains is to analyze it. . . .

B.5 Conclusion

Forensic computing does not often yield black-and-white choices or unambiguous conclusions about a past incident. Like its counterpart in the physical realm of criminal investigations, forensic computing depends most on the quality and integrity of the investigators and laboratories involved. The tools and methodologies used will continue to improve significantly into the future.

Forensic computing is a field that perhaps should be taken more seriously than other disciplines in computer science. According to one agent, "fifty percent of the cases the FBI now opens involve a computer" (Kansas City Star 2002). The percentage is surely rising. Programs and people involved in the gathering and analysis of evidence must take special care, because their results can seriously affect people's freedoms, lives, jobs, and more.

Nothing is certain, but while probabilistic forensics does have a negative sound to it, it's what we now have. However, much has been written and achieved in the short time this field has been around, and we fervently hope that progress continues, because it will benefit us all. With best luck to the future,

Dan Farmer
Wietse Venema

REFERENCES

Abell, Victor A. 2004. The `lsof` (list open files) tool.
ftp://lsof.itap.purdue.edu/pub/tools/unix/lsof/

Anderson, Ross, Roger Needham, and Adi Shamir. 1998. "The Steganographic File System." In *Information Hiding, Second International Workshop, IH'98,* edited by D. Aucsmith. Springer-Verlag.
http://www.ftp.cl.cam.ac.uk/ftp/users/rja14/sfs3.pdf

Arbaugh, W. A., D. J. Farber, and J. M. Smith. 1997. "A Secure and Reliable Bootstrap Architecture." In *Proceedings of the 1997 IEEE Symposium on Security and Privacy,* pp. 65–71. May.
http://www.cs.umd.edu/~waa/pubs/oakland97.pdf

Argus. 2004. The Argus Web site.
http://www.qosient.com/argus/

ASR. *See* Avalon Security Research.

Avalon Security Research. 1996. The `amodload` kernel loader for SunOS 4.
http://ftp.cerias.purdue.edu/pub/lists/best-of-security/110

Balas, Edward, et al. 2004. The Sebek program.
http://project.honeynet.org/tools/sebek/

CAIDA. *See* Cooperative Association for Internet Data Analysis.

Caloyannides, Michael A. 2004. *Privacy Protection and Computer Forensics.* 2nd ed. Artech House.

Card, Rémy, Theodore Ts'o, and Stephen Tweedie. 1994. "Design and Implementation of the Second Extended Filesystem." In *Proceedings of the First Dutch International Symposium on Linux.* Amsterdam, December 8–9.
http://web.mit.edu/tytso/www/linux/ext2intro.html

Carrier, Brian. 2004a. The Sleuth Kit.
http://www.sleuthkit.org/

Carrier, Brian. 2004b. The Autopsy Forensic Browser.
http://www.sleuthkit.org/

Cesare, Silvio. 1999. "Runtime Kernel kmem Patching."
http://www.google.com/search?q=Silvio+Cesare+Runtime+kernel+kmem+Patching

Cheswick, Bill. 1992. "An Evening with Berferd, In Which a Cracker is Lured, Endured, and Studied." In *Proceedings of the Winter USENIX Conference*. San Francisco, January.
http://research.lumeta.com/ches/papers/berferd.ps

Chow, Jim, Ben Pfaff, Tal Garfinkel, Kevin Christopher, and Mendel Rosenblum. 2004. "Understanding Data Lifetime via Whole System Simulation." In *Proceedings of the 13th USENIX Security Symposium*.
http://suif.stanford.edu/collective/taint.pdf

Cifuentes, Cristina. 1994. The dcc decompiler.
http://www.itee.uq.edu.au/~cristina/dcc.html

Coffman, K. G., and A. M. Odlyzko. 2002. "Internet growth: Is there a 'Moore's Law' for data traffic?" In *Handbook of Massive Data Sets*, edited by J. Abello, P. M. Pardalos, and M. G. C. Resende, pp. 47–93. Kluwer.

Common Vulnerabilities and Exposures. 2000. Entry CVE-2000-0666.
http://cve.mitre.org/

Cooperative Association for Internet Data Analysis. 2003. The CAIDA network telescope project.
http://www.caida.org/analysis/security/telescope/

CVE. *See* Common Vulnerabilities and Exposures.

Cymru. 2004. The Team Cymru Darknet project.
http://www.cymru.com/Darknet/index.html

Dasan, Vasanthan, Alex Noordergraaf, and Lou Ordorica. 2001. "The Solaris Fingerprint Database: A Security Tool for Solaris Operating Environment Files." Sun BluePrints OnLine, May.
http://www.sun.com/blueprints/0501/Fingerprint.pdf
http://sunsolve.sun.com/pub-cgi/fileFingerprints.pl

Drake, Chris, and Kimberley Brown. 1995. *Panic! UNIX System Crash Dump Analysis*. Prentice Hall.

Dunlap, George W., Samuel T. King, Sukru Cinar, Murtaza Basrai, and Peter M. Chen. 2002. "ReVirt: Enabling Intrusion Analysis through Virtual-Machine Logging and Replay." In *Proceedings of the 2002 Symposium on Operating Systems Design and Implementation (OSDI)*. December.
http://www.eecs.umich.edu/CoVirt/papers/

FAQ. *See* The UNIX FAQ.

Farmer, Dan, and Wietse Venema. 2004. The Coroner's Toolkit.
http://www.fish.com/tct/
http://www.porcupine.org/tct/

FIRE. *See* Forensic and Incident Response Environment.

Forensic and Incident Response Environment. 2004. Bootable CD.
   http://fire.dmzs.com/

Garfinkel, Simson L., and Abhi Shelat. 2003. "Remembrance of Data
   Passed: A Study of Disk Sanitization Practices." *IEEE Security &
   Privacy* 1 (1).
   http://www.computer.org/security/v1n1/garfinkel.htm

Garfinkel, Tal. 2003. "Traps and Pitfalls: Practical Problems in System
   Call Interposition Based Security Tools." In *Proceedings of the Internet Society's 2003 Symposium on Network and Distributed System
   Security (NDSS 2003).*
   http://www.stanford.edu/~talg/papers/traps/traps-ndss03.pdf

Garner, George. 2003. Forensic Acquisition Utilities. Includes dd for
   Windows.
   http://users.erols.com/gmgarner/forensics/

Goldberg, Ian, David Wagner, Randi Thomas, and Eric A. Brewer. 1996.
   "A Secure Environment for Untrusted Helper Applications: Confin-
   ing the Wily Hacker." In *Proceedings of the 6th USENIX Security
   Symposium*. San Jose.
   http://www.cs.berkeley.edu/~daw/papers/janus-usenix96.ps

Grugq [pseud.] and Scut [pseud.]. 2001. "Armouring the ELF: Binary
   encryption on the UNIX platform." *Phrack* 58.
   http://www.phrack.org/show.php?p=58

Guidance Software. 2004. The EnCase forensic tool.
   http://www.encase.com/

Gutmann, Peter. 1996. "Secure Deletion of Data from Magnetic and
   Solid-State Memory." In *6th USENIX Security Symposium Proceedings*. San Jose, July 22–25.
   http://www.cs.auckland.ac.nz/~pgut001/pubs/secure_del.html

Gutmann, Peter. 2001. "Data Remanence in Semiconductor Devices." In
   10th USENIX Security Symposium. Washington, D.C., August 13–17.
   http://www.cryptoapps.com/~peter/usenix01.pdf

Hinden, R., and S. Deering. 1998. "IP Version 6 Addressing Architecture." RFC 2373. The Internet Society.
   http://www.ietf.org/

Hobbit [pseud.]. 1996. Netcat version 1.10.
   http://coast.cs.purdue.edu/pub/tools/unix/netutils/netcat/

Hoglund, Greg, and Gary McGraw. 2004. *Exploiting Software: How to
   Break Code*. Chapter 8. Addison-Wesley.

The Honeynet Project. 2001. The Honeynet Project's Forensic
   Challenge. January.
   http://project.honeynet.org/challenge/

The Honeynet Project. 2004. *Know Your Enemy.* 2nd ed. Addison-Wesley.

IMS. *See* University of Michigan.

Internet Systems Consortium. 2004. ISC Internet Domain Survey.
http://www.isc.org/

ISC. *See* Internet Systems Consortium.

Jbtzhm [pseud.]. 2002. "Static Kernel Patching." *Phrack* 60.
http://www.phrack.org/show.php?p=60&a=8

Kansas City Star. 2002. Scott C. Williams, supervisory special agent for
the FBI's computer analysis and response team in Kansas City, as
quoted by David Hayes. April 26.

Karger, Paul A., Mary Ellen Zurko, Douglas W. Bonin, Andrew H.
Mason, and Clifford E. Kahn. 1991. "A Retrospective on the VAX
VMM Security Kernel." *IEEE Transactions on Software Engineering*
17 (11), November.

Kato, Ken. 2004. "VMware's Back." Web site.
http://chitchat.at.infoseek.co.jp/vmware/

Kernighan, B. W., and P. J. Plauger. 1976. *Software Tools.* Addison-Wesley.

Kleiman, S. R. 1986. "Vnodes: An Architecture for Multiple File System
Types in Sun UNIX." In *Proceedings of the 1986 USENIX Summer
Technical Conference,* pp. 238–247.
http://www.solarisinternals.com/si/reading/vnode.pdf

KNOPPIX. 2004a. Linux Live CD.
http://www.knoppix.org/

KNOPPIX. 2004b. KNOPPIX Security Tools Distribution.
http://www.knoppix-std.org/

Known Goods. 2004. The Known Goods search engine.
http://www.knowngoods.org/

Kouznetsov, Pavel. 2001. "Jad—the fast JAva Decompiler."
http://www.kpdus.com/jad.html

Liang, Zhenkai, V. N. Venkatakrishnan, and R. Sekar. 2003. "Isolated
Program Execution: An Application Transparent Approach for
Executing Untrusted Programs." In *19th Annual Computer Security
Applications Conference.* Las Vegas, December 8–12.
http://www.acsac.org/2003/papers/99.pdf
http://www.seclab.cs.sunysb.edu/alcatraz/

Mandia, Kevin, and Keith J. Jones. 2001. Carbonite forensic software.
http://www.foundstone.com/

McDonald, Andrew D., and Markus G. Kuhn. 1999. "StegFS: A Steganographic File System for Linux." In *Information Hiding, Third International Workshop, IH'99*, edited by A. Pfitzmann. Dresden, Germany, September 29–October 1. Springer-Verlag.
http://www.cl.cam.ac.uk/~mgk25/ih99-stegfs.pdf

McKusick, Marshall K., William N. Joy, Samuel J. Leffler, and Robert S. Fabry. 1984. "A Fast File System for UNIX." *ACM Transactions on Computer Systems* 2 (3): 181–197.
http://docs.freebsd.org/44doc/smm/05.fastfs/paper.pdf

McKusick, Marshall Kirk, and George V. Neville-Neil. 2004. *The Design and Implementation of the FreeBSD Operating System*. Addison-Wesley.

MemTool. 2004.
http://playground.sun.com/pub/memtool/

Microsoft Developer Network. 2004. System Structures: Kernel-Mode Driver Architecture: Windows DDK.
http://msdn.microsoft.com/library/default.asp?url=/library/ en-us/kmarch/hh/kmarch/k112_3de98e8c-d842-45e9-a9bd-948276e f1b87.xml.asp

Miller, Barton P., et al. 2000. "Fuzz Revisited: A Re-examination of the Reliability of UNIX Utilities and Services." Computer Sciences Department, University of Wisconsin.
http://www.cs.wisc.edu/~bart/fuzz/fuzz.html

MSDN. *See* Microsoft Developer Network.

Murilo, Nelson, and Klaus Steding-Jessen. 2003. The Chkrootkit rootkit-detection tool.
http://www.chkrootkit.org/

National Institute of Standards and Technology. 2004. The NIST National Software Reference Library.
http://www.nsrl.nist.gov/

Nemeth, Evi, Garth Snyder, Scott Seebass, and Trent R. Hein. 2000. *UNIX Administration Handbook*. 3rd ed. Prentice Hall.

Nemeth, Evi, Garth Snyder, and Trent R. Hein. 2002. *Linux Administration Handbook*. Prentice Hall.

Neuman, Mike. 2000. The TTY-Watcher program.
http://www.engarde.com/software/

NIST. *See* National Institute of Standards and Technology.

OpenSSH. 2004. The OpenSSH remote connectivity software.
http://www.openssh.org/

PLAC. 2004. The Portable Linux Auditing CD.
http://sourceforge.net/projects/plac

Plaguez [pseud.]. 1998. "Weakening the Linux Kernel." *Phrack* 52.
http://www.phrack.org/show.php?p=52&a=18

Plasmoid [pseud.]. 1999. "Solaris Loadable Kernel Modules." The
Hacker's Choice Web site.
http://www.thc.org/papers/slkm-1.0.html

Pragmatic [pseud.]. 1999. "Attacking FreeBSD with Kernel Modules."
The Hacker's Choice Web site.
http://www.thc.org/papers/bsdkern.html

Provos, Niels. 2003. "Improving Host Security with System Call Policies."
In *Proceedings of the 12th USENIX Security Symposium*. Washington,
D.C., August.
http://www.citi.umich.edu/u/provos/papers/systrace.pdf
http://www.systrace.org/

Ptacek, T., and T. Newsham. 1998. "Insertion, Evasion, and Denial of
Service: Eluding Network Intrusion Detection." Secure Networks,
Inc. January.

Ritchie, D. M., and K. Thompson. 1974. "The UNIX Time-Sharing System."
Communications of the ACM 17 (7): 365–375.
http://cm.bell-labs.com/cm/cs/who/dmr/cacm.html

Robbins, Daniel. 2001. "Advanced filesystem implementor's guide."
IBM developerWorks, June.
http://www.ibm.com/developerworks/library/l-fs.html

Robin, John Scott, and Cynthia E. Irvine. 2000. "Analysis of the Intel
Pentium's Ability to Support a Secure Virtual Machine Monitor." In
Proceedings of the 9th USENIX Security Symposium. Denver, August.
http://www.usenix.org/publications/library/proceedings/sec2000/
robin.html

Saferstein, Richard. 2003. *Criminalistics: An Introduction to Forensic Science.*
Prentice Hall.

Saint Jude. 2002. The Saint Jude Kernel-Level IDS Project.
http://sourceforge.net/projects/stjude/

Sanfilippo, Salvatore. 1998. "about the ip header id." BugTraq mailing
list posting, December.
http://www.securityfocus.com/archive/1/11562

SCAT. *See* Solaris Crash Analysis Tool.

Schneier, B., and J. Kelsey. 1998. "Cryptographic Support for Secure
Logs on Untrusted Machines." In *Proceedings of the 7th USENIX
Security Symposium*, pp. 53–62. January.
http://www.counterpane.com/secure-logs.html

Schulz, Michal. 2002. "VRAM Storage Device: How to use the memory on GFX board in a different way." *Linux News*, September 3.

Sd [pseud.] and Devik [pseud.]. 2001. "Linux on-the-fly kernel patching without LKM." *Phrack* 58.
http://www.phrack.org/show.php?p=58&a=7

Simpson, Duncan. 2001. The Checkps rootkit detector.
http://sourceforge.net/projects/checkps/

Solaris Crash Analysis Tool. 2004.
http://wwws.sun.com/software/download/products/3fce7df0.html

Song, Dug. 2002. "Trojan/backdoor in fragroute 1.2 source distribution." BugTraq mailing list posting.
http://www.securityfocus.com/archive/1/274927

Stevens, W. Richard. 1997. As cited in the Raw IP Networking FAQ.
http://www.faqs.org/faqs/internet/tcp-ip/raw-ip-faq/

Stoll, Clifford. 1989. *The Cuckoo's Egg*. Doubleday.

Sun Microsystems. 2004. "Solaris Zones." BigAdmin System Administration Portal.
http://www.sun.com/bigadmin/content/zones/

Truff [pseud.]. 2003. "Infecting loadable kernel modules." *Phrack* 61.
http://www.phrack.org/show.php?p=61&a=10

Turing, Alan M. 1950. "Computing Machinery and Intelligence." *Mind* 59 (236): 433–460.

University of Michigan. 2004. The Internet Motion Sensor project.
http://ims.eecs.umich.edu/

The UNIX FAQ. 2004. The FAQ currently resides here:
http://www.faqs.org/faqs/unix-faq/faq/

U.S. Department of Justice. 2004. "Forensic Examination of Digital Evidence: A Guide for Law Enforcement." National Institute of Justice Special Report, Office of Justice Programs.
http://www.ojp.usdoj.gov/nij/pubs-sum/199408.htm

U.S. DOJ. *See* U.S. Department of Justice.

van Doorn, L., G. Ballintijn, and W. A. Arbaugh. 2001. "Signed Executables for Linux." Technical Report CS-TR-4259, Department of Computer Science, University of Maryland, June.
http://www.cs.umd.edu/~waa/pubs/cs4259.ps

Veeco. 2004. Veeco Instruments Web site. You can find images of semiconductors and magnetic patterns, as well as Veeco's NanoTheatre.
http://www.veeco.com/

Venema, Wietse. 1992. "TCP Wrapper, network monitoring, access control and booby traps." In _UNIX Security Symposium III Proceedings_. Baltimore, September.
ftp://ftp.porcupine.org/pub/security/tcp_wrapper.ps.Z

VMware. 2004. Virtual machine monitor host software for Linux and Microsoft Windows.
http://www.vmware.com/

VServer. 2004. The Linux VServer project.
http://www.linux-vserver.org/

Wikipedia. 2004. "Library of Alexandria."
http://en.wikipedia.org/wiki/Library_of_Alexandria

Williams, Michael A. 2002. "Anti-Trojan and Trojan Detection with In-Kernel Digital Signature testing of Executables."
http://www.trojanproof.org/

Zwicky, Elizabeth D. 1991. "Torture-testing Backup and Archive Programs: Things You Ought to Know But Probably Would Rather Not." Lisa V Proceedings. San Diego, September 30–October 3.

INDEX

A

A record, DNS, 28–30
Accuracy *versus* ambiguity, 9
Alcatraz, isolated execution with, 131
Analyzing forensic data
    See also capturing forensic data
    See also malware analysis
    See also timeline reconstruction
    See also virtual memory analysis
    from existing files, 70–73
    honeypots, 82–84
    identifying unusual activity, 4–5, 32
    OOV (order of volatility), 5–8, 20
    preparing for, 60–61
    process creation rate, 14
    replaying an incident, 120
Anonymous memory, 163
Anonymous memory pages, 165
Archaeology *versus* geology, 13–15
Architecture of computer systems, 88–89
Argus system, 21–25
Articles. *See* books and publications.
atime attribute
    description, 18–20
    disabling update, 20–21
    example, 150
Autonomous processes *versus* user control, 13–15
Avoiding intrusions. *See* evading intrusions.

B

Backing up suspect files, 20, 61
Barney intrusion
    DNS, and time, 28–31
    first signs, 17–18
    timeline reconstruction, 23–25, 28–31

Bind (Berkeley Internet Name Daemon), 28–31
Birth time, 50
Bitmaps, file system, 54, 76, 147, 157
"Black-box" dynamic analysis, 117
Block device files, 47
bmap command, 57
Books and publications
    The Cuckoo's Egg, 83
    "An Evening With Berferd," 83
    Software Tools, 29
Brute-force persistence, 149–151
Buffer memory, 163
Bypassing the file system, 55–56

C

Capturing forensic data
    See also analyzing forensic data
    accuracy *versus* ambiguity, 9
    archaeology *versus* geology, 13–15
    file system information, 61–63
    gaps in process IDs, 14
    honeypots, 82–84
    layers and illusions, 8–9
    perceptions of data, 9
    recovering encrypted file contents, 172–173
    timelines. *See* timeline reconstruction.
    traps set by intruders, 10–11
    trustworthiness of information, 10–11
    user control *versus* autonomous processes, 13–15
    virtual memory, 165–171
Case studies and examples
    atime attribute example, 150
    Barney intrusion
        DNS, and time, 28–31